AN ACTION PLAN FOR

OUTCOMES ASSESSMENT IN YOUR LIBRARY

Peter Hernon

Robert E. Dugan

AMERICAN LIBRARY ASSOCIATION
Chicago and London
2002

Project editor: Joan A. Grygel

Cover: Tessing Design

Text design: Dianne M. Rooney

Composition by ALA Editions in Janson Text and Univers 55 using QuarkXpress for the PC

Printed on 50-pound white offset, a pH-neutral stock, and bound in 10-point coated cover stock by McNaughton & Gunn

The paper used in this publication meets the minimum requirements of American National Standard for Information Sciences—Permanence of Paper for Printed Library Materials, ANSI Z39.48-1992.

ISBN: 0-8389-0813-6

Printed in the United States of America.

06 05 04 03 02   5 4 3 2 1

CONTENTS

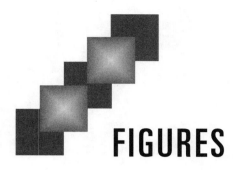

FIGURES

PREFACE

A body of literature is forming on learning, research, and operational outcomes assessment, and that literature offers good direction to anyone pursuing such assessment. Much of this literature is outside the realm of library and information science as it often appears on Web sites of institutions and in ERIC publications. There is little monographic literature devoted to the topic, and no other work offers the total picture presented here. *An Action Plan for Outcomes Assessment in Your Library* presents the policies of regional accrediting bodies for higher education; the activities of colleges and universities (including their libraries) in conducting assessment; guidelines developed by the Association of College and Research Libraries (ACRL); and the assessment plan and data collection activities of the Mildred F. Sawyer Library, Suffolk University, Boston, as it prepared for its self-study for the accreditation visit in 2002.

As with *Assessing Service Quality* (ALA, 1998) and *Delivering Satisfaction and Service Quality* (ALA, 2001), this book has a practical focus and provides data collection instruments that libraries can adapt to meet their local needs. It also speaks to both academic and public libraries. Although outcomes assessment has occurred, thus far, only within academic librarianship, it is not a subject that public libraries should ignore. The service responses of the public library planning process would undoubtedly benefit from the application of outcomes assessment.[1]

An Action Plan for Outcomes Assessment in Your Library discusses both learning and research outcomes and differentiates between the two, tries to clarify confusing terminology, and explains the research process with clear examples of each component. Furthermore, it includes experimental research that shows librarians and others one way to produce insights relevant to outcomes assessment. Experimental research, "the most rigorous of all research methods," uses comparison groups and is "capable of supporting causal relationships" between or among variables.[2] Finally, the book links outcomes assessment to accountability and argues that service quality and user satisfaction should be regarded as integral to, not separate from, outcomes assessment.

As chapter 1 explains, assessment differs from evaluation. Both rely on planning documents. In the case of assessment, the focus is on local improvement rather than a comparison with peer institutions. Some questions critical to outcomes assessment include the following:

- How have users of our library changed as a direct result of their contact with our collections and services? Are they more information literate, likely to engage in lifelong planning, and more effective and efficient in using search strategies?
- What evidence is used to address the above two questions (in the context of formally stated outcomes)? What is the quality of that evidence?

This book will address these questions and, in so doing, should appeal to librarians engaged in or planning to engage in outcomes assessment. It should also be of value to those groups with whom libraries partner to realize their assessment plan. As well, academic institutions and municipalities developing an assessment plan may appreciate the discussion and the reminder that the planning process should include the library. The library should be a central and critical player in the assessment process.

Notes

1. Sandra Nelson, *The New Planning for Results: A Streamlined Approach* (Chicago: American Library Assn., 2001), 8, 145–200.
2. Ronald R. Powell, *Basic Research Methods for Librarians*, 3d ed. (Greenwich, Conn.: Ablex, 1997), 123, 141.

ACKNOWLEDGMENTS

We wish to thank Betsy Carter at The Citadel for letting us reproduce some of the data collection instruments and for informing us of its approach to outcomes assessment. We also appreciate the support provided by the Mildred F. Sawyer Library staff, the Suffolk University New England Association of Schools and Colleges Standard 7 Self-Study Committee, and the faculty members of the College of Arts and Sciences' library committee. Ronald R. Powell of Wayne State University offered invaluable comments on chapter 7. We especially thank Peg Menear and Elinor Hernon for their patience and support as we worked on this book.

Chapters 1 and 7

"Understanding Faculty Productivity: Standards and Benchmarks for Colleges and Universities," Michael F. Middaugh, © Wiley, 2001. Reprinted by permission of Jossey-Bass Inc., a subsidiary of John Wiley & Sons, Inc.

Chapter 4

Montana State University Libraries. Student Outcomes Assessment Policy: draft. Bozeman, Mont. Available: http: //www.montana.edu/aircj/policy/Assessment Policy.html.

Chapter 5

David N. Ammons, "Overcoming the Inadequacies of Performance Measurement in Local Government: The Case of Libraries and Leisure Services," *Public Administration Review* 44 (Jan.–Feb. 1995): 37–47. Reprinted with permission from *Public Administration Review* © by the American Society for Public Administration (ASPA). 1120 G Street NW, Suite 700, Washington, DC 20005. All rights reserved.

Chapter 10

Neal, James G. "The Entrepreneurial Imperative Advancing from Incremental to Radical Change in the Academic Library," *Portal* 1, no. 1 (2001), 9. © The Johns Hopkins University Press.

1

A New Day Is Here

Higher education exists in the United States
as a public trust and a public good.[1]

For a number of years, higher education paid limited attention to assessment and accountability, but this is now changing. Libraries, too, are now being asked to link these terms to their planning and evaluation in a conscious effort to participate in the quality dimensions that stakeholders, accrediting bodies, and others expect academic institutions to prize and deliver on. Indeed, a "new day" is here as these groups see assessment as providing both the framework for and evidence of accountability. This chapter briefly reviews the basis for the increasing emphasis on accountability that has, in turn, led to the application of outcomes assessment. Neither assessment nor outcomes assessment looks at how libraries and institutions compare with their peers. Rather, the focus is on making institutions accountable for the improvement of learning and research productivity (e.g., effective student learning and making the library more relevant to the teaching and research needs of the faculty). The chapter also shows how regional accrediting agencies have incorporated accountability, assessment, and outcomes into their expectations of institutional performance and, specifically, how these expectations relate to academic libraries.

Accountability

For a long time higher education, like librarianship, looked on the performance measure movement as "a response to the failures of institutions to provide clear, verifiable productivity information." Productivity was defined as more than faculty focusing their energies on graduate education, research, publishing, and the receipt of grants.[2] Productivity started to deal with quality: that of graduating students and of the work that faculty produce. Furthermore, quality is now linked to accountability. For example, a number of consumer-related surveys and polls have rated colleges and universities on a variety of quality and cost measures in part because educational institutions have provided only anecdotal evidence of their successes in advancing student learning while underreporting or ignoring mediocre performance and failures. Complicating matters, universities have not always placed adequate resources into undergraduate education. Federal and state government, the private sector, and the consumers of higher education (students and parents) want educational institutions to be more accountable for the funds, time, and other resources allocated and expended in the education process, especially when the pursuit of an undergraduate degree is often expensive. More people are now asking if the benefits of an education at a particular institution equal or exceed its cost. Clearly, people are willing to bear the costs if they think the results are worth the expenditure.

A focus on accountability has resulted in increased attention being given to measures of institutional effectiveness. For decades, the oft-used measures employed were inputs (the materials used to provide services such as facilities, staffing, and equipment, usually described in financial terms) and outputs (measures quantifying workload undertaken or completed, such as the number of students enrolled in courses). Most recently, the application of outcomes has increased in importance as colleges and universities demonstrate their effectiveness through efficiency and quality. As a result, there is growing interest in answering such questions as

What should students learn?

How well are they learning it?

What measures and procedures does the institution use to determine that its programs are effective?

To what extent does the institution offer evidence that demonstrates its effectiveness to the public and to those paying for the tuition?

What does the institution plan to do with the evidence gathered to improve its performance?[3]

These questions are results-oriented and would benefit from the application of outcomes assessment as a measure of institutional effectiveness. Institutional effectiveness is concerned, in part, with demonstrating accountability (e.g., institutional fiscal efficiency) and educational quality and in the improvement of performance (e.g., student learning) and the production of faculty research.

Terminology

Although the terms "assessment" and "accountability" are often used interchangeably, they differ. According to Richard Frye, planning analyst for the office of institutional assessment and testing at Western Washington University, "In general, when an educational institution or one of its components assesses its own performance, it's assessment; when others assess performance, it's accountability."[4] More specifically, "assessment is a set of initiatives the institution takes to review the results of its actions, and make improvements; accountability is a set of initiatives others take to monitor the results of the institution's actions, and to penalize or reward the institution based on the outcomes."[5]

The regional agencies responsible for accrediting higher education institutions now emphasize outcomes assessment as a crucial component of an institution's self-study that demonstrates institutional effectiveness. During preparation of the self-study, an institution conducts assessment for both accountability and educational quality. Frye notes that

> Assessment for accountability is essentially an internal regulatory process, designed to assure institutional conformity to specified norms. Various performance measures, which attempt to measure institutional effectiveness, particularly with regard to fiscal efficiency and resource productivity, have been created and applied to universities and colleges and have been largely focused on aggregate statistics for entire schools. [On the other hand, assessment for educational quality] is an information feedback process to guide individual students, faculty members, programs, and schools in improving their effectiveness.[6]

Data collection efforts for assessment address numerous self-evaluative questions related to how well the institution accomplishes its education mission and goals. Clearly, the presence of a mission statement and goals are not luxuries but are essential for the accomplishment of assessment planning.

Student learning is integral to (not the byproduct of) the mission of higher education. Accountability applies processes of internal assessment related to educational effectiveness (i.e., student outcomes) and uses the results as indicators of educational quality. To increase accountability, regional accreditation bodies "are placing more pressure on higher education institutions to measure what students learn through assessment processes."[7]

Student outcomes and student learning outcomes are not the same. The former generally refer to aggregate statistics on groups of students (e.g., graduation rates, retention rates, transfer rates, and employment rates for a graduating class). Such outcomes are institutional outcomes and might be used to compare institutional performance. They do not measure "changes in students themselves due to their college experience."[8] These outcomes tend to be outputs and to reflect what the institution has accomplished; they do not reflect what (or how much) students learned.

In contrast, student learning outcomes encompass assorted attributes and abilities, both cognitive and affective, that reflect how the experiences at an institution supported student development as individuals. Cognitive outcomes include the demonstrable acquisition of specific knowledge and skills:

- What do students know that they did not know before?
- What can they do that they could not do before?

Affective outcomes probe how the college experience influenced students' values, goals, attitudes, self-concepts, world views, and behaviors. As Frye questions, "How has that experience molded their potential as an educated person? How has it enhanced their value to themselves, their families, and their communities?"[9]

Regional Accrediting Agencies and Assessment Requirements

As higher education reporter Beth McMurtrie acknowledges, "the regional accrediting agencies agree that measuring what students are learning will continue to gain importance. By focusing on results, rather than counting heads and library books, the regionals say, they are holding colleges accountable. Right now, it seems that the accrediting agencies are trying to get higher education to understand the new assessment framework and ease [institutions of higher education] into it."[10] Presumably, the next time that an institution prepares its self-study, it will be in a better position to show that its expectations for student learning have been achieved and that the results gathered were indeed used to improve performance. Thus, it seems that a new day in assessment is present.

Higher education institutions are individually accredited by regional accrediting bodies, for instance, the Commission on Colleges of the Northwest Association of Schools and Colleges; the Western Association of Schools and Colleges; the North Central Association of Colleges and Schools, Commission on Institutions of Higher Education; the Middle States Commission on Higher Education; and the Southern Association of Colleges and Schools. In turn, the Council for Higher Education Accreditation (CHEA), a national organization concerned with accreditation of higher education institutions, recognizes these regional accrediting agencies. Presidents of American universities and colleges established CHEA in 1996 to improve higher education through strengthening the accreditation of higher education institutions. CHEA affirms that standards and processes of accrediting organizations are consistent with the quality, improvement, and accountability expectations that CHEA has established.

The regional accrediting agencies have incorporated CHEA's guidelines as they develop their own sets of standards by which to evaluate institutions. Responding to the need to increase accountability and educational quality, CHEA expects accrediting organizations to advance academic quality and to demonstrate accountability.

> Accrediting organizations need standards that advance academic quality in higher education; that emphasize student achievement and high expectations of teaching and learning, research, and service; and that are developed within the framework of institutional mission.

> The purpose is to show that accrediting organizations have standards that ensure accountability by communicating the results of educational efforts to the public, higher education community, and stakeholders in a consistent, clear, and coherent manner.[11]

Assessment Requirements

The following sections illustrate the assessment requirements of the regional accrediting agencies for higher education institutions. Key policy documents are also noted.

Commission on Colleges of the Northwest Association of Schools and Colleges

In its current standards document, the Northwest Association of Schools and Colleges (Northwest) has a section on planning and effectiveness that specifies the following requirements concerning institutional effectiveness:

- The institution clearly defines its evaluation and planning processes. It develops and implements procedures to evaluate the extent to which it achieves institutional goals.

- The institution engages in systematic planning for, and evaluation of, its activities, including teaching, research, and public service consistent with institutional mission and goals.

- The institution uses the results of its systematic evaluation activities and ongoing planning processes to influence resource allocation and to improve its instructional programs, institutional services, and activities.

- The institution integrates its evaluation and planning processes to identify institutional priorities for improvement.

- The institution uses information from its planning and evaluation processes to communicate evidence of institutional effectiveness to its public.[12]

To strengthen these requirements, Northwest demands evidence that demonstrates the analysis and appraisal of institutional outcomes. Examples of these outcomes include

- annual goals and assessment of success in their accomplishments
- studies of alumni and former students
- studies regarding the effectiveness of programs and their graduates
- studies that indicate the degree of success in placing graduates
- test comparisons that reveal beginning and ending competencies
- surveys of student, alumni, and employee satisfaction[13]

Standard 2, educational program and its effectiveness, spells out the requirements for student learning outcomes assessment in standard 2.B—educational program planning and assessment:

Educational program planning is based on regular and continuous assessment of programs in light of the needs of the disciplines, the fields or occupations for which programs prepare students, and other constituencies of the institution.

- The institution's processes for assessing its educational programs are clearly defined, encompass all of its offerings, are conducted on a regular basis, and are integrated into the overall planning and evaluation plan. These processes are consistent with the institution's assessment plan as required by policy 2.2: educational assessment. . . . While key constituents are involved in the process, the faculty have a central role in planning and evaluating the educational programs.

- The institution identifies and publishes the expected learning outcomes for each of its degree and certificate programs. Through regular and systematic assessment, it demonstrates that students who complete their programs, no matter where or how they are offered, have achieved these outcomes.

- The institution provides evidence that its assessment activities lead to the improvement of teaching and learning.[14]

Policy 2.2 on educational assessment, referenced in standard 2.B.1, was adopted in 1992, and, in part, "expects each institution and program to adopt an assessment plan responsive to its mission and its needs." The policy statement clearly defines student learning outcomes (not outputs):

As noted in standard 2, implicit in the mission statement of every postsecondary institution is the education of students. Consequently, each institution has an obligation to plan carefully its courses of instruction to respond to student needs, to evaluate the effectiveness of that educational program in terms of the change it brings about in students, and to make improvements in the program dictated by the evaluative process.

The assessment of educational quality has always been central to the accreditation process. In the past, this assessment focused on process measures and structural features; as a result, considerable emphasis was placed on the resources available to enhance students' educational experiences (e.g., the range and variety of graduate degrees held by members of the faculty, the number of books in the library, and the quality of specialized laboratory equipment). More recently, while still stressing the need to assess the quantity and quality of the whole educational experience, the communities of interest served by the accreditation enterprise emphasize the validity and usefulness of output evaluations, assessment, and input measures.

Nearly every postsecondary institution engages in outcomes assessment. Some efforts are more formalized, quantified, developed, and used than others. The intent of commission policy is to stress outcomes assessment as an essential part of the ongoing institutional self-study and accreditation processes, to underline the necessity for each institution to formulate a plan which provides for a series of outcomes measures that are internally consistent and in accord with its mission and structure, and to provide some examples of a variety of successful plans for assessing educational outcomes.[15]

The policy statement also lists acceptable, although not required, measures that document outcomes assessment:

Central to the outcomes analyses or assessments are judgments about the effects of the educational program upon students. These judgments can be made in a variety of ways and can be based upon a variety of data sources. The more data sources that contribute to the overall judgment, the more reliable that judgment would seem to be. There follows a list of several outcomes measures which, when used in appropriate combinations and informed by the institutional mission, could yield an efficacious program of outcomes assessment. This list is intended to be illustrative and exemplary as opposed to prescriptive and exhaustive:

> student information
>
> midprogram assessments
>
> end-of-program assessment
>
> program review and specialized accreditation
>
> alumni satisfaction and loyalty
>
> dropouts/noncompleters
>
> employment or employer satisfaction measures[16]

The Western Association of Schools and Colleges

The Western Association of Schools and Colleges (WASC) has accreditation standards that its membership approved on November 2, 2000. Teaching and learning in standard 2: achieving educational objectives through core functions includes criteria for review. Parts 2.3 through 2.7 of those criteria are concerned with assessment plans:

2.3 The institution's expectations for learning and student attainment are clearly reflected in its academic programs and policies. These include the organization and content of the institution's curricula, the institution's admissions and graduation policies, the organization and delivery of advisement, the use of its library and information resources, and (where applicable) in the wider learning environment provided by its campus and/or cocurriculum. (The use of information and learning resources beyond textbooks is evidenced in syllabi throughout the undergraduate and graduate curriculum.)

2.4 The institution's expectations for learning and student attainment are developed and widely shared among its members (including faculty, students, staff, and, where appropriate, external stakeholders). The institution's faculty takes collective responsibility for establishing, reviewing, fostering, and demonstrating the attainment of these expectations.

2.5 The institution's academic programs actively involve students in learning, challenge them to achieve high expectations, and provide them with appropriate and ongoing feedback about their performance and how it can be improved.

2.6 The institution demonstrates that its graduates consistently achieve its stated levels of attainment and ensures that its expectations for student learning are embedded in the standards faculty use to evaluate student work.

2.7 In order to improve program currency and effectiveness, all programs offered by the institution are subject to review, including analyses of the achievement of the program's learning objectives and outcomes. Where appropriate, evidence from external constituencies such as employers and professional societies is included in such reviews. (The institution incorporates in its assessment of educational objectives results with respect to student achievement, including program completion, license examination, and placement rates results.)[17]

Question 8 from the section on institutional engagement of the standards asks: "To what extent does the institution ensure that students develop expected core learning abilities and competencies before they graduate?"[18] Although the core learning abilities are not identified, it is likely that WASC's higher education institutions identify these expectations in its academic programs and polices as required in standard 2.3.

North Central Association of Colleges and Schools, Commission on Institutions of Higher Education

The North Central Association (NCA) has been working on student learning outcomes assessment since 1989. After a decade of effort, associate director Cecilia L. Lopez concluded that, "in short, NCA's emphasis upon the assessment of student learning is helping transform an academy focused on what institutions and faculty *offer to* or *do for* students, to an academy focused on what students can demonstrate they *know* and can *do*."[19] To further that transformation, in March 2000, the NCA added requirements titled "Assessment of Student Academic Achievement: Levels of Implementation" to the second edition of its handbook concerning accreditation. The levels of implementation are tools to

1. assist institutions in understanding and strengthening their programs for assessment of student academic achievement
2. provide evaluation teams with some useful characteristics, or descriptors, of progress to inform their consultation and their recommendations related to those programs

The clusters of characteristics contained in "Levels of Implementation" emerge from rigorously applied research analysis of content found in team reports, the source of consultant-evaluators' discussion of assessment at scores of institutions. The term "levels of implementation," as used in this document, is to be understood as descriptive and not definitive. Therefore, the levels of implementation provide markers of the progress institutions have made in developing their assessment programs. As institutions and teams use the levels, it is unlikely they will find any assessment program exhibiting all of the characteristics associated with a particular level at any given time. Moreover, not every assessment program will progress through each level before it becomes an effective, ongoing system of processes that results in the continuous improvement of student learning. The commission's research continues, and as its learning grows, these characteristics will undoubtedly be modified.[20]

As illustrated in charts, the levels of implementation—patterns of characteristics are:

Level 1. Beginning implementation of assessment program

Level 2. Making progress in implementing assessment programs

Level 3. Maturing stages of continuous improvement that include

      I. Institutional change
         A. Collective/shared values
         B. Mission

     II. Shared responsibility
         A. Faculty
         B. Administration and board
         C. Students

    III. Institutional support
         A. Resources
         B. Students

    IV. Efficacy of assessment[21]

Obviously, the NCA is committed to the continuous improvement of student learning.

From this commitment come all of its efforts to engage institutions in the assessment of student learning. It is also committed to the tenet that assessment of student academic achievement is the key to improving student learning [and that assessment] is critical to . . . the educational accomplishment of students now and in the future.[22]

Middle States Commission on Higher Education

Among the several documents that the Middle States Commission on Higher Education (Middle States) uses concerning assessment include Characteristics of Excellence in Higher Education, Designs for Excellence: Handbook for Institutional Self-Study that updates the Characteristics document, and the Framework for Outcomes Assessment.[23] In the first source, Middle States relates student learning outcomes to institutional goals and institutional effectiveness and requires an institutional assessment plan:

Mission, Goals and Objectives

Educational goals particularly need to be stated in terms of outcomes they seek to achieve, e.g., the changes and/or competencies they seek to foster in their students. A statement of institutional goals describes the effects that the educational and related programs are designed to have, such as a sense of responsibility in students for their own development as well as an awareness of their obligation as contributing members of the institution and ultimately of society.

Institutional Effectiveness and Outcomes

Institutions should develop guidelines and procedures for assessing their overall effectiveness as well as student learning outcomes. The deciding factor in assessing institutional effectiveness is evidence of the extent to which it achieves its goals and objectives. The process of seeking such evidence and its subsequent use helps to cultivate educational excellence. One of the primary indications of the effectiveness of faculty, administration, and governing boards is the skill with which they raise questions about institutional effectiveness, seek answers, and significantly improve procedures in light of their findings.

Outcomes assessment involves gathering and evaluating both quantitative and qualitative data that demonstrate congruence among the institution's mission, goals, and objectives and the actual outcomes of its educational programs and activities. The ultimate goal of outcomes assessment is the improvement of teaching and learning. The approaches may vary and need not be elaborate or dependent on quantitative criteria, but they should be systematic and thorough. They should assess the outcomes at all levels, linking course goals to program goals and both to institutional goals. An institution should be able to demonstrate that the information obtained is used as a basis for ongoing self-renewal. The process through which faculty and staff conduct such analyses should produce results that will encourage institutional improvement.[24]

According to the Middle States, "The plan for the assessment of outcomes should attempt to determine the extent and quality of student learning. The basic process begins with a thorough review of the institution's programs, curricula, courses, and other instructional activities." Any assessment should include frequent appraisals of the academic progress and student achievement, the progress of graduates, and alumni opinions. In addition, "institutions should seek ways to assess the degree to which students' attitudes, social and ethical values, interests, and commitment to scholarship and lifelong learning develop as a result of their education."[25]

Building upon Characteristics of Excellence in Higher Education, in 1996 Middle States developed a policy statement, "Outcomes Assessment" and a "how to" handbook for implementing outcomes assessment at the institutional level, Framework for Outcomes Assessment; in 1998 it developed Outcomes Assessment Plans: Guidelines for Developing Outcomes Assessment Plans at Colleges and Universities. The Framework handbook has a clear statement of the purpose

> [T]o examine and enhance an institution's effectiveness, not only in terms of teaching and learning, which rest at the heart of the mission at colleges and universities, but also the effectiveness of the institution as a whole.
>
> [With respect to teaching and learning, the Framework document provides strategies that can assist colleges and universities to]
>
> > identify the knowledge and skills that students should learn and be able to apply after completing their college education
> >
> > ascertain the personal attributes that students should acquire or develop at an institution of higher education
> >
> > consider and decide upon various methods for measuring student academic achievement and personal development
> >
> > select or develop the best instruments for measuring student academic achievement and personal development
> >
> > collect and analyze the assessment data required to judge the effectiveness of teaching and learning
> >
> > develop a system for communicating assessment results and utilizing the findings to improve teaching and learning, now and in the future
>
> . . . The ultimate goal of outcomes assessment is to examine and enhance an institution's effectiveness. Four objectives must be met in order to reach this goal. They are to improve teaching and learning, to contribute to the personal development of students, to ensure institutional improvement, and to facilitate accountability. The challenge for colleges and universities is to develop an assessment plan that achieves a balance among these various objectives in reaching the ultimate goal.[26]

The Framework carefully differentiates between assessment for educational quality and assessment for accountability. According to the document, the former promotes self-reflection and evidence-based thinking about teaching, learning, and student growth. Not only can it lead to improvements in both the quality and quantity of learning by students, it also responds to their needs for personal development. Regarding assessment for accountability, it is important that institutions respond fully and accurately to a variety of public demands for accountability regarding both learning and institutional quality and effectiveness.[27]

Accountability and Effectiveness

Accountability is integral to effectiveness. By employing their current standards for accreditation or strengthening them through recent revisions, regional accrediting bodies expect higher education institutions to become more accountable. These accrediting bodies believe that outcomes assessment measures institutional effectiveness and that effectiveness can be defined in terms of achieving student learning outcomes and improving educational quality.

While the regional accrediting agencies are strengthening the requirements concerning accountability, they are also revising their accreditation standards to be less prescriptive, providing higher education institutions with more options for demonstrating their institutional effectiveness to the accreditors and the public (private sector, government bodies, and consumers). The less prescriptive efforts are evident in the revisions or planned revision of existing standards, such as the Southern Association of Colleges and Schools (to be discussed next), and in the development of alternative accrediting processes such as the North Central Association of Colleges and Schools' Academic Quality Improvement Project (AQIP).[28]

Regional Accrediting Agency's Standards Applied to Academic Libraries

Two important questions for librarians are "How do they view the standards?" and "How do the standards emphasizing accountability and outcomes assessment apply to academic libraries?" First, in most instances, librarians prefer the prescriptive standards to the more vague, institutionally based standards. For example, college librarian Larry Hardesty laments the proposed changes in the Southern Association of Colleges and Schools' standards that would reduce the prescriptive standards with the dozens of "must" statements to three "comprehensive requirements."[29] Academic librarians have, in the past, used the more prescriptive standards to leverage additional resources from their institutions to comply with the standards. Second, in addition to revising standards into less prescriptive measures, several regional accrediting agencies have recognized the need for information literacy, especially as it relates to student learning outcomes, in their revised standards.

An excellent example of the trend to less prescriptive library standards can be illustrated with the draft of revised standards of the Southern Association of Colleges and Schools. Southern's existing standards (written in 1998 and presented in appendix A) are very detailed, concerned mostly with inputs such as funding and staffing levels and outputs oriented toward ensuring process, structure, and accessibility.

In September 2000, Southern produced draft standards that would reduce standard 5.1, library and other learning resources, to three requirements under learning resources. For example, "the institution provides facilities and instructional support services appropriate to the courses or programs and adequate to support the institution's mission and to contribute to the effectiveness of learning."[30] The proposed standards are far less prescriptive than the existing 1998 standards. The word "library" has been dropped from the original standards and is replaced by "learning and information resources." However, information literacy as it may apply to academic libraries, or learning and information resources for that matter, is not mentioned among the replacement provisions for standard 5.1.

Northwest's standards also are not prescriptive. Rather, they enable member institutions to examine both their infrastructure and long-term sustainability within the context of their educational mission. Consequently, the standards seek a balance between the infrastructure and sustainability, shape Northwest's approach to outcomes assessment, and address program priorities. Clearly, an institution must provide evidence of how it accomplishes its mission, but it has latitude regarding what evidence it provides. Northwest seems to focus on three key questions:

1. Does the institution have the infrastructure to support its educational mission?
2. Does that infrastructure have sustainability? In other words, is it adequate to support the achievement of the mission?
3. Is the institution achieving its intended results—outcomes?

Northwest's current standards cover information resources and services, facilities and access, personnel and management, and planning and evaluation. Most importantly, libraries must provide supporting documentation as "required exhibits" for standard 5 that centers on

printed materials that describe for students the hours and services of learning resources facilities such as libraries, computer labs, and audiovisual facilities

policies, regulations, and procedures for the development and management of library and information resources, including collection development and weeding

statistics on use of library and other learning resources

statistics on library collection and inventory of other learning resources

assessment measures used to determine the adequacy of facilities for the goals of the library and information resources and services

assessment measures to determine the adequacy of holdings, information resources and services to support the educational programs both on and off campus

data regarding number and assignments of library staff

charts showing the organizational arrangements for managing libraries and other information resources (e.g., computing facilities, instructional media, and telecommunication centers)

comprehensive budget(s) for library and information resources

vitae of professional library staff

formal, written agreements with other libraries

computer usage statistics related to the retrieval of library resources

printed information describing user services provided by the computing facility

studies or documents describing the evaluation of library and information resources [31]

The assessment measures referred to in the required exhibits are output oriented, and the word "evaluative" could be replaced with "assessment" throughout the section. Neither information literacy nor identifying a need for student outcomes is mentioned. Although the standards focus on processes and structures concerning the delivery and use of library services, the evidence supplied through the supporting documentation deals with infrastructure. The question becomes "How does the library and its institution link that information to sustainability and its outcomes?" Clearly, Northwest's standards enable institutions to demonstrate how they use their resources to accomplish their mission.

Academic librarians tried to influence the development and revision of WASC Standards on information literacy.[32] Although WASC did not fully incorporate those recommendations into the standards approved in November 2000, a number of librarians got information literacy included in the text for the standards. Some of the standards' elements are prescriptive, whereas others are not. For instance, "Standard 3: Fiscal, Physical, and Information Resources," question 5 in questions for institutional engagement, focuses on information literacy and the library staff:

> How does the institution ensure that its members develop the critical information literacy skills needed to locate, evaluate, and responsibly use information? How does it utilize the special skills of information professionals to support teaching, learning, and information technology planning?[33]

Perhaps the strongest statements concerning libraries and information literacy are found in the standards of the Middle States. In Characteristics of Excellence in Higher Education, Middle States emphasizes:

> The services, resources, and programs of libraries, broadly defined, are fundamental to the educational mission of an institution and to the teaching and learning process. They support the educational program. They facilitate learning and research activities among students, faculty, and staff.[34]

In this same section, Middle States takes a less prescriptive approach, discussing the need for the institution to think beyond the physical library and ensuring that library services are proportional to institutional needs:

> The scope of library/learning resources, the types of services, and the varieties of print and nonprint and electronic media depend on the nature of the institution. They must be in reasonable proportion to the needs to be served, but numbers alone are no assurance of excellence. Of more importance are the quality, accessibility, availability, and delivery of resources on site and elsewhere; their relevance to the institution's current programs; and the degree to which they are actually used. The development of services and collections must relate realistically to the institution's educational mission, goals, curricula, size, complexity, degree level, fiscal support, and its teaching, learning, and research requirements.
>
> An institution should provide access to a broad range of learning resources, at both primary and off-campus sites. Although access to these resources is customarily gained through a library/resource center, an attempt should be made to think beyond the physical confines of the traditional library in regard to information access. A variety of contemporary technologies for accessing learning resources and instruction in their use should be available. In addition to providing broad access to the diffuse world of electronic information, institutions should provide critical reference and specialized program resources at or within easy reach of each instructional location. Where appropriate, institutions should also expand access for users at remote sites, such as extension centers, branch campuses, laboratories, clinical sites, or students' homes.[35]

Middle States strongly emphasizes information literacy and the role of the library, with the goal of having students become independent learners:

> Each institution should foster optimal use of its learning resources through strategies designed to help students develop information literacy—the ability to locate, evaluate, and use information in order to become independent learners. It should encourage the use of a wide range of nonclassroom resources for teaching and learning. It is essential to have an active and continuing program of library orientation and instruction in accessing information, developed collaboratively and supported actively by faculty, librarians, academic deans, and other information providers.[36]

Middle States also prescribes in Characteristics the desired library resources for interlibrary collaboration and resource sharing activities, materials selection, library staff competence, and the library facility. In the final section, however, Middle States identifies the development of "independent, self-directed learners" as a student learning outcome and expects libraries to contribute to that effort.

> Careful evaluation of all learning resources, on-site or elsewhere, should be an ongoing process. A system for assessing the effectiveness of library and learning resources should be available. It should focus on utilization, accessibility, availability, and delivery of materials. Quality and relevance of the collections, effectiveness of reference and referral services, and adequacy of funding for resources and their use are essential. Ultimately, the most important measure will be how effectively students are prepared to become independent, self-directed learners. [37]

In Designs for Excellence, Middle States reinforces its emphasis on the role of the library in increasing information literacy. Framework for Outcomes Assessment places outcomes assessment in the context of teaching and learning. Clearly, libraries have a role in meeting the goal of general education of students. Middle States goes on to identify four student learning outcomes competencies:

> The analysis of student achievement with respect to general education utilizes different measurement objectives for assessing competencies in four broad areas:
>
> - cognitive abilities (critical thinking, problem solving)
> - content literacy (knowledge of social institutions, science and technology)
> - competence in information management skills and communication
> - value awareness (multicultural understanding, moral and ethical judgment)[38]

With the regional accrediting agencies emphasizing student learning outcomes and identifying a role for libraries in achieving information literate students, the Association of College and Research Libraries' *Information Literacy Competency Standards for Higher Education*, coupled with its "Standards for College Libraries 2000 Edition," provide academic librarians with a framework for active participation in institutional efforts.[39] (Both of these documents are discussed in chapters 3 and 6.)

Conclusion

In response to increasing public scrutiny of the benefits of higher education as the costs of an education escalate and as segments of the public (e.g., the business community) view higher education as inadequately preparing graduates to participate in careers and society, an increased emphasis on institutional accountability has surfaced. Regional accrediting bodies that are responsible for accrediting institutions of higher education are involved in a nationwide effort to ensure that academe becomes more accountable. They are doing so by requiring institutions to demonstrate their overall effectiveness: both institutional efficiencies (e.g., fiscal responsibilities) and educational quality. Accrediting agencies are strengthening their requirements about accountability, revising their standards to be less prescriptive (providing higher education institutions with more options to present in their self-study report), and requiring the application of outcomes assessment measures, especially regarding educational quality and its continuous improvement.

These trends affect academic libraries. First, librarians do not like the generality associated with less prescriptive accrediting standards. Second, some regional accrediting agencies have revised their standards to emphasize information literacy as a student learning outcome, and they have suggested roles for academic libraries to play. Fortunately, the Association of College and Research Libraries has created several documents that provide excellent assistance for librarians as they adapt to the changing accreditation landscape.

The ultimate goal of outcomes assessment is to examine and enhance an institution's effectiveness.[40]

Notes

1. Western Assn. of Schools and Colleges, *Handbook of Accreditation 2001* (Alameda, Calif.: The Assn., 2001), 4. Available: http://www.wascweb.org/senior/handbook.pdf. Accessed 23 March 2001.

2. Michael F. Middaugh, *Understanding Faculty Productivity: Standards and Benchmarks for Colleges and Universities* (San Francisco: Jossey-Bass, 2001), 26.

3. Middle States Commission on Higher Education, Framework for Outcomes Assessment (1996), 2. Available: http://www.msache.org/msafram.pdf. Accessed 14 Dec. 2000.

4. Richard Frye, *Assessment, Accountability, and Student Learning Outcomes* (Bellingham, Wash.: Western Washington University, n.d.), 1. Available: http://www.ac.wwu.edu/~dialogue/issue2.html. Accessed 17 Nov. 2000.

5. Ibid.

6. Ibid.

7. Beth McMurtrie, "Accreditors Revamp Policies to Stress Student Learning," *Chronicle of Higher Education* (7 July 2000), A29.

8. Frye, *Assessment, Accountability, and Student Learning Outcomes*, 5–6.

9. Ibid.

10. McMurtrie, "Accreditors Revamp Policies," A30.

11. Council for Higher Education Accreditation. Available: http://www.chea.org/About/Recognition.cfm. Accessed 7 Dec. 2000.

12. Northwest Assn. of Schools and Colleges, Standard One—Institutional Mission and Goals, Planning and Effectiveness. Available: http://www.cocnasc.org/policyprocedure/standards/standards1.html. Accessed 7 Dec. 2000.

13. Ibid.

14. Northwest Assn. of Schools and Colleges, Standard Two—Educational Program and Its Effectiveness. Available: http://www.cocnasc.org/policyprocedure/standards/standard2.html. Accessed 7 Dec. 2000.

15. Ibid.

16. Ibid.

17. Western Assn. of Schools and Colleges, *Handbook of Accreditation 2001*, 21.

18. Ibid., 22.

19. Cecilia L. Lopez, A Decade of Assessing Student Learning: What We Have Learned; What's Next?, 42. Available: http://www.ncahigherlearningcommission.org/AMpastmaterial/ASSESS10.PDF. Accessed 23 March 2001.

20. North Central Assn. of Colleges and Schools, Commission on Institutions of Higher Education, Addendum to the Handbook 2d ed. (March 2000), 6, 8–12. Available: http://www.ncahigherlearningcommission.org/resources/Handbook_Supplement.pdf. Accessed 23 March 2001.

21. Ibid.

22. Cecilia L. Lopez, Assessing Student Learning: Using the Commission's Levels of Implementation, 3–4. Available: http://www.ncahigherlearningcommission.org/resources/assessment/Lopez_Levels_2000.pdf. Accessed 23 March 2001.

23. Middle States Commission on Higher Education, Characteristics of Excellence in Higher Education (1994), 7. Available: http://www.msache.org/msachar.pdf. Accessed 10 Dec. 2000. Middle States is currently in the process of revising Characteristics of Excellence in Higher Education. The revision goes into effect in spring 2002 subject to membership approval December 2002. See a proposed draft at http://www.msache.org/special.html. The redrafting of the Middle States accreditation standards was announced in a letter to members dated 1 Nov. 2000. Available: http://www.msache.org/chmemo. Accessed 27 May 2001. The proposed document, Characteristics of Excellence: Standards for Accreditation (Draft for Discussion), is dated 14 Feb. 2001. Available: http://www.msache.org/chpd. Accessed 27 May 2001. Middle States Commission on Higher Education, Designs for Excellence. Available: www.msache.org/msadesign.pdf. Accessed 27 July 2001. Middle States Commission on Higher Education, Framework for Outcomes Assessment.

24. Middle States Commission on Higher Education, Characteristics of Excellence in Higher Education (1994), 7.

25. Ibid., 16.

26. Middle States Commission on Higher Education, Framework for Outcomes Assessment, 1, 4.

27. Ibid., 5.

28. North Central Assn. of Colleges and Schools, Commission on Institutions of Higher Education, Academic Quality Improvement Project. Available: http://www.AQIP.org/criteria.html. Accessed 23 March 2001.

29. Larry Hardesty, "Libraries Dropped from Accreditation Criteria," *College & Research Libraries News* 61 (Nov. 2000), 888.

30. Commission on Colleges of the Southern Assn. of Colleges and Schools, Accreditation Review Project, Principles and Requirements for Accreditation—PROPOSAL (Sept. 2000), 18. Available: http//www.sacscoc.org/COC/AccrProposal.htm. Accessed 14 Dec. 2000.

31. Northwest Assn. of Schools and Colleges, Standard Five—Library and Information Resources. Available: http://www.cocnasc.org/policyprocedure/standards/standards5.html. Accessed 9 Jan. 2001.

32. CARL Task Force to Recommend Information Literacy Standard to WASC, *Recommended Texts for Consideration Related to Information Literacy* (Sept. 1997). Available: http://www.carl-acrl.org/Reports/rectoWASC.html. Accessed 9 Jan. 2001.

33. Western Assn. of Schools and Colleges, *Handbook of Accreditation 2001*, Section II The Standards, 25–6.

34. Middle States Commission on Higher Education, *Characteristics of Excellence in Higher Education*, 14.

35. Ibid., 14–15.

36. Ibid., 15.

37. Ibid., 16.

38. Middle States Commission on Higher Education, *Framework for Outcomes Assessment*, 18.

39. ACRL, *Information Literacy Competency Standards for Higher Education* (Chicago: American Library Assn., 2000). Available: http://www.ala.org/acrl/lintro.html. Accessed 5 March 2001. ACRL, "Standards for College Libraries 2000 Edition," *College and Research Libraries News* 61, no. 3 (March 2000), 175–82. Available: http://www.ala.org/acrl/guides/college.html. Accessed 5 March 2001.

40. Middle States Commission on Higher Education, *Framework for Outcomes Assessment*, 18.

2

Assessment Plans, Reports, and Guides in Institutions of Higher Education

Assessment focuses attention on students and learning. It helps the university focus on its mission, concentrate its resources on instruction, monitor progress toward planning goals, and demonstrate institutional integrity and high-quality education.[1]

As discussed in the previous chapter, the regional accrediting bodies of higher education institutions are placing an increasing emphasis on the application of outcomes assessment, oftentimes stressing the need for (and value of) student learning outcomes, to satisfy demands from governments and education consumers for proof that institutional effectiveness complies with accountability requirements. Regional accrediting bodies expect institutions to prepare assessment plans that measure outcomes within the institution. This chapter reviews examples of guides that colleges and universities have created to assist those responsible for assessment in developing internal plans and in applying the results from assessment activities. In addition, the relationship between four institutions with assessment plans and their respective academic libraries are briefly presented.

Guides Developed by Institutions to Assist in Assessment Planning

Many institutions have written guides to assist their colleges, programs, departments, and faculty in the preparation of assessment plans. The following examples highlight approaches taken to develop an assessment plan, including the structures and content of that plan.

Ball State University

Ball State University (Muncie, Indiana) has an Assessment Workbook composed of a series of chapters designed for those faculty and administrators responsible for assessment.[2] Most of the chapters include informative questions and answers that are quite detailed and useful along with recommendations for other resources to consult (found under "for further reading").

Designing a Department Assessment Plan, another document produced at the university, suggests how to identify the department's assessment needs and explores assessment tools and activities that are available to departments. It includes examples of assessment plans, and example 2 presents a table that identifies the program objective, outcome criteria, assessment measure and population.[3] A checklist in Designing a Department Assessment Plan asks:

- What are we assessing?
- What do we want to know?
- From whom are we collecting the data?
- Who will see the resulting information?
- How will the data be used?
- How often will the data be collected?[4]

Furthermore, the checklist includes sample assessment plans and identifies four characteristics that these plans must accomplish if they are to be effective. First, assessment flows from the mission statement and needs to be both ongoing and built into the department's program. Second, assessment should use multiple measures, both qualitative and quantitative, rather than relying on one instrument or activity. Third, faculty must assume ownership and responsibility for the plan and the underlying assessment program because it is the faculty who are directly involved in the process of student learning. Fourth, identifiable assessment activities should lead to improvement and be regarded as a means rather than as an end.[5]

Still another document, Shaping Department Goals and Objectives for Assessment, defines and discusses the differences among goals, objectives, outcomes, and assessment. The reader is taken through a process of writing departmental goals and objectives, differentiating between "mastery" and "developmental" objectives. A series of learning outcomes for writing instructional objectives focuses on knowledge, application, thinking skills, general skills, attitudes, interests, appreciation, and adjustments.[6]

Two other documents offer suggestions for the construction of questionnaire items, present a lengthy and detailed account of applying external and locally developed tests to assessment, explain how to calculate test item difficulty and discrimination, and show how to analyze the quality of a test.[7] There is also a discussion of performance-based assessment such as the use of portfolios (collected examples of student work over time), performance measures (using samples of students' writing, presentations, or projects for assessment), and the assessment center method (simulation of real-life situations in which expert judges evaluate student performance).[8]

Finally, a guide discusses the preparation of assessment reports and the use of the results of outcomes assessment. It asks "To whom are we reporting our results?" and identifies the following uses of the results:

primary uses (accreditation reports and reviews, general studies evaluations, and curriculum review)

secondary uses (recruiting, alumni newsletter, publications in which assessments results can be shared with other institutions, and career services)[9]

Columbia Basin College

Columbia Basin College (Pasco, Washington) has a detailed guide for those faculty, staff, and administrators responsible for assessment. Chapter 1 of the guide discusses designing a department assessment plan, offers a checklist to identify the design process, reviews existing information useful to academic departments in conducting assessment, and identifies what types of information the departments could generate by using various methods of data collection. The elements that an outcomes assessment plan addresses include, for instance, outcomes related to content learning, written and oral skills, quantitative and literacy/verbal skills, lifelong learning, and social awareness. Measures that provide evidence of the expected outcome include standardized tests, competency examinations, locally developed achievement tests, attitude inventories, surveys, observation of performance, and license/certification.[10] The guide's appendixes contain the worksheets and forms used throughout the assessment process.

Montana State University–Bozeman

Montana State University in Bozeman provides a comprehensive list of techniques and activities used to collect evidence of student learning in a subject major.[11] Some of the techniques repeat or build on those previously mentioned; others add new perspectives. Following are some examples:

Conduct focus group interviews with students at different levels of the major to obtain student feedback on advising, courses, and curriculum.

Develop a checklist and rating scale for expected knowledge and skills. Have three faculty use these tools to evaluate major works such as senior projects, theses, and dissertations. Although many of these undertakings receive an *A* grade, reviewing content for specific knowledge and skills may reveal areas that, although acceptable, are consistently below expectations.

Invite outside examiners from business, industry, and the professions to provide feedback on students' presentations or projects.

Assign a research/creative project to be evaluated by several faculty members.

Administer the ACAT, CLEP, MFAT, or a locally developed proficiency examination to test factual knowledge in the major.[12]

Administer a nationally normed, general education exam such as College BASE, ACT COMP, or CAAP or develop one specifically tailored to institutional objectives.[13]

Use "real-world" assignments such as case studies, in-basket exercises, recitals, and exhibits to evaluate whether students can integrate knowledge and skills developed throughout their progress in the major.

Analyze performance on licensure and qualifying examinations for professional or graduate school. (Remember the percent passing is an accountability number; it does not relate to program improvement. Bragging about a high pass rate does nothing to improve the program. Program improvement comes by focusing on the failures (e.g., determining why students failed) and taking steps to correct any problems identified.

Design one or two final exam questions to capture cumulative learning in the major and provide an in-depth assessment.

See chapters 6 and 8 of this book for an amplification of these and other techniques.

Concordia College

Recognizing that academic departments and faculty may not want to review a vast number of assessment planning documents, Concordia College (Moorhead, Minnesota) developed Assessment for People Who Don't Have Enough Time to Do Assessment. It presents a five-step approach to developing an assessment plan.

1. Develop and agree on clear learning goals for your program.
2. Develop an assessment plan that matches your goals as closely as possible.
3. Develop a plan such that it will give you results that will be useful.
4. Develop a plan that will be practical to implement.
5. Use the results of your assessment plan.[14]

Assessment Plans and Reports

Many institutions have created and implemented assessment plans reflecting their individual institution's mission, culture, and planning processes. The following subsections review some examples of existing planning and reporting efforts.

St. Louis Community College

St. Louis Community College's (SLCC, St. Louis, Missouri) five-year assessment plan (through academic year 2002–2003) offers principles of assessment, one of which states that "assessment is about improving learning not judging teaching."[15] The assessment process includes the mission and goals taken from the strategic plan; intended outcomes for the program, course, service, and so on; means of assessment (the mechanism by which student achievement of the outcome is ascertained); results of assessment; and use of the results. The results are applied to a review of the intended outcomes, thereby revitalizing the process. The plan emphasizes that the "outcome need *not* be quantifiable, merely verifiable."[16]

The means of program and course assessment are divided into qualitative techniques (in which assessment tools are used to demonstrate the scope of a student's achievement with information that usually cannot be quantified or counted) and quantitative techniques (in which assessment tools are used to produce numerical data that can be aggregated to indicate performance). Qualitative tools include portfolios, public performances, juried competitions, oral examinations or the defense of a thesis, and interviews; quantitative means include standardized tests, locally developed tests, licensure exams, surveys, and observations.[17]

Under this five-year plan, SLCC has identified assessable skills for general education that include communicating effectively; thinking critically; appreciating aesthetic expression; interacting productively; and understanding, analyzing, accessing, and using information.[18] The assessment plan identifies staffing needs, staff development, resources needed, and supervision of assessment and includes forms for faculty and the administrators of programs and services to complete.[19]

New Mexico State University

New Mexico State University (NMSU, at Las Cruces) has an outcomes assessment program that is "intended to provide an ongoing review of the institution's effectiveness."[20] Assessing institutional effectiveness includes documenting the university's accomplishments in achieving defined purposes and using the information gathered for institutional planning and program improvement.

> [NMSU's broad assessment efforts include] a commitment to evaluate institutional effectiveness throughout the teaching and learning process and the environment which supports it. Initial implementation of the program has focused primarily on the assessment of student learning and academic achievement—both because [they are] central to the institutional mission and because of the size and long-term nature of implementation, involving as it does all colleges and academic departments within the university. However, all aspects of institutional performance are receiving their share of assessment attention as implementation proceeds.[21]

Montana State University–Bozeman

One of the stated goals of Montana State University–Bozeman is to provide quality undergraduate and graduate educational programs.

> Toward this end, the university has established a program of student outcomes assessment with the goal of improving student learning and performance. . . . [Furthermore, the university sees assessment as] an ongoing collaborative effort by faculty and administrators. In conjunction with guidelines published by the Northwest Association of Schools and Colleges, faculty have established learning objectives for all undergraduate degree programs and developed departmental

plans for evaluating the extent to which students are achieving the stated objectives. The university follows a decentralized approach to assessment, with departments responsible for assessing specific academic programs and appropriate faculty groups responsible for assessing general education. The administration's role is to coordinate and document assessment activities taking place at the department level as well as to conduct surveys and provide data of institutional scope.[22]

It merits mention that each academic department has its own assessment plans and reports.[23]

Truman State University

Truman State University (Truman, at Kirksville, Missouri), formerly known as Northeast Missouri State University, has conducted assessment since the 1972–1973 academic year, with accountability being the catalyst for assessment.

> The university master plan calls on the university to "assess" its assessment procedures, to encourage faculty involvement in assessment, to develop a comprehensive assessment plan, to expand its use by administrators and by faculty in reviewing their own disciplines, to increase scholarly activity in the area, and to increase its use in the graduate program areas. The plan . . . sets specific quantifiable goals for almost all areas of the university's work. Assessment needs to continue to demonstrate accountability for use of the state's resources and provide evidence of student learning—the basis of awarding "degrees with integrity."[24]
>
> [At Truman, assessment] helps the university focus on its mission, concentrate its resources on instruction, monitor progress toward planning goals, and demonstrate institutional integrity and high-quality education.[25]

Truman's assessment methods and instruments collect data that measure the breadth of liberal arts learning, the nationwide competitiveness of a major, and student satisfaction. Designed to evaluate the institution's effect on the student's progress and personal experiences, the assessment program gathers data annually from each student.

Truman reports that as a result of the assessment process the curriculum has been revised. Moreover, a growing number of faculty have embraced outcomes assessment and the use of portfolios. For example, in 1999, Truman reported the following:

> Portfolio assessment continues to grow both in terms of the number of students turning in portfolios and the number of faculty who have participated in portfolio evaluation. Faculty evaluation of student work found in portfolios has led to important changes to the new liberal studies program—particularly in regard to interdisciplinary work (by adding the junior interdisciplinary seminar course) and in regard to quantitative reasoning (by adding a statistics requirement). Portfolio assessment has also moved toward a more objective method of judging interdisciplinarity through inter-rater reliability. Beginning in fall 1999, all entering students will be required to submit a portfolio prior to graduation.[26]

The value of assessment to the university is evident in a blunt statement about its disappointment with some of the assessment findings:

> The most discouraging assessment results for this year, as they were last year, are found in the freshmen–junior testing area, designed to see if students are improving

their knowledge and skills in general education areas. The CAAP tests show lower scores for juniors as compared to their freshmen scores in four out of the five areas. The academic profile for FY 1999 shows lower scores in all areas except for critical thinking. When faced with these results, the faculty may have several responses: (1) the tests are not testing appropriate skills and knowledge; (2) our students are arriving with such high scores that gains are unlikely (the ceiling effect); (3) the juniors have become more cynical about the assessment program and are putting in less effort; and/or (4) the curriculum is not consciously developing the skills [that] are tested. Any or all of these factors may be at work. The university has changed its general education program and perhaps this will help. On the other hand, the new liberal studies program may demonstrate even less of a "match" for the tests given, and scores may decline more. In any event, the assessment committee and the faculty discipline committees will need to review these tests for appropriateness. Many believe that motivation to do well is a strong factor and that we may never do particularly well unless students are given reason to do well.[27]

University of Colorado at Boulder

The University of Colorado at Boulder (CU–Boulder) applies outcomes assessment to comply with accountability requirements from state government and from the North Central Association of Colleges and Schools, its regional accrediting body.[28] A report, Assessment Methods Used by Academic Departments and Program, discusses the various methods used.[29] (See chapters 6 and 8 of this book for further discussion.) All academic programs produce self-studies as part of a seven-year review.

Similar to Truman, CU–Boulder has implemented curriculum changes as a result of a faculty review of student performance. For example, the English department, "disturbed by the number of minor grammatical errors in even the best of student writing, added a writing component to two introductory courses."[30]

Academic Libraries and University Assessment Planning

As discussed in chapter 1, standards applied by the regional accrediting bodies that pertain to academic libraries are becoming increasingly less prescriptive while the role of information literacy is becoming more pronounced. ACRL has developed *Information Literacy Competency Standards for Higher Education* (see chapter 6 of this book) and "Standards for College Libraries 2000 Edition" to assist academic libraries in articulating their roles within their institution.[31] The four institutions included in the following subsections have responded to the role of the academic library and information literacy differently.

St. Louis Community College

In its assessment plan, St. Louis Community College's statement on general education identifies "access, analyze, understand, and use information" as a set of assessable skills. It defines these as follows:

Information is stored in a variety of formats and locations. One must understand the need for information and have the ability to identify what type of information is needed before one can access, evaluate, and effectively use information for life-long learning. The student

> understands how information and information sources are identified, defined, and structured
>
> evaluates sources and information in terms of quality, currency, usefulness, and truthfulness
>
> understands the variety of ways information sources are physically organized and accessed
>
> incorporates a variety of tools to search for necessary information
>
> uses technology to access, retrieve, and communicate information
>
> gathers information for planned purposes[32]

While the academic library is not specifically assigned a role in conducting assessment, the library could apply ACRL's aforementioned tools to become an active participant in measuring the outcomes specified in these skills related to information literacy.

Montana State University–Bozeman

In spring 1997, the core curriculum committee at Montana State University–Bozeman developed a core curriculum survey to help assess general education. A report of survey findings stated that there were inadequate information resources in the library (using the word "impoverish") and that some courses did not require the use of the library. As a result, the report recommended that faculty require library research in their courses and proof students used the library. It stated that using the library should be a basic "general core criterion" and that learning to use the library should become a goal of the university.[33]

New Mexico State University and University of Colorado–Boulder

Goal 4 in the strategic plan of NMSU's library identified the following information literacy objectives:

> Develop instructional initiatives/programs to support the university mission, extending from basic information literacy competencies to lifelong learning skills. To do this the library will
>
> - develop competencies for NMSU students
> - offer more sections of information literacy course
> - provide more course-integrated library instruction
> - allocate instructor time
> - provide electronic classrooms
> - provide computer assisted instruction
> - develop programs for distance education
> - promote services to faculty and students[34]

UC–Boulder's strategic plan contains strategic directions. These state that the libraries should do the following:

> Maintain an information literacy program based on the libraries' student-centered learning approach where inquiry is the norm, problem solving is the focus, and critical thinking is the key element. This program should be designed to prepare students to
>
> - determine the nature and extent of the information needed
> - access needed information effectively and efficiently
> - evaluate information and its sources critically and incorporate selected information into their knowledge base and value system
> - use information effectively to accomplish a specific purpose
> - understand the many economical, legal, and social issues surrounding the use of information, while accessing and using information ethically and legally[35]

Both NMSU and UC–Boulder libraries have written mission statements and strategic plans with goals and objectives inclusive of information literacy initiatives. Objectives from NMSU's goal 4 are more output-based; whereas CU–Boulder's objectives, for the most part, are stated as student learning outcomes.

How does CU–Boulder determine that it successfully (or, for that matter, unsuccessfully) meets the strategic directions covering its information literacy program? While the objectives appear to be assessable as outcomes, measures were not evident in the library's published work reviewed. As a result, the question cannot be answered as of this writing.

Conclusion

Some colleges and universities have developed written guides to help their faculty and staff develop and implement assessment plans, and these guides can be useful elsewhere as more institutions prepare assessment plans. At the same time, colleges and universities are conducting assessments and making the results available internally and externally, adding to the modest body of literature and knowledge concerning assessment practices and processes. Many of these writings, however, have not appeared in the literature of library and information management. While objectives and learning skills covering information literacy appear in institutional assessment and library strategic plans, few outcomes assessment measures for information literacy have been publicized. Still, as this chapter and book reflect, there is now some guidance in how to interpret outcomes assessment measures and how to collect relevant data. The next chapter adds a practical and needed perspective. It presents one academic library's evolving assessment plan for student learning outcomes on specific, basic competencies and skills for information literacy.

> *Outcomes assessment examines the quality and effectiveness of academic programs through examination of student learning.*[36]

Notes

1. Truman State University, Chapter III: History and Philosophy of Assessment at Truman, 12. Available: http://www2.truman.edu/assessment99/99CH3HIS.pdf. Accessed 21 Jan. 2001.

2. Ball State University, Assessment Workbook. Available: http://www.bsu.edu/IRAA/AA/WB/contents.htm. Accessed 28 Oct. 2000.

3. Ball State University, Designing a Department Assessment Plan, Example 2. Available: http://www.bsu.edu/IRAA/AA/WB/ch1_ex2.htm. Accessed 28 Oct. 2000.

4. Ball State University, Designing a Department Assessment Plan. Available: http://www.bsu.edu/IRAA/AA/WB/chapter1.htm. Accessed 28 Oct. 2000.

5. Ibid.

6. Ball State University, Shaping Department Goals and Objectives for Assessment. Available: http://www.bsu.edu/IRAA/AA/WB/chapter2.htm. Accessed 28 Oct. 2000.

7. Ball State University, Using Surveys for Assessment. Available: http://www.bsu.edu/IRAA/AA/WB/chapter3.htm. Accessed 28 Oct. 2000. See also Ball State University, Using Tests for Assessment. Available: http://www.bsu.edu/IRAA/AA/WB/chapter4.htm. Accessed 28 Oct. 2000.

8. Ball State University, Using Performance-Based Measures for Assessment. Available: http://www.bsu.edu/IRAA/AA/WB/chapter5.htm. Accessed 28 Oct. 2000. See also Ball State University, Other Assessment Techniques. Available: http://www.bsu.edu/IRAA/AA/WB/chapter7.htm. Accessed 28 Oct. 2000.

9. Ball State University, Reporting and Using Results. Available: http://www.bsu.edu/IRAA/AA/WB/chapter8.htm. Accessed 28 Oct. 2000.

10. Columbia Basin College, Office of Institutional Research and Marketing, *Columbia Basin College: Assessment Resource Guide* (Pasco, Wash.: Columbia Basin College, 1999), 4–11.

11. Montana State University–Bozeman, Assessment Techniques and Activities. Available: http://www.montana.edu/aircj/assess/Techniques.html. Accessed 21 Jan. 2001.

12. ACAT is an examination from the Accreditation Council for Accountancy and Taxation. Information is available at http://www.acatcredentials.org. Accessed 6 Feb. 2001. CLEP is the College Level Examination Program from Educational Testing Service. Information is available at: http://www.ets.org. Accessed 6 Feb. 2001. MFAT is the Major Field Assessment Test, developed by Educational Testing Service. Information is available at http://www.ets.org. Accessed 6 Feb. 2001.

13. College BASE stands for broadly based achievement test. Information is available at http://www.arc.missouri.edu/collegebase. Accessed 6 Feb. 2001. ACT COMP is the College Outcomes Measures Program produced by ACT, Inc. (formerly American College Testing Program). The COMP appears to have been replaced by the CAAP, the Collegiate Assessment of Academic Proficiency examination from ACT, Inc. Information is available at http://www.act.org/caap/index.html. Accessed 6 Feb. 2001.

14. Concordia College, Assessment for People Who Don't Have Enough Time to Do Assessment. Available: http://www.cord.edu/dept/assessment/Wkshp99_00Time.htm. Accessed 17 Nov. 2000.

15. St. Louis Community College, *The Assessment Plan and a Five-Year Plan for Full Implementation of Assessment at St. Louis Community College* (St. Louis, Mo.: St. Louis Community College, 1999), 3.

16. Ibid., 7.

17. Ibid., 9–10.

18. Ibid., 18–19.

19. Ibid., 24–9.

20. New Mexico State University, Institutional Outcomes Assessment Plan & Progress Report: Focus on Student Learning. Available: http://www.nmsu.edu/Research/iresearc/outcomes/assessmentplan.html. Accessed 27 Oct. 2000.

21. Ibid.

22. Montana State University–Bozeman, Student Outcomes Assessment Policy: Draft. Available: http://www.montana.edu/aircj/policy/AssessmentPolicy.html. Accessed 21 Jan. 2001.

23. Montana State University–Bozeman, Assessment of Undergraduate Majors, AY98-AY99. Available: http://www.montana.edu/aircj/assess/majors/majors9899. Accessed 21 Jan. 2001.

24. Truman State University, Assessment Almanac—Chapter XX: Conclusion. Available: http://www2.truman.edu/assessment99/99CH20CON.pdf. Accessed 21 Jan. 2001.

25. Truman State University, Assessment Almanac—Chapter III: History and Philosophy of Assessment at Truman. Available: http://www2.truman.edu/assessment99/99CH3HIS.pdf. Accessed 21 Jan. 2001.

26. Truman State University, Assessment Almanac—Chapter XX.

27. Ibid. The CAAP is the Collegiate Assessment of Academic Proficiency examination from ACT, Inc. Available: http://www.act.org/caap/index.html. Accessed 6 Feb. 2001.

28. University of Colorado at Boulder, History of CU–Boulder's Outcomes Assessment Program. Available: http://www.colorado.edu/pba/outcomes/ovview/oahist.htm. Accessed 16 Nov. 2000.

29. University of Colorado at Boulder, Assessment Methods Used by Academic Departments and Programs. Available: http://www.colorado.edu/pba/outcomes/ovview/mwithin.htm. Accessed 26 Oct. 2000. See also University of Colorado at Boulder, Assessment and Accountability Practices at CU–Boulder. Available: http://www.colorado.edu/pba/qis/current/cc8.htm. Accessed 26 Oct. 2000.

30. University of Colorado at Boulder, Assessment and Accountability Practices at CU–Boulder. Available: http://www.colorado.edu. Accessed 26 Oct. 2000.

31. ACRL, *Information Literacy Competency Standards for Higher Education* (Chicago: American Library Assn., 2000). Available: http://www.ala.org/acrl/lintro.html. Accessed 5 March 2001. ACRL, "Standards for College Libraries 2000 Edition," *College & Research Libraries News* 61, no. 3 (March 2000), 175–82. Available: http://www.ala.org/acrl/guides/college.html. Accessed 5 March 2001.

32. St. Louis Community College, "Appendix C" of *The Assessment Plan and a Five-Year Plan for Full Implementation of Assessment at St. Louis Community College* (St. Louis, Mo.: The College, 1999), 4.

33. Montana State University–Bozeman, The Core Course Survey, April 1998. Available: http://www.montana.edu/wwwprov/core/CoreSurvey.html. Accessed 21 Jan. 2001.

34. New Mexico University Library, Strategic Plan 1997–2002. Available: http://lib.nmsu.edu/aboutlib/straplan.html. Accessed 16 Jan. 2001.

35. University Libraries at Boulder, Strategic Plan. Available: http://www.libraries.colorado.edu/do/lsp/frontpage.htm. Accessed 26 Oct. 2000.

36. University of Colorado at Boulder, Overview: Undergraduate Outcomes Assessment. Available: http://www.colorado.edu/pba/outcomes/ovview/ovview2.htm. Accessed 26 Oct. 2000.

3
Developing an Assessment Plan for Measuring Student Learning Outcomes

Teaching library and information literacy skills is viewed as directly affecting student outcomes because these skills support such general/liberal education outcomes as critical thinking, computer literacy, problem solving, and lifelong learning.[1]

Based on the requirements of the regional accrediting body and on standards and reports by ACRL, staff of the Mildred F. Sawyer Library at Suffolk University in Boston (hereafter referred to as the Sawyer Library) decided to create a student learning assessment plan. They reviewed information from articles and reports from other libraries and higher education institutions to identify and determine a process by which they would write the first formal assessment plan for the library. This chapter discusses the development effort, and appendix B includes the resultant assessment plan for student learning outcomes.[2] A similar effort produced the library's first faculty assessment plan as shown in appendix C.

Recognizing the Need for an Assessment Plan for Student Learning Outcomes

The requirements of the New England Association of Schools and Colleges (NEASC) concerning assessment of institutional effectiveness is most succinctly stated in its Policy of Institutional Effectiveness. "An institution's efforts and ability to assess its effectiveness and use the obtained information for its improvement are important indicators of institutional quality." Its policy states that assessment enhances institutional effectiveness but notes that assessment efforts can vary among institutions. Furthermore, it asserts that assessment is not a one-time activity; rather, it is evolutionary, ongoing, and incremental. Finally, the policy notes that "assessment and accreditation share the common goal of enabling the institution to reach its fullest academic potential by providing the highest quality education possible. In pursuing that goal, institutional autonomy should be preserved, innovation encouraged, and the distinct character of each institution recognized and honored."[3]

The six library and information resources standards presented in NEASC's 1992 *Standards for Accreditation* are input, output, and process based.[4] In 1998–1999, NEASC studied its current *Standards for Accreditation* and found that technology should either comprise a separate standard or be subsumed under standard 7: "Library and Information Resources." While NEASC did not incorporate the student learning assessment findings from this study in a draft revision of the existing standards, a memorandum concerning proposed revisions in the standards for accreditation stated that revisions in standard 7 "are meant to address the significant changes wrought by technology on information resources at member colleges and universities."[5]

The proposed changes in standard 7 are clear: First, the emphasis of the revision is reflected in the shift of the title of the standard from "Library and Information Resources" to "Information Resources and Services." The phrase "library and information resources" in standard 7 was often replaced by "library, information resources, and services." NEASC also added a new emphasis on information literacy. In standard 7.4, one sentence has been changed to "The institution provides appropriate orientation and training for use of these resources, *as well as instruction in basic information literacy*" (the italics denote the addition to this sentence). The revisions also strengthened standard 7.5 on resource sharing with other institutions to include "appropriate support for distance education learning students and faculty."[6]

The proposed NEASC revisions are silent on library assessment. Using the revised standard 7.4 on information literacy and existing standard 7.6 on usage, together with the Policy on Institutional Effectiveness, the staff decided to leverage both points as a stated need for the Sawyer Library to become a stronger institutional partner regarding the assessment of information literacy and student learning outcomes.

ACRL documents were invaluable when identifying the possible components of an outcomes assessment plan. A most useful document was the 1998 report from the Task Force on Academic Library Outcomes Assessment, which provided and discussed definitions that clarify the context of assessment:

> Outcomes, as viewed by the task force are *the ways in which library users are changed as a result of their contact with the library's resources and programs.* Satisfaction on the part of a user is an outcome. So is dissatisfaction. The task force considers simple satisfaction a facile outcome, however, too often unrelated to more substantial outcomes that hew more closely to the missions of libraries and the institutions they serve. The important outcomes of an academic library program involve the answers to questions like these:
>
> > Is the academic performance of students improved through their contact with the library?
> >
> > By using the library, do students improve their chances of having a successful career?
> >
> > Are undergraduates who used the library more likely to succeed in graduate school?

Does the library's bibliographic instruction program result in a high level of "information literacy" among students?

As a result of collaboration with the library's staff, are faculty members more likely to view use of the library as an integral part of their courses?

Are students who use the library more likely to lead fuller and more satisfying lives?

Questions like these are difficult to answer. That is to say, empirically rigorous measurement of academic library outcomes is hard to do. This task force firmly posits, however, that it is *changes in library users* such as the ones addressed in these questions that comprise the outcomes with which academic librarians should be concerned. It may be that these outcomes cannot be demonstrated rigorously, or in a short period of time, or even by very many institutions. The task force believes that they can be measured, however, and their relationship to resource inputs and program inputs can be meaningfully determined through careful and lengthy research.[7]

For the most part, academic libraries have been successfully measuring inputs and outputs. However, this report provides this sharp distinction:

"Outputs" serve to quantify the work done, i.e., number of books circulated, number of reference questions answered. They are valuable measures for making decisions about staffing levels, setting library hours of operation, and so forth. However, they do not relate these factors to the overall effectiveness of the library in affecting user outcomes. It is important to track the library's outputs, but insufficient for assessing outcomes.[8]

The task force determined that outcomes assessment conducted by libraries should be user, not institution, centered; that it needed to measure the contributions that the library made to the educational mission of the university or college; and that the use of a variety of methodologies to corroborate conclusions drawn was necessary.[9] Outcomes assessment measures changes in library users as a result of their contact with a library's programs, resources, and services as related to the stated educational goals of the parent institution.

A second ACRL document providing direction is "Standards for College Libraries 2000 Edition." Definitions of outcomes, outputs, and inputs were taken from the aforementioned Task Force on Academic Library Outcomes Assessment *Report*. The standards also provide a rationale for increasing the role of the academic library in the educational process:

While electronic publications have increased in number, publications on paper and microtext have continued, making it necessary for librarians to store, provide, and interpret information in multiple formats. With the increase in the availability of information, user expectations have risen substantially. Librarians are increasingly expected to assist users in evaluating the information they receive. These changes evince an evolving role for college librarians, one that suggests a closer partnership with users and a greater responsibility for the educational process.[10]

These standards also provide guidance on the relationships between library planning and assessment: Outcomes assessment measures how and what library goals and objectives achieve, provides accountability for student achievement, and serves as a mechanism for improving library practices.

Furthermore, academic librarians should provide assistance to users concerning methods of information retrieval, evaluation, and documentation, thereby facilitating student academic success and encouraging lifelong learning.[11]

ACRL also released *Information Literacy Competency Standards for Higher Education* in 2000. The standards define information literacy thus:

> [Information literacy is] a set of abilities requiring individuals to recognize when information is needed and have the ability to locate, evaluate, and use effectively the needed information. . . . Information literacy forms the basis for lifelong learning. It is common to all disciplines, to all learning environments, and to all levels of education. It enables learners to master content and extend their investigations, become more self-directed, and assume greater control over their own learning.[12]

Developing lifelong learning is central to the mission of higher education institutions. In turn, information literacy is a contributor to lifelong learning.[13]

The second part of this document identifies five standards and twenty-two performance indicators that focus upon the information literacy needs and skills of university and college students. In addition, the standards list potential outcomes as "guidelines for faculty, librarians, and others in developing local methods for measuring student learning" concerning progress toward the attainment of information literacy.[14] In using the *Information Literacy Competency Standards for Higher Education*, the staff of the Sawyer Library reviewed the standards and performance indicators, choosing those immediately supportable by the library's existing resources for inclusion in its outcomes assessment plan.

ACRL released Objectives for Information Literacy Instruction: A Model Statement for Academic Librarians in early 2001.[15] These helpful objectives, intended as suggestions for creating institutional goals and performance objectives and identifying appropriate institutional responsibilities, support the *Information Literacy Competency Standards for Higher Education* document. Staff of the Sawyer Library referred to those objectives as they developed objectives for their student learning outcomes assessment plan.

Sawyer Library staff also reviewed articles and reports from academic librarians concerning bibliographic instruction and information literacy. A study at The Citadel's Daniel Library found that outcome-focused library instruction appears to lead to skill development, improved efficiency, and a positive attitude change. The Hutchins Library at Berea College and the Jeremy Richard Library of the University of Connecticut at Stamford found that codevelopment of outcomes-based instruction by course and library faculty may be an effective approach to improving students' skills in navigating numerous library and digital resources.[16]

Two recent articles helped the Sawyer Library focus on specific student information skills needs. A study at the University of California–Berkeley found that students' perceptions about their ability to gain access to information and conduct research exceeded their actual ability to do so.[17] A study by Deborah J. Grimes and Carl H. Boening found that, at most, students only superficially evaluate Web sites and use unauthenticated Web resources rather than taking advantage of databases or Web guides provided by the library. Grimes and Boening suggest that librarians need to emphasize evaluative criteria, help students find "good" Web resources by including links to librarian-reviewed sites in the library's online public access catalog, and provide individual training for faculty members about Web resources so that they are better prepared to instruct students concerning appropriate use of the Web.[18]

In "Defining and Measuring the Library's Impact on Campuswide Outcomes," Bonnie Gratch Lindauer makes a convincing case for academic librarians to undertake outcomes assessment to "measure the ways that the library, learning resources, and computer services units make a real difference in the academic quality of life for students and faculty." Lindauer goes on to succinctly argue that the teaching of information literacy skills directly affects student outcomes, contributing to the student's development of critical thinking and instilling such values as lifelong learning.[19]

In a 2000 report for the Association of Research Libraries (ARL), Kenneth R. Smith, the distinguished service professor of economics and faculty associate to the provost at the University of Arizona, states that institutions are changing:

> [They are] moving from a model in which we package knowledge around the expertise of the faculty to a model based on the learning outcomes realized by students. These outcomes include not only what students know but also the skills they develop, what they are able to do, and the attitudes of mind that characterize the way they will approach their work over a lifetime of change. . . . [Furthermore, the institutional focus on learning] involves looking at the academic program not from the perspective of its subject matter content but from the perspective of the competencies to be developed by students. [Therefore, the library] must move from a content view (books, subject knowledge) to a competency view (what students will be able to do). Within the new environment, we need to measure the ways in which the library is contributing to the learning that the University values.[20]

Smith refers to the student learning outcomes in ACRL's *Information Literacy Competency Standards for Higher Education* while identifying additional student learning outcomes compiled from focus groups on his campus.

Identifying the Processes and Components of an Assessment Plan for Student Learning Outcomes

There is no shortage of recommendations concerning the process of creating and developing the format for assessment plans. Librarians Lois M. Pausch of the University of Illinois at Urbana–Champaign and Mary Pagliero Popp of Indiana University–Bloomington recommend that assessment plans begin with a mission statement and purpose followed by statements of expected student achievements and information concerning performance measures, evaluation, and use of the evaluative results.[21] A paper from the Schreyer Institute for Innovation in Learning, Pennsylvania State University (PSU), states that a "well-designed assessment plan starts with identifying the goals for the course or program as they relate to such areas as student learning, student attitudes, cost effectiveness, and program implementation. The student learning goals should be phrased in terms of what the students should be able to do at the end of the course."[22] Once all the goals and areas (student learning, student attitudes, cost effectiveness, and program implementation) are determined, the methods of assessment should be identified. Gloria Rogers and Jean Sando of the Rose-Hulman Institute of Technology outline eight steps to developing an assessment plan:

1. identify goals
2. identify specific objective(s) for each broad goal
3. develop performance criterion(criteria) for each objective
4. determine the practice(s) to be used to achieve goals
5. select assessment methods for each objective
6. conduct assessments
7. determine feedback channels
8. evaluate whether the performance criteria were met and the objectives achieved[23]

California Polytechnic State University's Student Learning Outcomes Assessment Model employs a similar eight-step process, but it emphasizes an evaluative feedback loop that takes the analysis and interpretation of the assessment findings from step 8 and determines "implications of results for program modification" by returning to step 3, which creates "educational objectives (EOs) for each program component."[24]

Assessment techniques and measures are difficult components to write in an assessment plan for student learning outcomes. Reflecting the literature on program and impact evaluation, PSU's Schreyer Institute for Innovation in Learning discusses formative assessment, which is the gathering of feedback during the semester, and summative assessment, which measures the course's overall success at its conclusion. Formative assessment relies on surveys, quality teams, peer evaluations, problem-solving tasks, or focus groups, while summative assessment uses multiple-choice tests, essay tests, pretest/posttest designs, control/experimental group designs, portfolios, poster sessions, presentations, case study analyses, concept maps, and interviews.[25] The Schreyer Institute also identifies assessment measures by performance objectives. For example, methods used to measure student attitudes include pretest and posttest surveys and surveys of student perceptions of how well-prepared they were for subsequent courses.[26]

The University of Wisconsin–Madison differentiates between direct and indirect learning indicators. Direct indicators include capstone course evaluation, course-embedded assessment, tests and examinations (both locally/faculty designed and commercially produced standardized tests), portfolio evaluation, pretest/posttest evaluation, thesis evaluation, and videotape and audiotape evaluation of performance. Indirect indicators rely on external reviewers, student surveying and exit interviewing, alumni surveying, employer surveying, and curriculum and syllabus analysis.[27]

An emphasis in most of the library assessment plans discussed concerns the involvement of faculty in focused information literacy instruction and outcomes assessment. Faculty involvement at the Daniel Library at The Citadel, the Hutchins Library at Berea College, and the Jeremy Richard Library of the University of Connecticut at Stamford have already been mentioned. Additionally, Pausch and Popp state the following:

Librarians should begin to work with other teaching faculty in assessment activities aimed at providing instruction in information literacy within the department's or school's curriculum. This could include helping to develop a set of learning goals and objectives that teaching faculty themselves can use in providing instruction and evaluating their students' abilities in finding and using information.

fostering a team-teaching partnership.

making a library lecture/workshop a regular part of a discipline-related course. This will require librarians to give up the idea that only they can teach the basic library information skills and . . . provide help and encouragement to teaching faculty as they incorporate the teaching of information literacy in their classes.[28]

The American Association for Higher Education's "Principles of Good Practice for Assessing Student Learning" looks at faculty-librarian collaboration in assessment from the institutional perspective:

Student learning is a campuswide responsibility, and assessment is a way of enacting that responsibility. Thus, while assessment efforts may start small, the aim over time is to involve people from across the educational community. Faculty play an especially important role, but [assessment] questions can't be fully addressed without participation by student-affairs educators, librarians, administrators, and students. Assessment may also involve individuals from beyond the campus (alumni/ae, trustees, employers) whose experience can enrich the sense of appropriate aims and standards for learning. Thus understood, assessment is not a task for small groups of experts but a collaborative activity; its aim is wider, better-informed attention to student learning by all parties with a stake in its improvement.[29]

Smith's ARL report also discusses the interaction of faculty and librarians. He contends that the student learning outcomes are often common to learning outcomes identified by faculty for departmental courses and programs. The library, he notes, could assist academic programs with student learning and assessment efforts by delivering "offerings," which are "units of learning materials designed to develop competency in specific learning outcomes that are considered important by the library and by other academic programs." The offerings, which should be incorporated into required courses, are a means to "give the library a curriculum (its own set of course segments) and an opportunity to connect this curriculum to other academic programs." Smith states that the library must internally develop these learning units and then proactively convince the faculty that the library can "contribute to the learning outcomes of the academic program," because it is unlikely that the academic department will formally request such assistance from the library.[30]

Creating the First Student Learning Outcomes Assessment Plan for the Sawyer Library

Taking all of the information and opinions gathered, the staff of the Sawyer Library began creating its student learning outcomes assessment plan. The learning outcomes that were sought should have a lifelong effect on students, and although that effect would be difficult to measure, there should be an effort to do so. While faculty involvement was essential, the staff wanted to identify and design learning modules that were in concert with their strengths and within the limits of available resources. Therefore, they identified a process by which to approach the effort to create the plan:

1. Create a rationale for the assessment effort based upon information literacy skills
2. Determine the learning outcomes (learning objectives) from the library's perspective required for student success:
    a. review the university mission statement
    b. revisit the Sawyer Library's strategic plan
    c. review other university/college planning and learning objectives documents
    d. use ACRL's documents concerning standards and information literacy
3. Determine methodologies for teaching the outcomes
4. Develop curriculum-based learning modules through which the library would present the methodologies as the effort to achieve the outcomes:
    a. understand the learning outcomes of academic degree programs
    b. create modules based upon the library's realized strengths and within its available resources
    c. determine how to convince the faculty that the library's learning modules may be integrated into academic courses to achieve shared outcomes
5. Identify ways to measure how well outcomes are being achieved (both directly and indirectly)
6. Collect data and measure the extent to which outcomes are achieved
7. Use the assessment results to improve academic programs (evaluative feedback) by incorporating results and analysis into a
    a. progress report
    b. modification/revision of the goals, objectives, and methods employed

The staff began by writing the rationale for the library's involvement in information literacy. Although they had been conducting bibliographic instruction for years, they wanted to formalize their relationship to the university's educational and learning mission and to increase the value of the library as a teaching/learning department for the faculty. Furthermore, Suffolk University is preparing for its reaccreditation in 2002; the regional accrediting body wants academic libraries involved in basic information literacy, and conducting assessment is one component of accountability for the accreditation review. As a consequence, the staff reviewed their instructional efforts and broadly identified that they offer

student orientation to library-held information resources and their role or use

explanations of the differences between scholarly and nonscholarly resources

demonstrations of the value of using Boolean searching strategies across all resources

evaluations of information sources, especially Web sites

explanations of the concept of collection development, including electronic resources

Next, it was decided to

> build on known strengths, formalizing what staff members do well into staff-taught instructional modules that they could offer the faculty

> conduct assessment practices (measures, analysis and interpretation of results, and evaluative feedback) to become familiar and comfortable with the effort made in information literacy

> develop additional learning modules as identified by library staff or requested by faculty

The rationale appears in a supporting statement, as follows:

> Outputs serve to quantify the work done, such as the number of books circulated or the number of reference questions answered. They are valuable measures for making decisions about staffing levels, setting hours of operations, etc. However, they do not relate to overall effectiveness of the library in affecting user outcomes. In addition, while it is important to track the library's inputs, they too are insufficient for assessing outcomes. In fact, the purpose of all inputs is to achieve outcomes.

> The focus to date has been on making information more accessible rather than addressing specifically the learning outcomes important to student success. The Mildred F. Sawyer Library is evolving from measuring only inputs (such as the annual and cumulative resources concerning collections, staffing, the physical facility, and installed information technologies) and outputs, to identifying and measuring learning outcomes (student known content, developed skills and abilities, and acquired attitudes and values). We need to measure the ways in which the library is contributing to the learning that the university values. Because of the nature of information access and availability, the major focus for the library concerns improving student information literacy competencies and skills.

> Student outcomes are statements about what students will know/think/be able to do as a result of library programs. They are not statements about what the library should/could do to bring about desired outcomes. Conducting student learning outcomes assessment is designed to improve services. The results may not be able to stand up to scientific scrutiny, but they should provide informed judgment on what does and does not work. Specifically, the staff want to identify the ways in which library users are changed as a result of their contact with library resources and programs:

>> Does the library's bibliographic instruction program improve students' information literacy?

>> Are students' learning attitudes improved through their contact with the library?

>> As a result of collaboration with the library staff, are faculty members more likely to view use of the library as an integral part of their courses?

Although group bibliographic instruction is one of the primary teaching methodologies, the staff still wanted to review how information literacy was being taught in higher education. First, they looked at the 1990 Comparative Data on Teaching Goals Inventory (commonly known as TGI) in Four-Year Colleges. Of the 52 TGI included in *Classroom Assessment Techniques: A Handbook for College Teachers*, two involve information literacy skills and attitudes. In cluster 1: higher-order thinking skills, 49 percent of faculty rated "develop ability to synthesize and integrate information and ideas" as essential. In cluster

4's liberal arts and academic values, 33 percent of faculty rated "develop a life-long love of learning" as essential. Furthermore, none of the classroom assessment techniques (CATs) presented in *Classroom Assessment Techniques* directly focused on information literacy.[31] Only CAT 39 (process analysis) could be adapted to the Sawyer Library's information literacy instruction process. As a result, the library staff decided to develop their own assessment techniques for the classroom.

Another difficult component in developing the assessment plan concerned the identification and application of direct and indirect measures. Although the staff had experience in conducting student and faculty satisfaction surveys, they had little experience in using direct measures. The direct measures identified in the assessment plan may not be adequate to reflect a change in student behaviors over their programs of study; only application and analysis will reveal weaknesses and strengths. As one example of the difficulty concerning the deployment of direct assessment measures, the staff identified and developed a measure that they thought directly contributed to improving lifelong attitudes:

> The statistics from the proxy server (which enables students and faculty to access and retrieve information from our subscription electronic databases from off-campus locations such as their homes) reveal that over 50 percent of use is from 9:00 P.M. until 1:00 A.M. This high level of use suggests that the Sawyer Library has made it convenient to use library resources from home. The timing of this heavy use could be interpreted as "family friendly." That is, hang out at home with the family. Then, once the children are in bed, log onto the library and do your course research work. By providing the proxy server, we are "changing" students' lives by enabling them to be at home for family hour and then access the library to do their work without leaving home.

However, this measure is indirect because there could be commitments other than family time; the life change is temporary (it only lasts for as long as they are students with access to the proxy server); and the proxy server is a means to the end, not the end in itself. The end is still information literacy because the students could be using the databases via the proxy server ineffectively and inefficiently.

The effort to create the Sawyer Library's student learning outcomes assessment plan involved library staff, faculty, the reaccreditation committee concerned with library and information resources and services, and the input of anyone willing to review it. It appears as appendix B.

Creating the First Faculty Support Outcomes Assessment Plan for the Sawyer Library

Students are the primary users of the Sawyer Library. However, faculty also use the library's resources, and efforts to provide them with services and support should also be assessed. Initially, library staff had not intended to develop a faculty support assessment plan; instead they focused their efforts only on students. However, faculty reviewing the student learning outcomes assessment plan wanted to be included. The first attempt at a faculty support assessment plan employed the same process used to create the initial draft of the student plan and incorporated faculty outcomes with student learning outcomes into one "grand" plan. The resulting document was unwieldy and not as easy to use as the staff wanted for their first, mission-critical assessment effort. Instead, they decided to use the same planning and development process used for the student plan and create a separate faculty support assessment plan.

Fortunately, there are several good articles from which to draw ideas concerning faculty outcomes. The previously mentioned study by Grimes and Boening concerning student use of the Web found that there is a gap "between what instructors expect of their students and what students are actually doing with Web resources." Those authors suggest that librarians "should direct in-service training, one-on-one collaboration, publicity, Web page design, and other activities toward faculty [and] encourage instructors to invite them to the classrooms and to bring their classes to the campus libraries."[32] Objectives for both of these suggestions can be planned, measured, and assessed. Pausch and Popp suggest that librarians help develop learning goals and objectives "that teaching faculty themselves can use in providing instruction and evaluating their students' abilities in finding and using information."[33] They also recommended Philip Pacey's suggestions of seven ways in which this specific objective and others may be accomplished: Librarians should:

1. keep a positive attitude toward other faculty who are willing to promote library skills themselves or in close partnership with librarians
2. make informal (and very subtle) efforts to foster, update, and develop library skills in other teaching faculty
3. incorporate library skills in in-house and other professional development programs offered to the faculty
4. continue to provide subject-oriented information skills training (especially true for subject librarians)
5. engage in more or less continuous programs of educating users through the promotion of services, especially new services (based on the commercial idea of selling your products)
6. recognize that students learn from one another often without the help of a professional
7. devote time and effort to the development of a possible common core curriculum unit devoted to various skills—information skills, study skills, etc.[34]

Lindauer identified two faculty-related library and learning resources objectives accompanied by several performance indicators. The objectives relate to "research, scholarly/creative works and community service [and] excellence in teaching and equivalent academic support roles."[35] ACRL's Task Force on Academic Library Outcomes Assessment *Report* includes a chart of selected good-practices outcomes with examples of outcomes, indicators, and data collection methods from a work of Lindauer about assessable changes in the skills and attitudes of faculty incorporating library and learning resources-based learning objectives.[36]

Sawyer Library's efforts to develop a faculty support outcomes assessment plan was similar to that of developing the student learning outcomes assessment plan. Because students are the primary users, creating the learning assessment plan initially received priority over that of the faculty plan (included as appendix C). However, both plans will be continuously developed and improved as the staff of the Sawyer Library learns more about conducting assessment.

Conclusion

Academic libraries must engage in assessment efforts to demonstrate the value of student learning and faculty support to the university community. Almost any institutional academic or administrative computing center could negotiate contracts with information providers, set up proxy servers to authenticate users, and provide access to electronic information resources. Students often state that everything is free on the Internet; they often do not see an immediate need for libraries and librarians. However, librarians have two important roles unduplicated elsewhere on the campus: They understand *quality* collection development and can teach about most, if not all, aspects of the information-seeking and evaluation process.

Assessment plans enable libraries to state formally and measure their efforts in supporting learning and research. Because of recent interests expressed by the accrediting bodies and library organizations (e.g., ACRL and ARL), information literacy is an excellent starting place for any student learning outcomes assessment effort. Academic libraries need to

create a mission statement

identify learning goals and objectives

write a strategic plan to quantify and qualify goals and objectives

advance instructional methods to support the learning objectives

develop learning modules (offerings) to deliver the methods

identify and apply outcomes measures

compile, analyze, and interpret information from application of these measures

use the evaluative results to revise learning objectives in the effort to improve teaching methods, modules, and student learning

While assessment plans for student learning outcomes should be the priority for the initial assessment effort, academic libraries should also consider developing a faculty assessment plan shortly thereafter.

Creating a library outcomes assessment plan is neither the easiest project a library staff will undertake nor is it the most difficult. There is a body of supportive library and higher education literature as well as library assessment workshops (especially from ACRL) and Web-based information from libraries that have successfully created and implemented plans. However, while the Sawyer Library staff were writing the assessment plan, it became clear that more efforts were needed to increase available library-based information focusing on identifying and applying practical outcomes assessment measures and on the development and application of successful instructional techniques that positively affect student learning.

Library assessment efforts should be integrated into the parent institution's efforts. What should a library do if the institution is not undertaking assessment efforts, or if the assessment efforts are not a priority? Librarians should assume a leadership role—develop and conduct an assessment program even if their institution's efforts are nonexistent or practically so. There is increasing understanding, knowledge, and support within the academic library community concerning student and faculty outcomes assessment—librarians will not be alone in this effort.

> *The primary change that outcomes assessment has caused,*
> *it seems, is to place responsibility on all institutional units*
> *for providing evidence of their contributions to desired*
> *educational outcomes and to incorporate outcomes assessment*
> *into organizational planning and improvement.*[37]

Notes

1. Bonnie Gratch Lindauer, "Defining and Measuring the Library's Impact on Campuswide Outcomes," *College & Research Libraries* 59, no. 6 (Nov. 1998), 549.

2. Bonnie Gratch Lindauer from the City College of San Francisco has developed a more general plan that covers performance objectives, performance indicators, and data sources to assess library instruction, resources, equipment, space, access, student learning outcomes, and staff requirements. Bonnie Gratch Lindauer, Assessing Community Colleges: Information Literacy Competencies and Other Library Services and Resources. Available: http://fog.ccsf.cc.ca.us/~bgratch/table.html. Accessed 11 March 2001.

3. New England Assn. of Schools and Colleges, Commission on Institutions of Higher Education, Policy on Institutional Effectiveness (22 Jan. 1992). Available: http://www.neasc.org/cihe/instuteffect.htm. Accessed 17 Dec. 2000.

4. New England Assn. of Schools and Colleges, Commission on Institutions of Higher Education, *Standards for Accreditation* (Bedford, Mass: New England Assn. of Schools and Colleges, Inc., Commission on Institutions of Higher Education, 1992), 23–4.

5. New England Assn. of Schools and Colleges, Commission on Institutions of Higher Education, Memorandum, 17 Nov. 2000. Available: http://www.neasc.org/cihe/memo_proposed_revision_standards.htm. Accessed 14 Dec. 2000.

6. New England Assn. of Schools and Colleges, Commission on Institutions of Higher Education. Standards for Accreditation: Draft. Available: http://www.neasc.org/cihe/draft_standards_for_accreditation.htm. Accessed 14 Dec. 2000.

7. ACRL Task Force on Academic Library Outcomes Assessment, *Report* (Chicago: American Library Assn., 27 June 1998). Available: http://www.ala.org/acrl/outcome.html. Accessed 5 March 2001.

8. Ibid.

9. Ibid.

10. ACRL, "Standards for College Libraries 2000 Edition," *College & Research Libraries News* 61, no. 3 (March 2000), 175–82. Available: http://www.ala.org/acrl/guides/college.html. Accessed 5 March 2001.

11. Ibid.

12. ACRL, *Information Literacy Competency Standards for Higher Education* (Chicago: American Library Assn., 2000). Available: http://www.ala.org/acrl/ilintro.html. Accessed 5 March 2001.

13. Ibid.

14. Ibid.

15. ACRL, Objectives for Information Literacy Instruction: A Model Statement for Academic Librarians. Available: http://www.ala.org/acrl/guides/objinfolit.html. Accessed 21 May 2001.

16. Timothy K. Daugherty and Elizabeth W. Carter, "Assessment of Outcome-Focused Library Instruction in Psychology," *Journal of Instructional Psychology* 24 (1998), 29–33; Susan Henthorn, Hutchins Library (Berea College) Bibliographic Instruction Program Evaluation. Available: http://www.berea.edu/library/BIEVAL/Pre-test-Post-test.html. Accessed 5 March 2001; Shelley Cudiner and Oskar R. Hamon, An Active Learning Approach to Teaching Effective Online Search Strategies. Available: http://www.thejournal.com/magazine/vault/A3223.cfm. Accessed 20 Dec. 2000.

17. Patricia Davitt Maughan, "Assessing Information Literacy among Undergraduates: A Discussion of the Literature and the University of California–Berkeley Assessment Experience," *College & Research Libraries* 62 (Jan. 2001), 83.

18. Deborah J. Grimes and Carl H. Boening, "Worries with the Web: A Look at Student Use of Web Resources," *College & Research Libraries* 62 (Jan. 2001), 20–1, 22.

19. Lindauer, "Defining and Measuring," 546, 549.

20. Kenneth R. Smith, New Roles and Responsibilities for the University Library: Advancing Student Learning through Outcomes Assessment (4 May 2000). Available: http://www.arl.org/stats/newmeas/outcomes/HEOSmith.html. Accessed 5 March 2001.

21. Lois M. Pausch and Mary Pagliero Popp, Assessment of Information Literacy: Lessons from the Higher Education Assessment Movement. Available: http://www.ala.org/acrl/paperhtm/d30.html. Accessed 26 Nov. 2000.

22. The Pennsylvania State University, Schreyer Institute for Innovation in Learning, Designing an Assessment Plan: The Case of Statistics 200. Available: http://www.inov8.psu.edu/news/assessplanforstat.htm. Accessed 5 March 2001.

23. Gloria M. Rogers and Jean K. Sando, Stepping Ahead: An Assessment Plan Development Guide. Available: http://www.rose-hulman.edu/IRA/IRA/steppingahead.html. Accessed 5 March 2001.

24. California Polytechnic State University, General Education, Student Learning Outcomes Assessment Model. Available: http://www.calpoly.edu/~acadprog/gened/modelasmt.htm. Accessed 5 March 2001.

25. The Pennsylvania State University, Schreyer Institute for Innovation in Learning, Assessment. Available: http://www.inov8.psu.edu/faculty/fassess.htm. Accessed 5 March 2001.

26. The Pennsylvania State University, "Designing an Assessment Plan."

27. University of Wisconsin–Madison, Office of the Provost, VI. Assessment Instruments and Methods Available to Assess Student Learning in the Major. Available: http://www.wisc.edu/provost/assess/manual/manual2.html. Accessed 5 March 2001.

28. Pausch and Popp, Assessment of Information Literacy.

29. Leon F. Gardiner and others, "Principles of Good Practice for Assessing Student Learning," in *Learning through Assessment: A Resource Guide for Higher Education* (Washington, D.C.: American Assn. for Higher Education (1997), 11–12. Available: http://www.aahe.org/assessment/principl.htm. Accessed 5 March 2001.

30. Smith, New Roles and Responsibilities.

31. Thomas A. Angelo and K. Patricia Cross, *Classroom Assessment Techniques: A Handbook for College Teachers*, rev. ed. (San Francisco: Jossey-Bass, 1993), 403–6.

32. Grimes and Boening, "Worries with the Web."

33. Pausch and Popp, "Assessment of Information Literacy."

34. Philip Pacey, "Teaching User Education, Learning Information Skills; or Towards the Self-Explanatory Library," *The New Review of Academic Librarianship* 1 (1995),100–2.

35. Lindauer, "Defining and Measuring," 567.

36. ACRL, Task Force on Academic Library Outcomes Assessment, *Report*.

37. Lindauer, "Defining and Measuring," 548.

Information Literacy Assessment Efforts of Some Academic Libraries

Assessment is a process in which goals and learning objectives of a program or course are identified and data are collected from multiple sources to document student, teacher, or program achievement of those goals and objectives.[1]

A number of efforts in academic libraries demonstrate accountability through the application of assessment, predominantly in information literacy programs. These efforts tend to concentrate on outputs, but some of them are starting to focus on student learning outcomes. Moreover, the tendency has been to collect indirect evidence that the outputs or outcomes have been achieved. Such evidence typically focuses on observation and the perceptions of students about what they have learned or their satisfaction with library instructional programs. Students' perceptions might be gathered by means of a focus group interview or questionnaire. Evidence might even come from the use of IPEDS (Integrated Postsecondary Education Data System)-type statistics of the U.S. Department of Education's National Center for Education Statistics.

Library-developed initiatives in assessment present a rationale for information literacy and focus on student learning outcomes applicable across programs and class levels. They also identify the library's role in the educational process, list the desired competencies that students should master, articulate a strategy for librarians to work directly with the teaching faculty, and provide instructional programs that develop and, it is argued, improve student skills in information seeking, evaluation, and use.

This chapter discusses what some libraries have done to advance the assessment of student information-literacy learning outcomes. It also highlights three approaches to assessment, those of Indiana University–Bloomington, the California State University system, and The Citadel. These approaches do not necessarily involve sophisticated, complex, and time-consuming data collection. In fact, some approaches and data collection efforts are highlighted for their simplicity in providing meaningful insights into the accomplishment of an assessment plan.

Some Libraries Accepting the Call for Assessment

As discussed in chapter 1, regional accrediting bodies and ACRL have encouraged academic institutions and, by extension, their libraries to engage in assessment and to demonstrate the extent to which student learning outcomes have been achieved. As a consequence, librarians have tried to determine different ways to measure institutional effectiveness and educational quality and have explored how to use the results to improve library services and operations in such a way that libraries play a more central role in the educational process—preparing students for graduation and for being lifelong learners.

Palomar College Library

Palomar College (San Marcos, California) Library, for instance, views outcomes in terms of guiding students "through the process of defining their information needs and locating and evaluating appropriate materials." As a result, students will:

- know that assistance is readily available in the library
- gain a comfort level in using the library
- know what resources are available in the library
- know how to use the library from their homes
- have success in completing assignments
- have information skills that they can employ throughout their lives[2]

As discussed in subsequent chapters, outcomes must be clearly and precisely framed so that there is no ambiguity in how they are interpreted. Clearly, the above-mentioned outcomes lack that degree of specificity.

The Palomar College Library identifies "information competent people" as ones who "have learned how to learn. They know how information is organized, how to find information, and how to use information in such a way that others can learn from them. They are people prepared for lifelong learning because they can always find the information needed for any task or decision that presents itself."[3] It merits mention that the outcome related to lifelong learning is supported by the library's Guidelines for Creating Library Assignments, which regards an effective library assignment as one that develops students' information competency by providing them with an opportunity independently to "add to their knowledge base and empower them throughout their lives."[4] To repeat, outcomes assessment seeks to provide evidence of the extent to which this competency has been gained and retained over time. In other words, has the library's instruction had a lasting impact on students' lives?

In its plan, the library has tried to "engage the entire college community in revising the mission of the college so that it includes information competency" and to integrate skills related to information competency in all subjects across the curriculum. The staff want to create a set of information skills that will be widely accepted as developing information competent students. They also want to strengthen the partnership between faculty and librarians, provide opportunities for faculty and staff development, and identify new ways of evaluating students' information competency.[5]

Ohio University Libraries

The University Libraries at Ohio University (Athens) maintain that information competency should be part of every general education course, and to this end, the staff have identified eight core information competencies. The provision of a basic education on the achievement of information competency, they maintain, "requires a minimum of two [student-library] encounters, one at the freshman level and a second at the sophomore or junior level."[6] Furthermore,

> The goal of student information competency can be embedded even more deeply into the curriculum by going beyond its introduction into general education requirement courses. To be most effective, information-seeking skills need to be course-specific and curriculum-specific at the time when students have a need for the information and instruction. Information competency education needs to be cumulative and so pervasive at Ohio University that it is inescapable.[7]

The librarians at Ohio University propose three possible scenarios to implement information competency skills: as an enhancement of an already established course in a discipline, as a discipline-specific course, or through assessed mastery.[8]

Iowa University Libraries

The university libraries and the faculty of the college of liberal arts of the University of Iowa (Iowa City) cosponsor the University of Iowa Information Literacy Initiative (UIILI), which is a specific initiative identified in the libraries' strategic plan. UIILI's core consists of a comprehensive set of general information literacy skills, or outcomes, that can be customized and integrated (depending on discipline or interdisciplinary area) into undergraduate courses. For example, for the completion of course assignments, there are Web links to clarify points and provide additional guidance if the students need it.[9]

A proactive effort to be institutionally involved in information literacy programs formally incorporates information competencies and skills into the goals and objectives of the library's strategic plan. For example, the University of Iowa identifies instructional services as a library goal and strategic direction:

> **GOAL 1**
>
> Provide instructional services for the university community that supports each individual's ability to use information resources effectively (supports University's goals 1, 2, and 3).
>
> *Strategic Direction*: Make information literacy an integral part of the undergraduate curriculum.[10]

There are outputs-based initiatives and indicators to measure progress toward success. The library also articulates information competence outcomes that may be incorporated into courses or curriculum goals:

An information literate individual will be able to

- articulate a problem statement

  develop a thesis statement

  explore information sources to become familiar with the topic

  introduce strategies for refining a topical assignment into a well formulated research question

- identify appropriate information sources

  understand the value of and differences among potential information sources in a variety of formats

  retrieve information from library catalogs, Web pages, and citation databases and compare results

- develop a search strategy

  select keywords and synonyms and related terms to use in the search

  construct search statements using limiters and Boolean operators

  refine the search strategy as needed

- evaluate the information retrieved

  determine if the information found satisfied the information need

  apply criteria to evaluate accuracy, authenticity, and worth of information to their problems

- organize, synthesize, and apply information to the problem

  read the materials found and select the main ideas

  synthesize the information found in order to construct new theories or concepts

  use quotes appropriately

- understand the scholarly communication system

  distinguish between scholarly and popular sources

  understand the peer review process.

- understand ethical use of information

  understand principles of academic freedom

  exercise both responsibilities and rights in their use of copyrighted information

  understand what constitutes plagiarism[11]

As will be discussed in chapters 6 and 8, these expectations exceed student learning outcomes and introduce another type of outcomes: research outcomes. Still, the perspective tends to focus on students, and outcomes have not been cast in terms of faculty and other groups. It would seem that libraries need to develop a set of broader learning and research outcomes.

Florida International University

Another example of a proactive effort is that of the Florida International University (FIU, Miami) Libraries. The libraries submitted a proposal to their university faculty senate recommending an information literacy requirement for all undergraduate students. The librarians directly related the need for the information literacy initiative specified in the standards set by the regional accrediting body and the university's strategic plan.[12] Information literacy would be integrated across the curriculum, and assessment would be conducted at the classroom and program levels.

FIU strategically places the need for information literacy in the libraries' mission statement:

> Information literacy enhances the pursuit of knowledge at the university by preparing students to think critically and use information for their academic, professional, and personal lives. The information literate individual can recognize the need for information, can locate it using a variety of media and technologies, and can evaluate information in order to use it effectively. Information literate students have the flexibility to take these skills from their formal education and use them throughout life as citizens and professionals and as a means toward continued learning. Colleges, schools, programs, and the libraries share the responsibility for helping students develop information literacy skills. Successful implementation of information literacy goals is achieved by integration across the curriculum and depends on active participation of all parties.[13]

To support the statement, the libraries specify eight goals and twenty-four information literacy objectives identifying skills for students to become information literate.[14] The libraries also identified student learning expectations and assessment measures that they linked to specific courses. Expectations are met when students accomplish specified tasks, such as "use the FIU Catalog to find resources in various formats and locations in the libraries. . . . Assessment of student learning. . . occurs through activities completed within class as well as out of class. Librarians and faculty may collaborate on the development of course assignments which may form the basis of course-embedded, performance-based assessment."[15]

University of Wisconsin–Madison

In October 1998, the Wisconsin Association of Academic Librarians (WAAL) adopted specific competencies for information literacy for statewide implementation. (See appendix D.) Individual campuses in the state were encouraged to consult the list of competencies when they develop instructional programs intended to help students become more proficient users of information. The library instruction program at the University of Wisconsin–Madison (UW–Madison), as one example, did this. Its rationale has a learning objective:

> Lifelong learning skills are essential in order for students to function successfully in today's global information society where the volume of information resources grows exponentially and where increasingly sophisticated information technologies proliferate. A critical component of lifelong learning is the ability to locate, evaluate and use information from a variety of sources. From primary school on, such information literacy skills need to be an integral part of students' learning experiences. Yet many students enter the university with minimal information literacy skills. Few have any understanding of information seeking as a systematic process or the critical thinking skills necessary to select and evaluate information

once they find it. Even students who have had formal instruction in information seeking in primary and/or secondary school have had little experience with a library system as complex and rich in resources—both print and electronic—as the UW–Madison's. As they progress through their academic careers, students need opportunities to learn and then apply increasingly complex research skills.[16]

UW–Madison envisioned a systematic approach to developing a sequence of information-seeking skills, beginning with freshmen and sophomores, progressing to juniors and seniors, and even to graduate students. Librarian- and faculty-developed programs included course-related lectures, exercises, hands-on computer instruction sessions, orientation tours and presentations, library guides, point-of-use instructional handouts, workshops, online tutorials and instructional assistance, and other approaches to instruction.

Examples of Assessment Plans for University Libraries

This section highlights the assessment plans developed by three university libraries. Appendixes E, F, and G reproduce some instruments that one of them uses to assess outcomes. The major attraction of these instruments is their simplicity: They do not require extensive amounts of time or knowledge of the research process (discussed in chapter 7) to use.

Indiana University–Bloomington Libraries

In their 1998–2002 long-range plan, the libraries at Indiana University (IU–Bloomington) include, as a "learning environment" goal, the development and use of "assessment mechanisms for services and for collections."[17] An assessment plan for information literacy supports this goal. That plan addresses basic and advanced information literacy. The basic level has two goals and seven measurable objectives. For example, the first goal is "appreciates the richness and complexity of the information environment" and one of the objectives is "You will be able to describe the wide array of information sources available and discuss their appropriateness for a given information problem."[18] Possible ways to measure the accomplishment of the objectives are through essay examination, oral reports, a practicum in the library, and a written evaluation assignment.

Advanced information literacy is defined thus:

As individuals move forward in their fields of study and specialization, their information needs change, and the level of information literacy they need changes as well. It is appropriate that academic departments take responsibility for advanced/research level information literacy in collaboration with library subject specialists and other librarians with specialized knowledge. The discipline-specific nature of these skills dictates that departments develop specific goals and objectives customized to the unique culture of their approach to teaching a specific discipline and preparing scholars in these fields.[19]

The assessment plan includes additional goals and measurable objectives for advanced information literacy.

Most interestingly, IU–Bloomington's assessment plan also identifies "learning strategies" for both basic and advanced information literacy. For example, basic information literacy "can be achieved through a combination of learning strategies. There is no one mix that works for all students in all situations." According to the assessment plan, some of the possibilities include the following options:

Offer a basic, one-credit course in information literacy, or develop a similar course within the department.

Schedule class library visits tied to a specific course assignment.

Develop specific information assignments that teach students basic literacy skills in the context of a particular course or assignment.

Develop a series of self-directed learning activities that teach basic information literacy in the context of a particular course or discipline.

Develop a course home page that links to useful information sources.

The IU–Bloomington Libraries also announced that they "have experience in all of these activities and will assist any department or faculty member who wants to incorporate one or more of these strategies. The libraries will be developing a package of resources that will be available to all departments."[20] In summary, IU libraries' assessment plan appears to be specifically directed at faculty in a proactive effort to convince them of the willingness and value of the libraries in strengthening information literacy skills for students at all levels.

California State University System

The libraries of the California State University (CSU) system have been involved with student outcomes assessment since April 1995, when the information competence work group was charged with developing an information competence program. In January 1997, the work group submitted a report to its institutional parent, the Commission on Learning Resources and Instructional Technology (CLRIT), identifying core information literacy competencies:

In order to be able to find, evaluate, use, communicate and appreciate information in all its various formats, students must be able to demonstrate the following skills:

1. Formulate and state a research question, problem, or issue not only within the conceptual framework of a discipline but also in a manner in which others can readily understand and cooperatively engage in the search.
2. Determine the information requirements for a research question, problem, or issue in order to formulate a search strategy that will use a variety of resources.
3. Locate and retrieve relevant information, in all its various formats, using, when appropriate, technological tools.
4. Organize information in a manner that permits analysis, evaluation, synthesis, and understanding.
5. Create and communicate information effectively using various media.
6. Understand the ethical, legal, and socio-political issues surrounding information.
7. Understand the techniques, points of view, and practices employed in the presentation of information from all sources.[21]

The CSU system empowered the Information Competence Initiative (ICI) to accept proposals and make grants to academic departments for "the purpose of incorporating information competence into the learning outcomes of their programs" to "ensure that all students graduate with a mastery of this vital skill."[22] "Requirements" to participate specify that learning outcomes should be included and should be consistent with ACRL information literacy standards:

> Activities must result in a statement of information competence as a required learning outcome for the degree program.
>
> Activities must result in assessments that certify that a student has met the information competence requirement.
>
> An appropriate member of the library faculty must play an integral role in the project activities.
>
> Specified learning outcomes must be consistent with the ACRL standards on information literacy for higher education. (See http://www.ala.org/acrl/ilcomstan.html.)[23]

To promote and increase the understanding concerning information literacy necessary to participate in ICI's grant opportunities, a comprehensive information literacy fact sheet was developed in October 2000 and made available. It defines information literacy, provides a rationale for why students need to be information literate, discusses responsibilities for information literacy teaching and learning, and identifies options for information literacy programs (e.g., orientation sessions, general education courses, and capstone classes in the major).[24]

The twenty-two campuses of the CSU system have a unified strategic plan that includes the following goal and strategy:

GOAL B   Instruction

The efforts of the CSU in information competence have been guided by a set of six key principles. These principles were developed through intensive consultation among library faculty, discipline faculty, and library administrators and were endorsed by the CSU Academic Senate.

1. Information competence should be taught across the curriculum.
2. Information competence needs to be addressed at all levels—freshman, introduction to the major, and graduate level.
3. There needs to be an articulation of information competence skills between the K–12 and the university.
4. Requirements for information competence at the freshman, transfer, and senior level should be considered.
5. Tools for faculty to teach information competence should continue to be developed.
6. Emphasis should be placed on faculty development opportunities in information competence. . . .

STRATEGY 1   Skills Development, Collaboration, and Assessment

Propose requirements for student information competence,
create instructional modules, and develop assessment plans.

Information competence is vital to success at all levels of a student's academic career. The ability to recognize an information need, develop effective search strategies, select the appropriate tools, [and] retrieve, evaluate, and organize the information is essential for all students. Library and discipline faculty will explore the possibility of information competence as entrance and exit requirements that will not increase units.

In order to determine the success of our information competence program, student skills will need to be assessed. First, an initial assessment will be conducted to determine the current skill level. Then, ongoing assessment will occur to determine student advancement in meeting targeted information competence skills. Discipline faculty will also be surveyed for their opinion of student progress.[25]

To meet this assessment need, the information competence work group formed a task force in 1998 to conduct a systemwide assessment of basic information competence skills.

[The assessment project design was to employ] a nonlinear method of data collection to determine information competence. The method is phone interviews based on a scenario corresponding to the CSU-identified information competencies and selected questions covering related areas. The scenarios (problems or tasks) are the heart of the assessment, and they are designed to allow students to demonstrate the steps they would take to solve the information problem presented by the scenario. The interviewers chart student's responses to the scenarios into a carefully designed matrix.[26]

The sample was to include about 3,300 students, and the phone interviews were to cover key demographics, work experience, and previous library instruction and were to take the interviewee through two core information competency scenarios. The interviewers read the hypothetical scenarios to the students and asked them about the strategies they would use in completing the hypothetical tasks. Their responses were recorded.[27]

The Citadel

The Citadel, in Charleston, South Carolina, has been conducting student learning outcomes assessment since the mid 1990s. It primarily employs three measures: pre/posttesting, focus groups, and reviewing class products. Librarians at the Daniel Library know that students need guidance in identifying, evaluating, and retrieving information resources effectively and in applying information searching strategies efficiently. Collaborating with faculty members, the librarians have developed outcome-focused instruction and have applied simple outcome assessment to measure changes in skill development, library usage efficiency, and perceptions about the library.[28]

Appendix E presents the pre/posttest instrument used in academic year 1999–2000 for first-semester freshmen. The test required students to document the steps they would use to find books on earthquakes and then to repeat the process to find journal articles. At the same time, they were asked about the use of their high school library and their comfort and skills in using that library. The librarians carefully measured each student's response about searching for materials on earthquakes against a "perfect" answer. Each correct step received one point. Students were given credit if they could adequately describe a process or resource so that the scorer could understand what they meant. The evaluated responses were summed, and a mean score for the freshman class was determined.

Following the pretest phase, cadets received library instruction on the use of the library and searching information resources. They were retested later in the semester on the same research question. This time, however, the page concerning high school library use was replaced with one asking essentially the same questions but directed at the use of the Daniel Library at The Citadel. Again, librarians measured the students' step-by-step responses about their search for materials on earthquakes against the same "perfect" answer applied in the pretest.

As measured by The Citadel in academic year 1999–2000, the mean pretest score was 2.15 on the pretest and 5.23 on the posttest. In other words, cadets prior to the receipt of library instruction got two steps in the search process as measured against the perfect process. After having received the instruction, they could complete five steps as measured against the perfect answer.

The Citadel revised the freshman pre/posttest for use during academic year 2000–2001. (See appendix F.) The two "how would you conduct the research" related questions remained. However, the scale applied to the questions concerning previous library experience were replaced from a "how true scale" to a "how many times"; this change is expected to yield more-useful information. A second set of perception questions were developed, and responses focus on the extent of agreement. The same "perfect response" is applied to the responses, and a class mean is calculated. Again, the posttest is given after the cadets receive library instruction. The library usage questions are also asked, but they are directed at the Daniel Library.

In addition to the freshman assessment, The Citadel measures progress for sophomores in two classes. During the second class period of Psychology 209, students receive a pretest concerning how they would find an article in a psychology journal on a specific topic. They are also given a questionnaire similar to the one provided to the freshmen concerning library usage and attitude. An outcome-focused library instruction follows. To complete the assessment, students are asked to complete the same questionnaire during the course's last class period and detail the search process for finding a psychology article on a specific topic. In addition, the library convenes a focus group of professors and current students.

Past assessments have showed that outcome-focused library instruction (for this particular course) improved searching skills, reduced the number of times that students visited the library because their efficiency at searching improved, and improved their perceptions of the Daniel Library.[29]

The librarians also conduct outcomes assessment in History 203. (See appendix G.) Students complete a questionnaire following three hours of library instruction. Then the librarians convene focus groups to discuss further students' reactions to the instruction. A review of the responses from the questionnaire and the discussion from the focus groups provide evaluative feedback, and the librarians use it to improve instruction sessions.

A review of the assessments from History 203 confirmed the conclusions drawn from Psychology 209: Searching skills improved, students made more efficient use of the library, and their perceptions of the Daniel Library improved following outcome-focused library instruction.[30] The Citadel's collaborative library-faculty approach, the applications of pre/posttests, the use of focus groups, and a review of courses illustrate a positive application of outcomes assessment. The appropriate and timely review of results discovered through the evaluative feedback loop resulted in changes made to both data collection instruments and the teaching methodologies used in the instruction sessions. Clearly, there is a joint library-faculty effort to improve instruction and student learning.

Conclusion

Academic librarians may proactively support, participate in, and sometimes lead efforts to develop and implement student learning outcomes on a campus. The most visible initiatives are the instructional-based goals and objectives contained in library strategic plans and the identification of information literacy competencies and skills, many of which have measurable objectives. However, the objectives may still require some refinement to make them more applicable to outcomes assessment. (See chapter 8.) Both the WAAL and ACRL have model lists of identified information literacy skills and competencies for higher education students. IU–Bloomington Libraries have an exemplary assessment plan. The libraries of the CSU system are leaders in creative and practical systemwide information literacy initiatives and in the large-scale assessment of student learning outcomes of graduate students. The Citadel's Daniel Library has applied simple yet effective pre/posttesting and focus groups for freshmen and specific sophomore courses that measure student improvement in information seeking and retrieval skills, efficiency in using the library, and students' image of the library after receiving outcomes-focused library instruction. The Citadel's feedback mechanisms are used to evaluate and improve the assessment instruments and library instruction on a continuous basis.

> *Information competent people have learned how to learn.*
> *They know how information is organized, how to find*
> *information, and how to use information in such a way that*
> *others can learn from them. They are people prepared for life-long*
> *learning because they can always find the information needed*
> *for any task or decision that presents itself.*[31]

Notes

1. Assessment Planning Committee, Indiana University Bloomington Libraries, An Assessment Plan for Information Literacy (1 May 1996). Available: http://www.indiana.edu/~libinstr/Information_Literacy/assessment.html. Accessed 8 Feb. 2001.

2. Palomar College Library, Bibliographic Instruction Classes. Available: http://daphne.palomar.edu/Library/infocomp/bi.htm. Accessed 29 Jan. 2001.

3. Palomar College Library, Why Do We Need Information Competency? Available: http://daphne.palomar.edu/Library/infocomp/whyic.htm. Accessed 29 Jan. 2001.

4. Palomar College Library, Guidelines for Creating Library Assignments. Available: http://daphne.palomar.edu/Library/infocomp/guidelines.htm. Accessed 29 Jan. 2001.

5. Palomar College Library, Palomar's Plan to Achieve Information Competency. Available: http://daphne.palomar.edu/Library/InfoComp/palomarplan.htm. Accessed 29 Jan. 2001.

6. University Libraries at Ohio University, Information Competency. Available: http://www.library.ohiou.edu/libinfo/librarydocs/infocomp/infocomp.htm. Accessed 29 Jan. 2001.

7. Ibid.

8. Ibid.

9. University of Iowa Libraries, Strategic Plan 2000–2004. Available: http://www.lib.uiowa.edu/lib/strategic-plan.html. Accessed 29 Jan. 2001. See also University of Iowa Libraries, The University of Iowa Information Literacy Initiative. Available: http://www.lib.uiowa.edu/user-ed/uiii/index.html. Accessed 29 Jan. 2001.

10. Ibid.

11. University of Iowa Libraries, Outcomes: Information Literacy Skills and Concepts. Available: http://www.lib.uiowa.edu/user-ed/uiii/outcomes.html. Accessed 29 Jan. 2001.

12. Florida International University Libraries, Information Literacy at Florida International University: A Proposal for Faculty Senate from Undergraduate Council. Available: http://library.fiu.edu. Accessed 8 Feb. 2001.

13. Florida International University Libraries, Information Literacy Mission Statement. Available: http://library.fiu.edu. Accessed 9 Feb. 2001.

14. Florida International University Libraries, Information Literacy Goals and Objectives. Available: http://library.fiu.edu. Accessed 9 Feb. 2001.

15. Florida International University Libraries, Information Literacy: Library Instruction Outcomes. Available: http://library.fiu.edu. Accessed 8 Feb. 2001.

16. University of Wisconsin–Madison, GLS Library Instruction Program, Achieving Information Literacy: Guidelines. Available: http://www.library.wisc.edu/libraries/Instruction/achinfolit.htm. Accessed 8 Feb. 2001.

17. The Indiana University Bloomington Libraries, Realizing Our Potential. Available: http://www.indiana.edu/~libadmin/mission.html. Accessed 8 Feb. 2001.

18. Indiana University Bloomington Libraries, Assessment Planning Committee, An Assessment Plan for Information Literacy (1 May 1996). Available: http://www.indiana.edu/~libinstr/Information_Literacy/assessment.html. Accessed 8 Feb. 2001.

19. Ibid.

20. Ibid.

21. California State University Northridge, University Library, Information Competence: A Set of Core Competencies. Available: http://library.csun.edu/susan.curzon/corecomp.html. Accessed 30 Jan. 2001.

22. California State University Northridge, University Library, Information Competence Initiative, Call for Proposals: 2001. Available: http:// library.csun.edu/susan.curzon/ic_call_for_proposals.html. Accessed 11 Feb. 2001.

23. Ibid.

24. California State University, Information Literacy Fact Sheet (2 Oct. 2000). Available: http://library.csun.edu/susan.curzon/fact_sheet.html. Accessed 11 Feb. 2001. An example of a link that describes information literacy projects conducted at several CSU campuses, including California Polytechnic State University at San Luis Obispo, Northridge, San Marcos, Monterey Bay, and California Polytechnic State University at Pomona is available from Dr. Susan C. Curzon, chair of the information competence work group and dean of the University Library at the Northridge campus. See http://library.csun.edu/susancurzon/infocmp.html.

25. CSU Council of Library Directors, California State University, *Working Together: A Strategic Plan for the CSU Libraries* (June 2000), 44–6. Available: http://www.calstate.edu/tier3/SLI/2000-Lib_Strategic_Plan.pdf. Accessed 11 Feb. 2000.

26. Kathleen Dunn, California State University, *Assessment Methodology*. Available: http://www.csupomona.edu/~kkdunn/Icassess/ictaskforce.html. Accessed 11 Feb. 2001.

27. Kathleen Dunn, California State University, *Background, and Methodology*. Available: http://www.csupomona.edu/~kkdunn/Icassess/ictaskforce.html. Accessed 11 Feb. 2001. See also California State University, *Information Competence Assessment Project*. Available: http://www.csupomona.edu/~kkdunn/Icassess/ictaskforce.html. Accessed 11 Feb. 2001; and Kathleen Dunn and Jo Bell Whitlatch, Poster Session: Assessing Student Information Competence in the California State University, California Academic and Research Librarians (CARL) Annual Conference, Long Beach, 6–7 Oct. 2000. Available: http://www.csupomona.edu/~kkdunn/frontpage.html. Accessed 8 Feb. 2001.

28. Elizabeth W. Carter and Timothy K. Daugherty, "Library Instruction and Psychology—A Cooperative Effort," *Technical Services Quarterly* 16, no. 1 (1998), 33–41; Timothy K. Daugherty and Elizabeth W. Carter, "Assessment of Outcome-Focused Library Instruction in Psychology," *Journal of Instructional Psychology* 24 (March 1997), 29–34.

29. Ibid.

30. Ibid.

31. Palomar College Library, *Why Do We Need Information Competency?*

5

Moving Public Libraries toward Outcomes Assessment

What will be different for the client?[1]

Public libraries are experiencing many of the same pressures as are academic libraries. For example, local government has increasingly demanded accountability among public libraries. Accountability is monitored through the application of performance measures that deal with outputs rather than simply measuring inputs and processes. In addition, public libraries have abandoned prescriptive national standards in favor of locally developed plans dealing with the effectiveness of library services and with service priorities specifically directed toward users. These plans incorporate goals and objectives, and they examine activities by means of measurable, evaluative results. Public libraries are increasingly applying surveys that reflect the extent of user satisfaction with library services as outputs and as an indirect assessment of outcomes. They use these surveys as evaluative data to suggest which services need improvement and as part of a planning cycle. It is presumed that accountability increases as performance measures are compiled, compared, and reported in a cross-jurisdictional manner and as the reported percentages increase.

Accountability

Institutions of higher education are not alone when they are expected to prove and improve institutional effectiveness as part of an increased demand for accountability. Educators Sheila S. Intner and Elizabeth Futas defined public library accountability as follows:

> Public money supports public libraries. Members of the public are held accountable in their own lives for their actions, including spending money, so they expect

the same from their institutions. And this is right and proper. As citizens we want to know where our money goes, how it gets there, and what it buys. We hold government officials accountable for how tax money is collected, contracted, and consumed. Libraries need to show how their expenditures of tax dollars benefit the public.[2]

At the same time that governmental fiscal accountability was on the rise, performance measure advocates urged government to report not only how much they spent but also how efficiently they expended taxpayer dollars and what their spending achieved.[3] At the same time, the public asked if it was getting sufficient value for the money expended.

> [In public libraries] we have also had a move in accountability away from measuring the resources that go into libraries and toward measuring services people receive from libraries. . . . [W]e are moving toward more service-oriented measures that help to show what the library accomplished with its money.[4]

Some librarians argued that application of performance measures would result in better management decisions, strengthen legislative oversight, and increase accountability.[5]

In 1980 the Public Library Association (PLA) of the American Library Association published *A Planning Process for Public Libraries* instead of a new edition of national, professionally determined prescribed standards.[6] PLA, in effect, was stating the following:

> We don't know what your library ought to look like in your community. We don't know enough about your situation to tell you, and we have an absence of theory to tell us what each library ought to look like. But we will give you a tool that will help you plan how to be the library your community needs.[7]

At that time, most public libraries defined *excellence* as meeting or exceeding state or national standards. However, library programs that exemplified excellence in one community may not be relevant in a neighboring community. For example, differing populations require differing library services, such as a locality with households of school-aged children would want different library services than seniors in a retirement community.[8] Public libraries consciously moved to empirically determined, locally developed standards to meet the demands for accountability by addressing the individual and unique library needs of communities at the local level.[9]

Excellence in public libraries is to be defined locally by each library determining its role in the community through an assessment of community needs. The local planning process that replaced the national standards refined its library service "roles" or "responses" over the years; roles or responses are defined in terms of "what a library does, or offers, to the public in an effort to meet specific community needs." Roles, or later responses, provide library planners with a mechanism for linking identified community needs with specific library services and programs.[10] Chapter 6 of this book discusses the thirteen services responses.

In applying the planning process, a public library selects and prioritizes appropriate service responses based upon identified and quantified community needs. The resultant planning document identifies the outcomes being achieved in general terms within the context of stated goals. Each objective supporting a goal specifies how a public library expects "to measure progress toward reaching the outcome, a standard against which to compare that measure, and a date or time frame by which time the standard should be met."[11] Therefore, the planning process uses output measures, and rather than being based upon national standards, performance measures are internally applied to answer the local questions "What are you trying to do?" and "Are you accomplishing it?"[12]

The public library planning process recognizes three primary measures: first, the number of people served by a service or program; second, users' opinion about how well the library services meet their needs. This opinion could be about either the quality or the impact of the service. The determination of quality is based on asking the people receiving the service to express what they think through a survey, a focus group, or a personal interview. Third, the library applies measures that determine the number of service units or service transactions that it provides. These measures reflect, for instance, circulation counts, the number of reference questions asked and answered, and the number of programs presented.[13]

Performance Measures and Standards

While the PLA and its members have operated without national standards for more than a decade, the abandonment of the prescribed standards has not necessarily been viewed as entirely positive. David N. Ammons, senior associate at the University of Georgia's Carl Vinson Institute of Government, believes that public interest in governmental services and accountability of operational efficiency and effectiveness increases when performance measures are reported within the context of comparative, cross-jurisdictional standards.[14] He noted that

> [PLA's standards have shifted] from initial efforts to prescribe appropriate levels of financial support and staff credentials to the formulation of qualitative library goals, and eventually expanded to include more quantitative standards pertaining to library collection, facilities, services, and performance. . . . [T]he standards prescribed acceptable travel time for library patrons, library operating hours, collection size and quality, collection maintenance practices, library staffing levels, and physical characteristics of the library facility and served the cause of librarians whose operations fell below the prescribed numbers and who wished to use the standards as a peg for demonstrating and remedying local deficiencies.
>
> [The standards could be easily applied as a basis to] compare local collection, staffing, and facility characteristics with national prescriptions and identify areas of conformance or deficiency.[15]

As a result, the measures emerging from the standards could also be used to compare one community with other communities in the nation.

Ammons identified two problems concerning governmental services and accountability. First, there is a lack of appropriately applied performance measures. He acknowledged four categories of performance measures: workload, efficiency, effectiveness, and productivity measures. Workload measures provide basic counts of activities or efforts (e.g., library visits or total circulation). The numbers may be examined over several reporting periods to identify trends or sometimes may be combined with other data to form more-revealing indicators of efficiency or effectiveness. Efficiency measures reflect the relationship between the quantity of outputs and the amount of resources consumed in the production or delivery of resources (e.g., unit costs or employee hours per library hour open). Effectiveness measures address the amount of service activity or the extent to which objectives are met (e.g., percentage of reference questions answered, circulation per capita, and registered patrons as a percentage of total population). Productivity measures combine efficiency and effectiveness in a single indicator.[16]

Despite the claims of local government officials to the contrary, most cities and counties place limited emphasis on and make little use of performance measures.[17] Ammons suggests that the lack of application of performance measures is, in part, because the "arguments extolling the usefulness of performance measurement simply have failed to convince many local government administrators."[18] In addition, "the lack of existence of valid and reliable measures of efficiency and effectiveness leads one to conclude that local governing bodies have not insisted on deploying adequate performance measurement systems."[19]

As for public libraries, Ammons points out that PLA's initiatives "emphasize the importance of community goal setting, management practices, and planning processes but tend to address outputs and results in a conceptual, rather than concrete, manner."[20] However, although PLA "has distanced itself from standards it once promoted," it now "publishes performance statistics that may be a richer source of evaluative data than the formally declared standards ever were."[21] Here, Ammons is referring to the *Public Library Data Service Statistical Report 2000*, designed to aid library managers to "identify top performing libraries, compare service levels and technology usage, and provide documentation for funding requests."[22] The data contained in the year 2000 report were collected from more than 700 public libraries. Categories include financial information, library resources and per capita measures, annual use figures, and technology in public libraries.

Ammons' second identified problem is that the public "is not engaged" in performance measures because such measures must be made interesting to the general public to gain its attention:

> How can performance measurement be made interesting to the general public? A logical place to begin, then, would be with the development of indicators that compare local performance with standards, norms, or the performance of other recognizable jurisdictions.
>
> [For example, the] average scores of local elementary and high school students on standardized tests are much more interesting when presented in comparison to national or state averages."[23]

He provides an example from a public library:

> Does it interest the people of Loveland, Colorado, for example, to know that their public library circulates 467,179 items and responds to 33,000 reference questions per year, as reported in that city's 1993 budget? Would it interest them—and the local media—more to know that the corresponding "per capita" rates of 11.99 and 0.87, respectively, place Loveland's public library in the nation's upper quartile for circulation and above its population category's median for reference transactions per capita? The raw numbers for circulation and reference questions would be unlikely to garner a headline in the local newspaper, but the refined figures and comparisons just might.[24]

Ammons states that public and media interest in standards-based ratings and cross-jurisdictional comparisons of performance indicators "may prompt greater attention to more customary measures of efficiency and effectiveness as a means of understanding the local standing" and may expand the number of comparisons of local government functions. "If so, that expansion would serve the interests of citizen education and participation, and would almost assuredly enhance accountability."[25]

Outputs to Outcomes: What Will Be Different for the User?

Although the literature on public library planning and evaluation discusses outcomes, most of the examples to date might be more appropriately characterized as outputs. The lifelong effect or impact of library services on the individual is infrequently measured. However, public libraries using PLA's planning process are developing standards that focus on the ends rather than the means, are now looking at outcomes as well as outputs, and are applying evaluative feedback to revise inputs in the ongoing effort to improve services.

The application of user surveys to gauge user opinions as an assessment of public library performance dates back at least to the 1980s. *ASQ: Alternative Tools for Information Need and Accountability Assessments by Libraries* was intended to make available to the California library community an approach to assess

- the information needs of patrons and potential patrons
- accountability, whether patron needs have been met[26]

Using the *ASQ* model, the data collected would

translate library experience and potential into human terms in several senses. One sense is that the approach talks to users and potential users in their own human terms, rather than in library or system terms. The other is that the resulting data is useful in translating library experience and potential beyond counts of library inputs and outputs and the sheer movement of nonhuman materials into the terms of human experience that speak eloquently to voters and policy makers. In essence, the research approach described here adds a "human interest" dimension to the repertoire of library research tools.[27]

Some *ASQ* surveys asked users to identify ways in which they were helped by the books, records, tapes, or magazines at a library. The data could then be turned into an outcome—that is, the resources helped them to

get ideas or gain an understanding of something

accomplish something

make contact with others

rest or relax

be motivated to do something

feel like they belonged or were not alone

get pleasure or be entertained[28]

The ASQ user survey methodology was clearly an early effort

> to move the library's attention on measuring what the library contains (inputs) and output measures such as counting library visits per capita, program attendance per capita, reference transactions per capita, reference completion rate, title fill rate, circulation per capita, and so on to the resources and services the library does provide, the things the person likes or dislikes about the library, and the activities the person would like the library to pursue.[29]

Another example of applying user surveys to gain a better understanding of library use was conducted in Connecticut. Survey data showed that people used public libraries primarily to borrow books and use reference services, that they used libraries in other towns to obtain more or better materials, and that the location of a public library was a factor in predicting use. Using the survey results, it was possible to conclude that a library in a convenient location will draw people; that librarians should emphasize collection development; and that to develop a society of library users the public would have to acquire the library "habit."[30]

PLA's planning process identifies information literacy as one of the service responses. This service response frames the provision of services to the user thus:

> The library will provide training and instruction in skills related to locating, evaluating, and using information resources of all types. Teaching the public to find and evaluate information will be stressed over simply providing answers to questions. The library will provide access to information in a variety of formats and will offer public Internet training and access. Library staff will be knowledgeable about how people seek information and learn.[31]

Using this service response, it is possible to identify possible measures to consider when developing objectives. These objectives could emphasize outputs that focus on the total number of users served, such as the number of people who attended information literacy classes, the number of people who accessed computer-based information modules, and the number of people assisted by library technology aides.[32] They might also address outcomes dealing with how well the service meets the needs of people served, such as the percentage of people who used information literacy services who indicated on a survey that the information was provided in a timely manner, the percentage of people who attended an information literacy class who indicated on a survey that the class was satisfactory or excellent, and the percentage of people attending a class on using technology who indicated that their confidence in their ability to use computerized reference tools has increased.[33] The first set of measures are quantifiable outputs, whereas the second set of measures are indirect outcomes based upon application of user satisfaction surveys. A higher level of outcomes—direct outcomes—would examine if (how) the contact with the library produced a change in users. Did that contact increase their ability to engage in critical thinking or problem solving?

Conclusion

Public libraries are gaining a greater acceptance of and, presumably, use of output measures. They are also looking at evaluation as a means to examine and demonstrate the effectiveness of their services and expenditures. As state librarian Amy Owen has remarked,

> I think there's an increasing awareness also that the role of evaluation is "not to prove, but to improve." This is an important insight. The notion of evaluation that we grew up with is that we were going to make a judgment. But if we look at evaluation not as making some final judgment on goodness or badness but as providing information to help us to do better, evaluation becomes a different kind of tool.[34]

As this chapter has indicated, public libraries are facing many of the same issues as are higher education institutions: demands for increased accountability; the introduction and application of local (community-based) standards in place of prescriptive (national, regional, and state) standards; a planning process emphasizing local service priorities; and the development of plans that contain goals, objectives, and activities with measurable performance results. While the most recent public library planning process primarily labels "outputs" as "outcomes," it is evident that some effort in the public library community has attempted to differentiate between the terms. Public libraries are employing indirect outcomes assessments when they ask their users about the difference that library collections, services, and programs make to their lives. It is only a matter of time before direct outcome assessment measures are deployed, and to this end, it is hoped that the next chapters will be as useful to public librarians as they should be to academic librarians.

. . . outcomes matter.[35]

Notes

1. Amy Owen, "So Go Figure: Measuring Library Effectiveness," *Public Libraries* 26 (spring 1987), 23.
2. Sheila S. Intner and Elizabeth Futas, "Evaluating Public Library Collections," *American Libraries* 25, no. 5 (May 1994), 410.
3. David N. Ammons, "Overcoming the Inadequacies of Performance Measurement in Local Government: The Case of Libraries and Leisure Services," *Public Administration Review* 55 (Jan.–Feb. 1995), 37.
4. Owen, "So Go Figure," 21.
5. Ammons, "Overcoming the Inadequacies of Performance Measurement," 37.
6. Vernon Palmour and others, *A Planning Process for Public Libraries* (Chicago: American Library Assn., 1980).
7. Owen, "So Go Figure," 21.
8. Sandra Nelson for the Public Library Assn., *The New Planning for Results: A Streamlined Approach* (Chicago: American Library Assn., 2001), 1.
9. Brenda Dervin and Kathleen Clark, *ASQ: Alternative Tools for Information Need and Accountability Assessments by Libraries* (Belmont, Calif.: The Peninsula Library System, 1987), 4.

10. Nelson, *The New Planning for Results*, 63–4.

11. Ibid., 142.

12. Owen, "So Go Figure," 22.

13. Nelson, *The New Planning for Results*, 83-4.

14. Ammons, "Overcoming the Inadequacies of Performance Measurement," 38.

15. Ibid., 39.

16. Ibid., 41.

17. Ibid., 41–2.

18. Ibid., 42.

19. Ibid., 43.

20. Ibid.

21. Ibid., 45.

22. American Library Assn., Public Library Assn., *Public Library Data Service Statistical Report 2000*. Information concerning the report is available at http://www.pla.org/plds.html. Accessed 4 Feb. 2001.

23. Ammons, "Overcoming the Inadequacies of Performance Measurement," 39, 43.

24. Ibid., 43.

25. Ibid.,43, 46.

26. Dervin and Clark, *ASQ*, 1.

27. Ibid.

28. Ibid., 205, 261.

29. Ibid., 6.

30. Alicia J. Welch and Christine N. Donohue, "Awareness, Use, and Satisfaction with Public Libraries," *Public Libraries* 33, no. 4 (May/June 1994), 151.

31. Nelson, *The New Planning for Results*, 205.

32. Ibid., 207.

33. Ibid., 208.

34. Owen, "So Go Figure," 22.

35. Nelson, *The New Planning for Results*, 137.

6

Outcomes as a Type of Assessment

Learning-outcomes assessments have been a long time coming and are, in many ways, a welcome and necessary change.[1]

For years, libraries have focused on collections and the provision of information to the communities they serve. Now, they are being asked to focus on what those communities (e.g., students and the general public) will be able to do from their use of these collections and other services provided. Assessment seeks to document how libraries contribute to the learning process and, in the case of universities, to the research enterprise. For public libraries, the focus is on the ways that the library meets its *service responses* and the extent to which these service responses are met. Outcomes, a part of the assessment process, focus on results (e.g., student achievement) and enable local institutions to settle on what is important to know and to develop strategies to determine the extent to which they have been successful in achieving their assessment plan.

Outcomes are indicators of quality, a multifaceted word that can look at collections and other services. Service quality and satisfaction are also quality indicators that underlie library users' receptivity to the learning process. ACRL's Task Force of Academic Library Outcomes Assessment has taken a contrary view of satisfaction. It has erroneously labeled satisfaction as follows:

> [Satisfaction is a] facile outcome, . . . too often unrelated to more substantial outcomes that hew more closely to the missions of libraries and the institutions they serve. The important outcomes of an academic library program involve answers to questions like these:
>
> > Is the academic performance of students improved through their contact with the library?

By using the library, do students improve their chances of having a successful career?

Are undergraduate students who used the library more likely to succeed in graduate school?

Does the library's bibliographic instruction program result in a high level of "information literacy" among students?

As a result of collaboration with the library's staff, are faculty members more likely to view use of the library as an integral part of their courses?

Are students who use the library more likely to lead fuller and satisfying lives?"[2]

The previous questions applying to academic library programs could be adapted for use by public libraries:

Is the academic performance of school students improved through their contact with the library? (This question could be rewritten to focus on other communities, e.g., business, consumers, senior citizens, and parents and their roles and needs.)

By using the library, do community residents improve their chances of having a successful career?

Are primary and secondary students who used the public library more likely to succeed in college?

Do the library's programs on information and computer literacy result in a high level of such literacy among community residents?

As a result of collaboration with the library's staff, are faculty members teaching continuing education programs more likely to include a library component in their courses?

Are community residents who use the library more likely to lead fuller and more satisfying lives?

Because the role of the library in lifelong learning is difficult to isolate and quantify with any degree of precision, such questions are not easily answered, except, for instance, through the perceptions of students and college graduates as they progress through their careers and through area employers of former students. Furthermore, as discussed in chapter 9, satisfaction and service quality contribute to the success of outcomes assessment and are an indirect measure of outcomes. People are more receptive to learning when they believe that the library is trying to make their experience a satisfying one and that the library is trying to meet their high-priority expectations.

The purpose of this chapter is to explain outcomes assessment and to encourage library staff to review their assessment plan and decide on those outcomes on which they want to concentrate their resources. A key question is "How will we determine whether or not an outcome was achieved and that the result was due to the library's intervention?" In answering that question, libraries should link outcomes to their assessment plan and that of the institution. As discussed later in the chapter, librarians should also consider partnerships with the classroom faculty and others to ensure that library goals and objectives are aligned with course and program goals and objectives.

Outcomes Defined

By slightly modifying the definition contained in "Standards for College Libraries 2000 Edition," outcomes reflect how library users have changed as a result of their contact with the institution's library and its resources, services, and programs.[3] Such a definition focuses on *change* and the gathering of evidence that, in effect, presents a picture of users' information-gathering knowledge and skills before and after contact with the library. What were the users like before the library tried to produce a positive change? Was change (if it occurred) truly due to contact with library resources, services, and programs? Is the change consistent with the library's mission and assessment plan?

Outcomes focus on either the competencies (knowledge, skills, values, perceptions, and an ability to learn) that students master as a result of the courses they take or the "collective success of the program in developing the competencies of the students in the program"—competencies, it is hoped, that will influence them throughout their lives.[4] What are the learning outcomes for a course (e.g., those related to library use), and how well can students meet them upon completion of the course? Who makes that determination, and what evidence is it based on? Similarly, what are the learning outcomes that students should have mastered at the time of graduation, and how well have they, indeed, achieved that mastery? Furthermore, can they demonstrate an ability to use the knowledge gained in unstructured situations?[5]

As noted in the "Standards for College Libraries 2000 Edition," "outcome[s] assessment will increasingly measure and affect how library goals and objectives are achieved."[6] Goals and objectives specify what results are preferable and achievable. Such results can be expressed as learning or research outcomes when they indicate and measure change due to contact with the library. (See the section on distinguishing between objectives and outcomes later in this chapter.)

> [Learning outcomes are statements] of learning achievement which may take the form of the acquisition of knowledge, understanding, an intellectual skill or a practical skill. . . . They provide a clear explanation of what is required to complete successfully a module in a [program] of study providing there are strong links between the learning outcomes, the assessment criteria, and the assessment methods.[7]

They reflect what students will know, think, or be able to do as a result of having used library resources, received library services, or participated in library programs. They are not statements about what the library should or could do to bring about the desired outcome. Learning outcomes for students relate to

content (what they know)

skills and abilities they develop (e.g., communicating their solutions, becoming proficient with information-handling technology and electronic resources, and developing information and technical literacy)

attitudes and values that characterize the way they will approach work and learning over a lifetime (e.g., becoming independent and lifelong learners, and having a willingness to learn)

Learning outcomes specifically address the following set of questions:

- What do the students need to learn?
- Is the library helping them to learn it?
- How is the library doing that?
- How well is the library doing it?
- How can the library sustain and improve its effort?[8]

Not all of these questions require the use of data that document change; rather, in some instances, it is possible to deal with perceptions of the communities served (e.g., students), the job placement of college and university graduates, and partnerships between librarians and classroom teachers regarding learning.

Some academic institutions will go beyond learning outcomes and expect students to meet research outcomes. Research outcomes focus on graduate students (e.g., those working on seminar papers, theses, and dissertations) and undergraduate students (e.g., those working on a senior thesis or seminar paper) and address the types of resources they actually used, how they evaluated and selected those resources, their problem-solving skills, their critical thinking skills, and the quality of the end product. Research outcomes do not relate to faculty productivity and publication unless students played a role in producing that scholarship and got some recognition for it. However, this perspective is difficult for faculty to accept as they rightly tend to think that research outcomes should not be defined solely in terms of student achievement.

Research outcomes for students might relate to problem solving and critical thinking and involve the application of a research design to problem solving. How well do students recognize and apply the steps of the research process? (See chapter 7.) In some instances, research outcomes might be a modification of learning outcomes. For instance, in standard 1 of ACRL's *Information Literacy Competency Standards for Higher Education*, "develops a thesis statement and formulates questions based on the information need" is a learning outcome, whereas "develops a problem statement, objectives, and hypotheses based on a given *problem*" is a research outcome. As another example, in standard 2, "develops a research plan appropriate to the investigative method" is a learning outcome, whereas "develops procedures (research design and methodology) appropriate to a given problem and set of objectives" is a research outcome.[9] (Appendix H, Information Literacy Standards, Performance Indicators, and Outcomes, identifies learning outcomes and indicates which ones could be converted to research outcomes related to the application of the research process. Clearly, those items in the appendix linked to research outcomes are measurable and relate to either problem-solving or critical-thinking ability.)

The critical issue will be for libraries to specify a role in meeting research outcomes. Most likely, that role will center on the retrieval of information and its inclusion in a research study. For example, in developing a problem statement, relevant literature might buttress the justification for conducting the proposed research; that is, can students find and incorporate relevant literature to strengthen the stated justification?

Given the complexity of conducting outcomes assessment, librarians should develop some "shared outcomes," especially where expertise in "the library complements the expertise of those in the academic programs."[10] As a result, they might concentrate their efforts on required and capstone courses and the major research projects (e.g., students' proposals for theses and dissertations). In so doing, they are trying to incorporate library outcomes into program outcomes and to share the responsibility for ascertaining the extent to which stated outcomes have been achieved. Once these initial efforts have been successfully implemented, librarians could explore other outcomes; however, an assessment plan must guide the setting of outcomes. To repeat, librarians should not be too ambitious and make more promises than they can realistically keep.

Not Limiting Outcomes to Students

As previously mentioned, outcomes assessment should not be limited to students. In the case of academic libraries, the faculty comprise another important group. Thus, an important question is "How does the library contribute to faculty teaching?" Conceivably, some learning outcomes might apply to new faculty members and help them adjust to a new environment, one that might be very dissimilar to the one from which they earned their doctorate.

Another question is "How do the library and its resources contribute to the research and scholarly production of the faculty?" Outcomes cannot look at changes in scholarly behavior and the mastery of competencies unless there are clear deficiencies that the library can identify and address. Rather, at least for now, the answer to the question might involve indirect evidence (faculty perceptions, for instance, of how their research benefited from the use of library resources and of the role of the library in enabling them to complete their research projects effectively and efficiently). Research outcomes might look at the institutional support that the faculty receive to produce a paper, book, or other manifestation of their creativity. (See appendix I.)

Finally, learning outcomes can relate to public libraries and the performance of those individuals enrolled in workshops or to the accomplishment of service responses. Research outcomes might focus on instruction related to genealogy and how well genealogists apply their critical thinking and problem-solving skills to tracing ancestral linkages.

The Balanced Scorecard

The balanced scorecard, a tool for strategic management developed by Robert S. Kaplan and David P. Norton, is a matrix of measures that reflects organizational performance from the perspective of its stakeholders and, it is hoped, from that of the organization's users. Organizations take financial measures (inputs) and convert them to factors that they can equate with success (the desired outcomes). Once they have identified the measures that reflect success, they can develop strategies to gather data showing the extent to which those measures have been accomplished. According to Kaplan and Norton, any measure represents "a balance between . . . the results from past efforts . . . and . . . [indicators] that drive future performance." The scorecard enables organizations "to gain clarification, consensus, and focus on their strategy, and then to com-

FIGURE 1
The Balanced Scorecard

municate that strategy through the organization," as they realize their mission and goals.[11]

Figure 1 depicts the balanced scorecard for a library. The management system operates within the context of "quality principles [that] are a personal philosophy and organizational culture" that measure outcomes and use systematic management techniques and collaboration to achieve an institution's mission.[12] Within the context of quality principles and the organization's mission, the library manages its resources and costs to serve its user community and to achieve its outcomes.

Measures

All types of libraries engage in collecting and reporting input and output measures as a percentage. As the "Standards for College Libraries 2000 Edition" explains, "inputs are generally regarded as the raw materials of a library program—the money, space, collection, equipment, and staff out of which a program [or service] can arise."[13] An input measure might be professional staff as a percentage of total staff, salary expenditures as a percentage of total expenditures, the number of volumes held in terms of the number of faculty, number of faculty per library staff member, expenditures for serials per faculty, or expenditures for library materials per student.[14] Other examples are the number of faculty publications (unless students are involved); the amount of time that students spend in class; the size of the library; the percentage of students enrolled in a distance education program in relation to the number enrolled in the institution, department, or program; and number of computer workstations per capita.

Outputs quantify the work done and report how busy the library is and the amount of use a particular service receives. Examples of outputs are the number of items loaned over the number borrowed, the number borrowed by a particular group in relation to the total number borrowed by everyone, the number of reference questions answered over the number asked, the number of library users in relation to the population of the community, and library computer workstation use rate. Some output measures might be framed in terms of cost (e.g., cost per log-in per electronic library service or cost per electronic document delivered per electronic library service).[15]

If a measure examines the speed by which the Web master responds in relation to the number of reference questions that distance students direct to the library's Web master, then the measure might be labeled a *customer measure*. Such a measure is one that has direct importance to library users. As Martha Kyrillidou, ARL's senior program officer for statistics and measurement, succinctly stated, "we need measures telling us our users' views" and what their expectations are.[16]

Danuta A. Nitecki, associate university librarian at Yale University, and Peter Hernon used quadrant analysis, a visual correlation technique, to identify high performance expectations and important expectations to improve performance.[17] The results of this analysis might be cast as customer measures. These measures would not necessarily require data collection directly from users. For example, the number of books reshelved promptly (within a specified time limit) in relation to the number of books waiting to be reshelved could be gauged periodically by monitoring reshelving. Perhaps a colored marker might be inserted into some books, and the length of time it takes for them to reappear on the shelves could be determined. Two other examples of customer measures are the mean waiting time for access to library computer workstations and failure to be able to log-in as a percentage of total log-ins.[18]

Academic institutions might ascertain the percentage of graduating seniors accepted to graduate school in relation to the number who want to go there (based on self-reporting surveys) or the number of graduating seniors not going to graduate school who gain employment. (Complicating the precision in the interpretation of the latter measure is the fact that some graduates may be unable to gain employment and instead attend graduate school.)

Outcomes measures may be too complex to express as a ratio and percentage, for example, the number of public library workshop participants whose information-gathering search behavior changed as a result of attending a program. Information seeking is a complex phenomenon that varies according to information need. Nonetheless, the ratio and percentage might be expressed as

$$\frac{\text{Number whose search behavior changed as a result of that workshop}}{\text{Number in attendance at the workshop}} = 0 \times 100 = \_\_\_\_ \%$$

Complicating an interpretation of this percentage are the following questions: "What is a change in behavior?," "How do the staff know that behavior actually changed?," and "Was that change temporary or lasting?" Clearly, such questions require use of the research process discussed in the next chapter.

Central to any statement of an outcome is the quality of the evidence gathered to document a change. Is the evidence reliable (accurate and reputable) and valid (measures or reflects what it is supposed to)? Given the complexity of outcomes assessment, it is important that librarians give careful consideration to which outcomes they want to use. The list of candidate outcomes should not be overly ambitious, especially as staff gain experience in applying outcomes assessment. Herein is the advantage of exploring shared outcomes (e.g., with the teaching faculty).

Phrasing Outcomes

Both Kenneth R. Smith and the *Information Literacy Competency Standards for Higher Education* (appendix H) frame their outcomes by using verbs. Smith has identified some learning outcomes that should be of interest to both faculty and librarians:

Become self-reliant (comfortable and confident) in information literacy skills including
- finding/locating information
- selecting relevant information
- assessing and evaluating information
- synthesizing information
- using information effectively
- presenting information

Understand and use the information search process (e.g., Kuhlthau model)

Understand different formats of information and deal with them effectively

Be aware (have an accurate mental model) of the structured nature of information

Understand how to evaluate bias and the credibility of information

Appreciate the way the quality of information varies along a historical continuum

Understand the social/ethical/political/economic implications of information and intellectual property

Understand the research process through which new knowledge is created

Understand the scholarly communications cycle and its application to scholarly research

Become self-confident and comfortable in information-rich environments

Develop attitudes of openness, flexibility, curiosity, creativity, and an appreciation of the value of a broad perspective[19]

Smith's list should be recast using more-concrete, action-oriented verbs (see below) and adding more specificity to whatever outcomes are actually adopted.

Information Literacy Competency Standards for Higher Education contains five standards and a set of performance indicators and outcomes for each standard. Verbs that frame outcomes include the following:

applies	differentiates	draws	organizes
analyzes	defines	evaluates	recognizes
compares	designs	identifies	selects
constructs	develops	implements	synthesizes
creates	distinguishes	maintains	translates

Using such verbs, staff can develop concrete statements that reflect what precisely they expect learners to know and be able to do to achieve an outcome. Furthermore, these action-oriented verbs are interactive and decision-focused —they are not ambiguous. Each expresses something that is measurable and clearly understood.

An examination of the five standards shows that some of the outcomes use less-concrete verbs:

articulates	determines	knows	reflects
assesses	discusses	manipulates	restates
chooses	disseminates	obtains	reviews
communicates	examines	participates	seeks
complies	explores	posts	stores
confers	extends	preserves	tests
considers	incorporates	reads	uses
demonstrates	integrates	realizes	utilizes
describes	investigates	records	

Such statements of outcome should be rewritten using more-specific action verbs that will offer a clearer indication of precisely what will be measured to show a change in behavior.

Distinguishing between Objectives and Outcomes

Once library staff have decided on the areas of information literacy for which they want to create outcomes, they need to convert objectives into measurable outcomes. Objectives lack the specificity of outcomes. For example, an objective might be to introduce students to the stages of the research process, whereas a learning outcome would be to distinguish between reflective inquiry and procedures and to identify the strengths and weaknesses of survey research. For the same objective, an example of a research outcome might be to differentiate between a problem statement and a statement of purpose.

Another objective might be to develop an appreciation of cultural diversity in the conduct of research. As Cheryl Metoyer, who is well-known for her research and sensitivity to culturally diverse communities, writes:

Any researcher who chooses to conduct legitimate research among culturally diverse populations must first recognize that, to these populations, one's motives for conducting such research are of paramount importance. Thus, the first question that the researcher should ask is not "How can I conduct the study?" but rather "Why am I, in this place and time, willing to devote weeks, months, or years to the project, to gaining community support, and to ensuring that the community sees benefits to itself from the proposed research?" If the researcher is not a member of the culturally diverse group to be studied, the second question becomes "Is it possible for me to conduct the research?"[20]

A learning outcome would be to identify reasons that the community might be unwilling to participate (in a study) and to evaluate different (ethically acceptable) strategies for possibly gaining community support. A research outcome for the same objective is to identify cultural differences that affect response rate to surveys and that undermine the reliability (accuracy and consistency of the data collected) and internal validity (ensuring that the data collection instrument measures what it is supposed to) of the study. Another research outcome for the same objective is to design a guide for the selection and training of interviewers that reflects sensitivity to the community to be studied and to translate the data collection instrument into the language of the community to be studied and ensure that the translation is reliable and valid.

Some Ways to Explore Outcomes

Initially, to assess a research outcome such as one relating to problem statements, librarians might, for instance, review senior and masters theses and doctoral dissertations and use content analysis to determine the extent to which the components of a problem statement are present and sufficiently developed. (See chapter 7 for a discussion of a problem statement.) Then, they could initiate a dialogue with the faculty in academic programs and see how they interpret a problem statement. Important research methods textbooks and other literature could be identified, and a departmental or program definition of a problem statement might be developed. That definition then becomes the basis for assessing a research outcome in the future.

Similarly, library staff might work with academic programs to review documentation for internship programs and to set a series of outcomes that students should master over time. The director of the internship program, together with the person overseeing the intern or an advisory panel, could determine the extent to which the outcomes have been met.

Some other methods of providing direct evidence of student learning include the following:

Capstone Course Evaluation As part of their program of study, students might have to complete a capstone course that culminates their educational experience, provides a final common educational experience in that discipline or field of study, and integrates the competencies associated with a program of study. The evaluation of students' written and oral work could deal with student outcomes, some of which might relate to information literacy. In those instances in which academic programs do not have a capstone course, a select group of courses might be designated to demonstrate the competencies that students majoring in that discipline or field must possess.

Course-Embedded Evaluation   As proposed by the University of Wisconsin–Madison:

> Such assessment is a separate process from that used by the course instructor to grade the exam, report, or term paper. Here, two or more faculty members evaluate student work or responses to specific questions on the assignments and determine how and what students are learning in the program and the classroom: Are they achieving the prescribed goals and objectives of the department?
>
> There are a number of advantages to using course-embedded assessment. First, student information gathered from embedded assessment draw[s] on accumulated educational experiences and familiarity with specific areas or disciplines. Second, embedded assessment often does not require additional time for data collection, since instruments used to produce student learning information can be derived from course assignments already planned as part of the requirements. Third, the presentation of feedback to faculty and students can occur very quickly creating a conducive environment for ongoing programmatic improvement. Finally, course-embedded assessment is part of the curricular structure, and students have a tendency to respond seriously to this method.

Evaluation across Courses   This would involve looking at a collection of courses that fit together as a program of study.[21]

Chapter 8 discusses different methods of data collection that can be used for outcomes assessment. These methods provide either direct or indirect evidence that specific outcomes have been accomplished.

Librarians and faculty might employ different methods of assessment in tandem. When librarians are not the course instructors, they might be involved in shaping the outcomes for the portion of the course or program related to information literacy. Where the assessment is performed by other than the classroom instructor, librarians might become part of the review or assessment panel or committee.

Public Library Outcomes

The Public Library Association's *The New Planning for Results: A Streamlined Approach* provides a framework to assist libraries, their stakeholders, and their community in making choices among service priorities. A key element of that framework is the thirteen service responses—defined as "what a library does for, or offers to, the public in an effort to meet a set of well-defined community needs. . . . [Service responses] represent the gathering and deployment of specific critical resources to produce a specific public benefit or result."[22] Following are the thirteen service responses:

Basic Literacy   A library that offers Basic Literacy service addresses the need to read and to perform other essential daily tasks.

Business and Career Information   A library that offers Business and Career Information service addresses a need for information related to business, careers, work, entrepreneurship, personal finances, and obtaining employment.

Commons   A library that provides a Commons environment helps address the need of people to meet and interact with others in their community and to participate in public discourse about community issues.

Community Referral   A library that offers Community Referral addresses the need for information related to services provided by community agencies and organizations.

Consumer Information   A library that provides Consumer Information service helps to satisfy the need for information to make informed consumer decisions and to help residents become more self-sufficient.

Cultural Awareness   A library that offers Cultural Awareness service helps satisfy the desire of community residents to gain an understanding of their own cultural heritage and the cultural heritage of others.

Current Topics and Titles   A library that provides Current Topics and Titles helps to fulfill community residents' appetite for information about popular cultural and social trends and their desire for satisfying recreational experiences.

Formal Learning Support   A library that offers Formal Learning Support helps students who are enrolled in a formal program of education or who are pursuing their education through a program of homeschooling to attain their educational goals.

General Information   A library that offers General Information helps meet the need for information and answers to questions on a broad array of topics related to work, school, and personal life.

Government Information   The library that offers Government Information service helps satisfy the need for information about elected officials and government agencies that enables people to participate in the democratic process.

Information Literacy   A library that provides Information Literacy service helps address the need for skills related to finding, evaluating, and using information effectively.

Lifelong Learning   A library that provides Lifelong Learning service helps address the desire for self-directed personal growth and development opportunities.

Local History and Genealogy   A library that offers Local History and Genealogy service addresses the desire of community residents to know and better understand personal or community heritage.[23]

There might be other service responses if the community has special needs or serves a unique customer group. "The service responses a library selects and the goals, objectives, and activities that are derived from those responses become the library's plan."[24] These, in turn, are part of the assessment plan.

Outcomes assessment complements *Managing for Results*, which provides library staff and managers with the tools they need to realize a library's plan.[25] Assessment applies to library programs and the extent to which a library's participation in service responses was responsible for change within the community.

For example, let us assume that the library selected Government Information as one of its service response priorities. Further, the staff realize that the response, as written in *The New Planning for Results*, means that libraries will fully integrate government information, regardless of the level of government producing the information, into its reference service. Integration of resources of the federal government, for instance, provides a real challenge because there are more than 20,000 government home pages relevant to various age groups, occupations, and socioeconomic groups (from students in elementary school to the elderly). Most importantly, the government offers assorted services (such as providing applications for benefits and forms for conducting business with the government). As a consequence, the resources that the government releases on the Web broadly enable citizens to participate in the democratic process as well as to lead full lives, and these resources may have no print counterparts. All of this suggests that the phrase "to participate in the democratic process" is very general. However, more activities of the federal government now occur on the Internet, thus "some possible components of government information service" should recognize more fully the electronic environment and the ability of the public to interact directly with government without the aid of an intermediary, such as a library. Nonetheless, two questions for library managers to ask might be "Did library educational programs and Web access improve the ability of the public to participate in democracy?" and "In what way?" Library staff could convert these questions into outcomes and complete the same type of analysis as shown in figure 2.

FIGURE 2
Relating Outcomes to the Assessment Plan

Objective: To introduce students to the stages of the research process.

OUTCOME (EXAMPLE)	WHERE THE OUTCOME WILL BE ADDRESSED	MEANS OF COLLECTING BASELINE DATA	LEVEL OF EXPECTATION	HOW THE OUTCOME WILL BE ASSESSED
Distinguish between a problem statement and a statement of purpose	Seminar leading to senior thesis Master's and doctoral proposal leading to thesis/dissertation Thesis/dissertation itself	Content analysis Test (performance) of ability to construct each Oral performance	Performance on the paper itself Performance on the test Oral communication performance	Grade (from a rating scale that faculty and librarians develop to grade performance) applied to the content analysis, test, or oral performance

Source: Columns 2, 3, and 4 adapted from work by Peggy L. Maki, Director of Assessment, American Association for Higher Education.

The New Planning for Results encourages public librarians to engage in satisfaction studies and to compile output measures, many of which are based on respondents' self-reports. As the manual implies, librarians also need to be concerned about the effectiveness of their programs and services. Ultimately, this will involve outcomes assessment that examines, for instance, how knowing certain information will improve the library's ability to enable the public to participate in a democratic process as explained in the government information service response.

Best Practices

Although libraries and other service organizations are now exploring outcomes assessment and determining how it will fit into an emerging culture of assessment, there has been no attempt to document best practices and to highlight those organizations that offer a model of best practices for others to emulate. As time goes on, efforts to identify and understand best practices in libraries will materialize. The goal should be to offer advice to libraries and others on how to develop strategies that are effective at the local level.

Assessment Plan

Outcomes assessment does not occur in a vacuum, but it is interrelated to the accomplishment of an assessment plan. Once the outcomes have been set, librarians, often together with the teaching faculty, will have to

establish a schedule for assessment (e.g., at the end of a specified semester, at the conclusion of a set of required courses, or upon graduation)

determine who will be assessed (e.g., those in certain programs or departments, culturally diverse students, or students completing specific program requirements)

determine who will do the assessment

link the results back to the assessment plan

Through the assessment plan (see chapter 3), the library conducts an organizational analysis, examining its constituent activities and services and how they relate to the provision of services, service quality, user satisfaction, and outcomes assessment. Outcomes assessment starts with the library and its stakeholders developing and agreeing on an assessment plan, then examining learning and perhaps research outcomes.

When first implementing a strategy of outcomes assessment, the evidence that libraries gather will likely be imperfect and contain substantial error. Instead of trying to reduce the imperfections and error immediately, librarians should gain some familiarity with outcomes assessment and the strengths and weaknesses of the evidence that they gather. They can then build from this modest beginning and select priority areas for more formal data gathering as they work toward lessening the imperfections and error.

Conclusion

Outcomes assessment is conducted as part of an overall assessment plan for a library; it provides an excellent opportunity for the library to be a partner with key members of the community served (e.g., faculty of academic institutions and schoolteachers). It is important that library objectives, where appropriate, be converted into learning or research outcomes and that librarians determine where an outcome will be addressed (e.g., in a required course, program of study, internship, or independent study). Furthermore, how will baseline data be collected? How will the data collected be used for continuous improvement of learning and research among the communities served?

Smith encourages higher education to set outcomes that "include not only what students know, but also the skills they develop, what they are able to do, and the attitudes of mind that characterize the way they will approach their work over a lifetime of change." He notes that librarians could target the "faculty responsible for the general education program as well as those responsible for many of the academic degree programs" as they are also "interested in critical thinking, the effective use of information and technology, the search process, and collaborative reasoning."[26] These become key areas for the development of partnerships and setting outcomes for both academic and public librarians.

Assessment of learning is an imperfect science, one that has not yet evolved into measures that are commonly understood and easily transferable to different types of institutions.[27]

Notes

1. Jane V. Wellman, "Accreditors Have to See Past 'Learning Outcomes,'" *The Chronicle of Higher Education* (22 Sept. 2000), B20.
2. ACRL, Task Force on Academic Library Outcomes Assessment, *Report* (Chicago: American Library Assn., 1998), 2. Available: http://www.ala.org/acrl/outcome.html. Accessed 28 Oct. 2000.
3. ACRL, "Standards for College Libraries 2000 Edition," *College & Research Libraries News* 61, no. 3 (March 2000), 175.
4. Kenneth R. Smith, New Roles and Responsibilities for the University Library: Advancing Student Learning through Outcomes Assessment (4 May 2000), 6. Available: http://www.arl.org/newsltr/213/assess.html. Accesseed 28 Oct. 2000.
5. Ibid., 7.
6. ACRL, "Standards for College Libraries 2000 Edition," 177.
7. Melvyn Dodridge, "Learning Outcomes and Their Assessment in Higher Education," *Engineering Science and Education Journal* 8, no. 4 (1999), 161.
8. See Smith, New Roles and Responsibilities for the University Library; and Kenneth R. Smith and Elena Berman, Advancing Student Learning through Outcomes Assessment. Available: http://www.arl.org/stats/newmeas/outcomes/HEOSmith.html. Accessed 28 Oct. 2000.
9. American Library Assn., Assn. of College and Research Libraries, *Information Literacy Competency Standards for Higher Education* (Chicago: ACRL, 2000). See also appendix H.
10. Smith, New Roles and Responsibilities for the University Library, 13.

11. Robert S. Kaplan and David P. Norton, *The Balanced Scorecard: Translating Strategy into Action* (Boston, Mass.: Harvard Business School Press, 1996), 10, 19.

12. Jann E. Freed, Marie R. Klugman, and Jonathan D. Fife, *A Culture for Academic Excellence: Implementing the Quality Principles in Higher Education*, ASHE-ERIC Higher Education Report 25, no. 1 (Washington, D.C.: George Washington University, Graduate School of Education and Human Development, 1997), iv.

13. ACRL, "Standards for College Libraries 2000 Edition," 175.

14. See Assn. of Research Libraries, "Developing Indicators 1995–96 and 1996–97" (Washington, D.C.: The Assn., n.d.). Available: http://www.arl.org/stats/arlstat/indi97.html. Accessed 28 Oct. 2000.

15. EQUINOX, Library Performance Measurement and Quality Management System, Initial Definition of Electronic Performance Indicators. Available: http://equinox.dcu.ie/reports/pillist.html. Accessed 28 Oct. 2000.

16. Martha Kyrillidou, "Research Library Trends: ARL Statistics," *Journal of Academic Librarianship* 26, no. 6 (Nov. 2000), 435.

17. Danuta A. Nitecki and Peter Hernon, "Measuring Service Quality at Yale University's Libraries," *Journal of Academic Librarianship* 26, no. 4 (July 2000), 264.

18. EQUINOX.

19. Smith, New Roles and Responsibilities for the University Library," 1, 4–5. For the Kuhlthau model, see Carol Collier Kuhlthau, *Seeking Meaning: A Process Approach to Library and Information Services* (Norwood, N.J.: Ablex, 1993).

20. Cheryl Metoyer, "Issues in Conducting Research in Culturally Diverse Communities," *Library & Information Science Research* 22, no. 3 (2000), 235.

21. University of Wisconsin–Madison, Office of the Provost, Outcomes Assessment VI: Assessment Instruments and Methods Available to Assess Student Learning in the Major, 2. Available: http://www.wisc.edu/provost/assess/manual/manual2.html. Accessed 30 Oct. 2000.

22. Sandra Nelson, *The New Planning for Results: A Streamlined Approach* (Chicago: American Library Assn., 2001), 146.

23. Ibid., 65.

24. Sandra Nelson, Ellen Altman, and Diane Mayo, *Managing for Results: Effective Resource Allocation for Public Libraries* (Chicago: American Library Assn., 2000), 2.

25. Ibid.

26. Smith, New Roles and Responsibilities for the University Library, 1.

27. Wellman, "Accreditors Have to See Past 'Learning Outcomes,'" B20.

7

The Research Process

If you can't measure it, you can't manage it.[1]

As libraries employ outcomes assessment, they try to determine the extent to which they have achieved their targets (i.e., benchmarks), goals, and objectives; these targets focus on how library users *changed* through their contact with the library and its collections, programs, or services. Have students, for example, mastered the learning outcomes that librarians and teaching faculty set? Can students demonstrate a plan for gathering information related to a researchable problem? As librarians address such questions, how much error—sampling and nonsampling error—will they tolerate as they interpret findings about changes in behavior and perceptions? Clearly, the intent at this time is to make the academic community, including librarians, familiar and comfortable with this new type of data collection, to encourage public and other libraries to explore outcomes assessment, and to reduce the error associated with the data collection and interpretation.

Outcomes assessment is a type of program evaluation and monitoring. It may involve the application of the research process to investigate systematically the effectiveness of learning intervention programs in producing change among library users and to ensure that the programs functioned as intended—that is, that they produced the intended result. Thus, this chapter provides an overview of the research process for outcomes assessment, identifying areas that will require strengthening over time as librarians reduce error and possible threats to reliability and validity.[2] Appendix I sketches the components of the research process but does not fully develop each one. The purpose is to illustrate the type of information that goes into a component and to clarify the discussion of this chapter. Chapter 8 expands on methods of data collection, and appendix J reports on an actual study used at Suffolk University for inclusion in its assessment plan and illustrates data collection and data presentation to assist those wanting to conduct a more complex type of outcomes assessment.

The research process consists of four separate, but interrelated, stages. The first, which is commonly known as *reflective inquiry*, sets up exactly what the study will focus on and provides the framework for data collection and interpretation. This stage converts the topic under consideration into a researchable *problem* (i.e., the problem statement) and conveys the literature review and theoretical framework, logical structure, objectives, research questions, and any hypotheses.

The second stage relates to study *procedures*, or, more specifically, research design and methodologies. In the case of outcomes assessment, the research design often includes a case study that uses quantitative methods and perhaps qualitative methods of data collection to assess a particular library program or service. The third stage involves actual data collection, data analysis, and data interpretation. The final stage relates to the presentation of the findings and their use to assess whether the intended outcome was achieved. If not, why? Is there a need to revise the outcome or the goals of a program or service? If there was a change in the performance, perceptions, or expectations of students or others, was the change anticipated?

Outcomes assessment is ongoing. Even if it is conducted with graduating students (in academic institutions) or individuals who have completed a series of instructional workshops (in academic or public libraries), the insights gained could be useful for setting the next set of outcomes—for incoming freshmen or individuals about to start a series of workshops.

A critical issue in outcomes assessment relates to the extent to which a change in user behavior can be attributed directly to contact with the library—its collections, programs, and services. Since people cannot be placed in a laboratory where their every movement, action, and thought might be monitored, it is impossible to eliminate all error and be absolutely certain that any positive change was due to library intervention. Nonetheless, libraries can tolerate error (even if it exceeds the probability level of .05 presented in research methods textbooks) and gather information useful for planning and decision-making purposes.

By offering an example of the components for stages one and two, appendix I clarifies the following discussion. Appendix I is selective in its coverage, but it illustrates the types of issues that both stages address.

STAGE 1
Reflective Inquiry

The reflective inquiry stage consists of five seamless and interrelated parts that are bonded together tightly and identify what the study will examine and how the data collected will be interpreted. The parts must be well thought out (reflecting reasoned judgment), and any weakness, inconsistency, or lack of clarity at any point must be resolved. Stage 2, procedures, provides a strategy that guides data collection to address the objectives, questions, and hypotheses established in stage 1.

Problem Statement

Because social science research focuses on the study of problems, the beginning step is to convert a study topic into a problem. A problem statement, which defines and guides the entire inquiry, has four components:

1. lead-in
2. declaration of originality
3. delineation of the direction the study will go (what will be examined, often expressed in the form of a purpose statement or overarching question[s])
4. justification of study (an expression of the study's significance or value)

The lead-in portion of the problem statement is specific to the organization or institution under examination and provides a context to the direction portion of the problem statement (component 3). The declaration of originality indicates that the study differs from all previous research, and the delineation of the direction indicates what exactly will be examined that has not been previously explored. A purpose statement, if used, is one component of the larger problem statement. A purpose statement adds clarity to the direction of the study. (See appendix I.) In the case of outcomes assessment, the declaration of originality is irrelevant. Outcomes assessment may involve replication and the identification of the extent to which a library's mission and goal have been met. The direction portion, which should not be confused with the study's objectives, must show that what is proposed to be studied is manageable with the resources likely to be allocated. It is essential that an organization or institution not adopt too many outcomes so that its resources are not spread too broadly and the staff do not spend an inordinate amount of time in data collection.

The justification of the study indicates that what was proposed is meaningful to the assessment plan. Quite frankly, a detailed justification becomes more important if the intent of the authors is to seek publication; in such a circumstance, they must explain the value of investigating the problem and why a journal and its readers would be interested in that study and its findings, especially if the study is a local one that focuses on a specific program or service. In other words, why would others—not necessarily just readers in the United States—be interested in the study and its findings? Whatever is examined must be very important to the library and the broader institution, as expressed in the assessment plan.

The problem statement must be clear, precise, and well written. It must identify key concepts and terms, articulate the study's boundaries or parameters, and avoid the use of value-laden words and terms.

Literature Review

The literature review neither summarizes findings of past studies nor identifies all of the literature produced on a topic. Instead, it focuses on landmark studies, but occasionally researchers make judgmental calls concerning which other studies to reference. Any review of the literature should relate how others have investigated that or similar problems. Such insights will help to guide the researchers in deciding on the objectives, research questions, and hypotheses, as well as on the procedures. The literature review identifies the variables that previous studies have investigated and indicates if some are more important than others. Furthermore, does masking (that is, some variables operating in combination with—or influencing—other variables) occur? What method of data collection was used? How successful were those methods?

In the case of outcomes assessment, the literature review should not be confined to the published literature of library and information science nor should it reflect geographical boundaries (e.g., only the literature produced in North America). Some libraries might have conducted a similar study and placed relevant information about that study on their home page; of course, such literature becomes quite difficult to discover.

The so-called *theoretical framework*, an extension of the literature review, expands the search for relevant literature to other disciplines, such as management, evaluation, and higher education. It also seeks out relevant models and theories to guide the data-collection process. In summary, the purpose of the literature review and theoretical framework is to seek out and relate relevant knowledge to guide the conduct of the proposed study (the one described in the problem statement). For example, the staff might believe that library anxiety is an impediment to academic achievement and, therefore, seek to reduce anxiety as a factor inhibiting change in user behavior and performance. The theoretical framework discusses what library anxiety is and if certain variables are linked to it. The literature review, on the other hand, identifies and relates studies within library and information science that have examined library anxiety. What methods of data collection were used? Did they work? Have some researchers presented ways that anxiety could be reduced or eliminated? Might their solutions apply to the proposed study?

Logical Structure

The logical structure moves the study from an abstract level to a practical level and enables researchers to visualize and conceptualize the components of the study so that each component can be addressed. The structure focuses on the directional segment of the problem statement. (See the *theme* and *who* portions in appendix I.) It also serves as a reminder that the researcher may have to deal with *where* and *when* components as well as *how* data will be collected.

The logical structure might be compared to a restaurant menu that lists the range of associated variables—things that might be investigated—and the concepts that might be investigated. (Note that the larger the number of variables identified, the more likely that the problem statement needs some revision and narrowing of its direction.) The literature review, as well as discussions with others, can help to produce the list of variables and ensure that masking is not likely to occur. As is evident, the logical structure "is both a clarifying and exclusionary step in the research process"; it depicts the "terms and relationships with which the problem is formulated and solved."[3]

Objectives

Once the list of variables has been identified, the researcher makes choices and determines which ones will guide the study. These are then cast as objectives. More than likely, a study assessing outcomes involves *descriptive* and *relational* objectives. Descriptive objectives look at the *theme* and *who* portions of the logical structure. Descriptive objectives are written in the following outline manner:

To (verb: do what?) (object: to what?)

The verb is descriptive and might be *depict, identify, determine,* or *describe.* The object is the variable selected from the logical structure. For example, from section A of the survey in appendix I, for the variable "frequency of use of online databases," a descriptive objective would be

To identify the frequency of use of online databases

A relational objective takes variables from both segments of the logical structure and relates (compares or contrasts) them according to the following outline:

To compare _____ and _____

Drawing again from appendix I, a relational objective would be:

To compare the frequency of use of library services for classroom assignments (teaching purposes) per month by faculty rank

This latter objective is measured in questions 1 and 8 of the questionnaire contained in appendix I.

Relating objectives for a true or quasi experiment (see the research design section later in this chapter) might be:

To compare posttest scores with pretest scores
To compare posttest scores (of the various experimental groups)

Any study might have multiple objectives; however, outcomes assessment is less likely to follow this pattern. It is more likely to favor relational objectives (changes in behavior or performance) and the number of objectives is likely to be small and, if an experimental study is conducted, to center on a comparison of posttest scores with one another or with pretest scores, perhaps by conducting repeated posttests and comparing scores over time.

Research Questions, Ratios, and Hypotheses

Descriptive objectives translate into research questions; relational objectives, for the purpose of data collection, become hypotheses. At times, library staff may prefer to collect descriptive data. Like input measures (reflecting resource allocation) and output measures (reflecting the volume of activity for library programs and services), simple outcome measures take those data, express them in the form of a ratio, and convert them into a percentage. (For example, see chapter 8 and the example of Boolean search operators.) However, more-complex outcomes (as discussed in the previous chapter) cannot be stated so simply; this is especially true for measuring or documenting change in user behavior and performance.

Outcomes should be reasonable (ones that the program or service can reasonably be expected to produce) and cast in such a way that they reflect change that occurred from preprogram to postprogram. Furthermore, as noted evaluators Peter H. Rossi, Howard E. Freeman, and Mark W. Lipsey explain, "The critical issue . . . is whether a program produces desired effects over and above what would have occurred either without the intervention or, in some cases, with an alternative intervention."[4] Consequently, the most interpretable outcome indicators are those that involve variables that only the program could affect to any appreciable degree. Rossi, Freeman, and Lipsey also remark that "the outcome indicator easiest to link directly to the program's actions is . . . customer satisfaction," whereas "the critical issue in impact assessment . . . is whether a program produces desired effects over and above what would have occurred either without the intervention or, in some cases, with an alternative intervention."[5]

A research question recasts a descriptive objective in the form of a question; any key term in an objective requires a definition if it could be open to varied interpretations. Research does not provide a definitive answer to questions. Researchers neither prove cause-effect relationships nor assume that additional samples drawn from the population would automatically produce similar findings. Research questions indicate a less-sophisticated and a more-exploratory framework, whereas hypotheses reflect a highly sophisticated and conceptual framework for the study.

Hypotheses, expectations about the nature of things based on generalizations about the assumed relationship between or among variables, flow from the conceptual framework. Hypotheses represent a narrowing of objectives and are subject to statistical testing. They enable researchers to determine whether something about the population is likely to be true or false on the basis of sample data. Since it is difficult in the social sciences to obtain unequivocal support for a hypothesis or to disprove a statement with certainty, researchers tend to be cautious and to emphasize that they are either *supporting* (not disproving, not rejecting) or *not supporting* (not proving, not accepting) that hypothesis. For outcomes assessment, hypotheses focus on whether the program or service produced the intended change. As well, can the findings be explained by some process not included within that program or service?

Outcomes assessment may explore relationships between (and among) variables. A variable may be, for instance, dependent or independent, or it may be controlled.

Independent variables determine, influence, or produce the change. This kind of variable is manipulated so that its effect on the dependent variable can be observed. In those research designs dealing with a determination of a causal relationship, the causes are the independent variables and the effects are dependent variables. When variables are not manipulated, it is impossible to distinguish between cause and effect.

Controlled variables are held constant or randomized so that their effects are neutralized or "controlled." Examples of controlled variables are gender and age.[6]

As educator and researcher Ronald R. Powell discusses, there are other types of variables and different forms in which hypotheses appear.[7] The null hypothesis is a statement of the absence of a relationship or a difference in the results; any relationship or difference is due to chance or sampling error. An example of a null hypothesis could be There is no statistically significant difference ($p = .05$) between the discipline taught by high school teachers and the number of times per month they use the library's services for developing classroom assignments. Every null hypothesis has an alternative form and, in some instances, more than one alternative form. By implication, by not supporting the null hypothesis, the investigation supports the alternative hypothesis as a true statement, assuming that there is only one logical alternative to the null hypothesis.

Hypothesis testing involves four steps, the first of which is to decide on the form of the hypothesis to use. Instead of selecting a null hypothesis, researchers, for instance, might use a directional hypothesis that specifies the direction of the expected findings; it expresses a relationship between the variables under study. Second, investigators specify the level of significance for hypothesis testing. A significance level gives the probability that the results of any analysis are due to chance or sampling error. Researchers in library and information science typically select from the 10 percent ($p \leqslant .10$), 5 percent ($p \leqslant .05$), or 1 percent ($p \leqslant .01$) significance levels to test whether the null hypothesis is or is not supported. The 5 percent level, which is the most commonly used of the three, says that researchers want to be at least 95 percent certain that a treatment worked, or a change occurred, before they are unwilling to support the null hypothesis. However, the investigators must factor in the possibility of making a Type I error—to reject the null hypothesis when it is true; in other words, to conclude falsely that a difference exists in the data when, in fact, it does not. They must also consider the possibility of making a Type II error—to accept the null hypothesis when it is false; in other words, to conclude falsely that a difference does not exist in the data when, in fact, it does. Most research methods textbooks offer guidance in whether, in a given situation, it is better to risk a Type I or Type II error, since the probability of one increases as the other decreases.

If the investigator selects the null hypothesis, the difference is expected to fall at either end (or tail) of the sampling distribution. Envision a normal bell-shaped curve in which each of its ends approaches (but never touches) the baseline; these ends are the tails. For instance, half of the 5 percent level of probability (.05), or .025, resides in each tail. The null hypothesis looks at both tails and states there is no difference, thus such a hypothesis involves the use of both ends of the curve. In contrast, if the hypothesis predicts the direction of the difference, the investigator looks only at one tail; the difference is expected to reside in one tail, not both. Thus, such a hypothesis involves the use of a one-tailed test. Explained another way, in estimating the value of the population mean, investigators might believe that the population mean can be on only one side of the sample mean. In such cases, they are dealing with only one tail of the sampling distribution (a one-tailed test).[8]

Third, researchers select the statistical procedure (e.g., chi-square test of independence or regression analysis) that will guide hypothesis testing and interpretation. Fourth, data are collected and analyzed, and the interpretation is applied; the hypothesis is either supported or not supported. Because the notion of probability underlies all statistical procedures in which inferences are drawn from the data, library evaluators, to repeat, cannot speak in terms of proving or disproving hypotheses.

STAGE 2
Procedures

The procedures, or the action plan (the study design and the methods by which researchers will study the problem), emerge from the reflective inquiry. In the case of outcomes assessment the study design could be complex, and there may be either quantitative or qualitative data collection or both.

However, since accrediting bodies appear to want academic institutions to adjust to the use of outcomes assessment and to view this adjustment period as a learning experience, they are unlikely, at this time, to expect libraries and academic programs to engage in the sophisticated types of designs presented in this section and in appendix J. The purpose for presenting these designs is to illustrate the direction that outcomes assessment is likely to move over time, once librarians and others have gained some understanding of (and experience with) the process of engaging in such assessment. Nonetheless, some librarians will find these designs useful now.

Research Design

Research design addresses five issues:

1. Who or what is studied—the entire population, or a sample of it? (Note that the sample might, or might not, be representative of the population.)
2. What are the major variables to be covered in the study? Will they be controlled or manipulated?
3. Are there experimental treatments that subjects will receive?
4. What is the time frame for data collection? Are sampling and repeated measures used?
5. What are the threats to reliability and validity?

A design can be looked at from three perspectives:

1. the type of study (e.g., true experiment, quasi experiment, or descriptive study)
2. whether or not a case study is used (an in-depth investigation of that program or discipline)
3. the examination of a sample or a population

All three perspectives might be included in an investigation of outcomes assessment and whether an intervention or treatment (e.g., the learning outcome)—the independent variable—produced the intended change once all confronting effects had been removed or controlled. (It is worth repeating that outcomes assessment examines whether any change in library users was the result of their use of the library's collections, services, or programs.)

Type of Study

A true or quasi experiment monitors change or the impact of the independent (experimental or treatment) variable on the dependent (subject) variable. An experiment aids in ruling out rival explanations, thereby offering protection against threats to internal validity. A true experiment involves the random assignment of subjects to control (no treatment received) and experimental (contrasting) groups, manipulation of the independent variable, and observation of its effect on the dependent variable. As Powell explains, the experimental group receives the experimental treatment whereas the control group does not, "thereby creating an independent variable with at least two values. The dependent variable is represented by the measurement of the effect of the experimental treatment, and several variables or measures of effect may be used."[9] Thus, it is the independent variable that is manipulated. When an investigation covers a broad time span—from preprogram to postprogram assessment—conditions become quite difficult to control and alternative explanations may account for any change in user behavior that occurred.

Randomization ensures that the groups are similar and that any difference between them is due to the independent variable, not to the participants themselves (e.g., their age, gender, and previous experience in using information-handling technology). Randomization may be achieved by random assignment, which involves the random placements of subjects in a control or treatment group.

Problems associated with the use of an experimental design are that it is time-consuming and costly to set up and conduct, requires extensive controls over the selection of subjects and the conduct of the treatments, calls for a sophisticated understanding of the research process and statistical procedures, and may lack generalizability to all disciplines and programs offered by the academic institution or to all participants of technology workshops offered by a public library during the calendar year. Yet, the use of such designs enables library staff to gain the best insights into the library's contribution to changes in user behavior.

As an alternative to the use of randomization, researchers might achieve equivalence by systematic assignment from serialized lists, provided that the ordering of these lists does not produce bias. By this method, students, for instance, could be assigned to a group based on whether their college identification number ended in an odd or even digit. However, prior to using this method, the researchers would have to verify that the institution did not assign numbers in a biased way. For example, they would want to ascertain that female students did not receive odd numbers and male students even ones.

Figure 3, which pertains to the use of an experimental design, characterizes how change—the outcome—is determined. Change for either the experimental or control group might be gauged by measuring any differences between pretest and posttest scores, differences between posttest scores, and by taking into account threats to validity, chance, and measurement error. Various types of experimental designs exist and have potential application in libraries. These designs either use a combination of a pretest and posttest or omit the pretest and rely on a posttest. They may also involve one or more control and experimental groups and may vary the type of test given to each.

With the pretest–posttest control group design, researchers randomly assign subjects to a control and experimental group and administer a pretest to both groups. Some time after the experimental group (but not the control group) has received the treatment, both groups complete the posttest.

FIGURE 3
Outcome in Experimental Design

OUTCOME =
Result of experimental group
(the one receiving the treatment)

MINUS
1. Result of the control group
2. Threats to validity

PLUS OR MINUS
Fluctuations attributed to chance
and measurement error

Or

OUTCOME =
Result of postprogram group
(the one benefiting from
the treatment over time)

MINUS
1. Result of the preprogram group
2. Threats to validity

PLUS OR MINUS
Fluctuations attributed to chance
and measurement error

Or

OUTCOME =
Result of postprogram group
(the one benefiting from the treatment
after a set time period)

MINUS
1. Result of the preprogram group
2. Threats to validity

PLUS OR MINUS
Fluctuations attributed to chance
and measurement error

FIGURE 4
Some Types of Experimental Designs

PLAN A   Pretest/Posttest Design with Control Group

	Pretest	Treatment	Posttest
Experimental group	✓	✓	✓
Control group	✓		✓

PLAN B   Pretest/Posttest Design without Control Group

	Pretest	Treatment	Posttest
Experimental group 1	✓	✓	✓
Experimental group 2	✓	✓	✓

PLAN C   Pretest/Posttest Design with Control Group

	Pretest	Treatment	Posttest
Experimental group	✓	✓	✓
Control group	*		*

PLAN D   Solomon Four-Group Design

	Pretest	Treatment	Posttest
Experimental group 1	✓	✓	✓
Experimental group 2		✓	✓
Experimental group 3	✓		✓
Control group			✓

PLAN E   Pretest–Posttest Design for Many Groups

	Pretest	Treatment	Posttest
Experimental group 1	✓	✓	✓
Experimental group 2	✓	✓	✓
Experimental group 3	✓	✓	✓

*The control group receives either the pretest or the posttest.

(In his book on research methods for librarians, Powell identifies a multivariate equivalent to the pretest–posttest control group design that accommodates more than one independent variable and one dependent variable.)[10] The result (the difference from the posttest and pretest for the experimental group and the difference from the posttest and pretest for the control group, minus the factors depicted in figure 3) is the change or outcome.

Nonetheless, for outcomes assessment, there is another change to monitor: any differences between posttest scores. Mortality—participants dropping out—is the most important potential problem. (See figure 4, which shows different design choices researchers have.) It is also critical that the researchers administer the pretest and posttest in the same way and that both groups have minimal contact with each other.

A variation of the basic experimental design shown in plan A of figure 4 is to have both groups receive different treatments; there is no control group. (See plan B of figure 4.) For example, library staff participating in information literacy programs might compare two methods of instruction without using a control group. The differential results of both forms of the treatment (difference from the posttest and pretest for the first group and the difference between the posttest and pretest of the other group, minus the factors depicted in figure 3) are compared. Again, for outcomes assessment, the key is any difference between posttest scores.

If library staff suspect that completion of a pretest might sensitize students about a knowledge or skill deficiency, the control group could receive *either* the pretest or posttest as shown in plan C of figure 4. The outcome is the difference between the results of the posttest and pretest for the experimental group and a comparison of this score to that of the pretest or posttest of the control group, minus the factors depicted in figure 3. For outcomes assessment, the key is any difference between *posttest* scores. An alternative to this design is to employ two control groups (one receives both the pretest and posttest and the other completes only the posttest).

The Solomon four-group design, which is a stronger design than the previous ones, is based on the premise that the pretest might sensitize participants to the treatment. If this occurred, study results could not be generalized, erroneous conclusions might be drawn, and the treatment could not be administered to people who have not received the pretest. As shown in plan D of figure 4, with this design subjects are randomly assigned to four groups. Two of these groups receive the experimental treatment and the posttest (but only one of the groups gets the pretest), while a third experimental group receives both the pretest and posttest, but not the experimental treatment. A control group receives the posttest but neither the pretest nor the treatment. Change is measured from a comparison of pretest and posttest results as well as a comparison of the results of the four posttests. This design controls the threats to internal validity and the interaction between the pretest and treatment (the pretest does not contaminate the effects of the treatment), thus providing external validity (generalizability).

Another possibility is a pretest–posttest design for many groups in which subjects are randomly assigned to three or more groups. Each group receives the pretest, a treatment, and the posttest as shown in plan E of figure 4. Change is determined from a comparison of the pretest and posttest scores as well as the posttest scores of each group, taking into account the threats presented in figure 3.

If the groups exist over time, it is possible to gather measures (conduct additional posttests and compare the scores with different sets of posttest scores). If groups dissolve, library staff might track some of the students over time and administer posttests to them. However, the staff must be careful about the purpose of such exercises. A key question for outcomes assessment to address is "How well do students retain what they had previously learned?" The central threat to validity is the extent to which other learning interventions (either self-taught or gained from other than the use of library collections, programs, and services) influenced posttest scores. It is possible that library staff might take individuals from some past groups, match them on certain attributes, and assign them to a new group. However, the purpose for such an exercise must be clearly identified, and students must be encouraged to participate. Nonetheless, the threats depicted in figure 3 become more pronounced because matching ensures only that the participants in each group are similar on the one characteristic. Matching is no substitute for randomization.

When randomization is not feasible and, for whatever reason, researchers work with preexisting or intact groups, the result is a quasi-experimental design. This design takes such groups (or classes) and applies a learning intervention, but the threats to validity (e.g., due to statistical regression and self-selection—letting people choose to participate or enter a group) and fluctuations due to chance and measurement error may be more pronounced.

Quasi-experimental designs may involve the use of pretest and posttest interventions in a time series so that treatments are removed or reintroduced at different times. (See figure 5, plan A.) Any change in the dependent variable is observed over time, and researchers have access to longitudinal data. That change is measured by giving the experimental group and the control group repeated pretests and posttests and then comparing the scores of both groups; researchers must consider the threats to validity, measurement error, and chance. Repeated testing serves as a check to some threats to validity (maturation, testing, and statistical regression) but not to history.

Similar to the pretest-posttest control group (figure 4, plan A), the nonequivalent control group compares two similar groups before and after the exposure of one group to a treatment. (See figure 5, plan B.) Researchers could take intact groups and randomly assign participants to one group or to subgroups, each of which might receive a different treatment. One subgroup

Figure 5
Some Quasi-Experimental Designs

PLAN A   Time-Series Design

	Pretest	Treatment	Posttest	Pretest	Treatment	Posttest	Etc.
Experimental group	✓	✓	✓	✓	✓	✓	. . .
Control group	✓		✓	✓		✓	. . .

PLAN B   Nonequivalent Control Group

	Pretest	Treatment	Posttest
Experimental group	✓	✓	✓
Control group	✓		✓

PLAN C   Pretest/Posttest Design

	Pretest	Treatment	Posttest
Experimental group 1	✓	✓	✓
Experimental group 2	✓	✓	✓
Experimental group 3	✓	✓	✓
Experimental group 4	✓	✓	✓

might not receive the pretest, or one subgroup might not receive a treatment. Change focuses on the difference between posttest and pretest scores for each group or subgroup and a comparison of the scores for both groups and the subgroups, factoring in threats to validity, measurement error, and chance. Each group should be as similar as possible. Any lack of similarity between the groups understates or overstates the change and, thus, should be recognized when study findings are interpreted.

Researchers might also examine different treatments but not compare the treatments with a control group. (See figure 5, plan C.) There are numerous variations of such a design, but the presence of a control group tends to reduce the threats to validity. Anyway, an interrupted time-series employing "switching replications" enhances external validity and controls for most threats to internal validity. Two nonequivalent groups could receive a treatment at different times. By continuing the process and rotating treatments between the groups, each group serves as the control group at different times.

Pseudoexperimental (or preexperimental) designs (e.g., the one-shot case study, one-group pretest and posttest, and the intact-group comparison) cannot rule out rival explanations for change or the lack of change in the dependent variable. Although the threats to validity are present, such designs may be useful in those instances in which library staff need to monitor ongoing programs and to gather data quickly and inexpensively. The one-shot case study, which lacks a control or comparison group, exposes a group to a treatment and measures the impact or change. Researchers must gauge the perceptions, attitudes, and competencies of the group before it received the treatment.

With the one-group pretest and posttest, researchers make observations before and after the group received the treatment. Regarding the intact-group comparison, let us assume that researchers take two groups, administer a treatment to one of them, but give the pretest and posttest to both. The group not receiving the treatment becomes the control group. With this design, participants are not randomly assigned to a group, and the groups might not be equivalent. If change in the dependent variable occurs, it might still be due to factors other than the assumed explanation.

Many descriptive designs center around the use of case studies, which are most appropriate for outcomes assessment. More than likely, the library wants to generalize any findings to a particular program or discipline. Researchers can take the results of different case studies and see if they apply to other settings (programs of that library and disciplines of that institution).

Finally, ex post facto studies can explore previously implemented programs and see if the insights gained might apply to a new program or discipline. However, any conclusions drawn are tentative at best. Nonetheless, such studies indicate that evaluation should not be ahistorical; it should place all insights gained within a historical (time) perspective.[11]

Sampling

Sampling is often preferable to the examination of an entire population, and a number of research designs require sampling. Statistical sampling produces a sample that is representative of a population. The population should be defined with care because this is the entire collection or group of items to which estimates and inferences apply. Once the population has been defined, researchers may see if there is a list of the population so that they can select a representative sample from it.

Random selection eliminates personal bias or subjectivity in the sample selection. By using this method, researchers ensure that the sample reflects the population within the limits of sampling error, which is the expected difference between the value found in a statistical sample and the value of the same characteristic that would have been found by examining the entire population with the same methodological procedures.

Examples of statistical sampling include the following:

Simple random sampling. Every item found in the sampling frame has an equal and known chance of inclusion, and the selection of one case or subject does not influence the selection of another. For example, all the students in a high school could be treated as a population. A simple random sample would be selecting the study participants in such a way that every student has a chance of being included.

Stratified random sampling. The universe is divided into two or more parts (e.g., faculty might be divided into the disciplines associated with the physical sciences, behavioral sciences, health sciences, humanities, and social sciences), and a sample (perhaps using simple random sampling) is selected from each part. Parts might be selected in proportion to their numbers in the population.

Systematic sampling. Each member of the population is not chosen independently. Once the first member has been chosen, other members are automatically determined. Such sampling centers on the selection of the *nth* case; in other words, the researcher might take every *nth* (e.g., fifth or tenth) person or item. The beginning *nth* number might be selected randomly from a table of random numbers.

Quota sampling. A proportion of the population is selected according to a specific characteristic (such as being a residential or commuter student or being a child or parent).

Cluster sampling. Instead of selecting individual items directly, researchers select groups of items (or clusters). Cluster sampling focuses on a naturally occurring group of individuals. Researchers divide the population into subdivisions or clusters of smaller units. These clusters might be randomly selected. If they are geographic subdivisions, this kind of sampling is known as *area sampling.* Given the detailed data available on households, it is possible to use geographic information systems (GISs) to identify specific clusters to investigate. The key issue relates to how closely researchers can match clusters to the population on certain attributes.

Determination of sample size can be quite complex. A number of guides discuss some approaches for making that determination.[12] At any rate, researchers specify the precision required, calculate the sample size needed to achieve that precision, and then estimate the cost or time required to collect the data for the computer sample size.

Methodology

Methodology refers to how data will be collected. Methods might be quantitative, in which data are reduced to numbers and statistical procedures are applied, or qualitative when no reduction to precise measurement is possible. Examples of data-collections methods follow. Each method has inherent strengths and weaknesses. The key is to select the method that has the most strengths and fewest weaknesses in the context of the problem statement and objectives.

QUESTIONNAIRES

Questionnaires might be presented as surveys that are mailed, e-mailed, attached to a Web site, or distributed in person to users of a library. They might also be used to conduct in-person interviews or focus group interviews. Printed questionnaires can be made available in different areas of the library for users to pick up and complete as they choose. In addition, outcomes assessment might use questionnaires that are administered on a pretest/posttest basis. An example of a questionnaire used to survey faculty as part of outcomes assessment appears in appendix I. That instrument can be modified to accommodate the needs of public libraries.[13] Furthermore, the Bureau of Labor Statistics (http://www.bls.gov) has categorized the public into occupational categories that could be inserted into the questionnaire.

CONTENT ANALYSIS

This method is a systematic analysis of the occurrence of words, phrases, and concepts in open-ended questions or documents.[14] For example, if we asked library users what they liked best about the library, we could categorize their answers based on the words *choice*, *frequency*, or *intensity*.

CITATION ANALYSIS

A type of bibliometrics study, citation analysis might examine the citations of student and faculty papers and characterize, for example, the extent of co-authorship, the type of document cited (e.g., article in scholarly printed or electronic journal, monograph, and government document), the age of the cited material, and the language of the material.

TRANSACTIONAL LOG ANALYSIS

Looking at the online public access catalog and, from the computer logs, characterizing the mistakes that users most likely made in conducting their search involves transactional log analysis. Log files from the library home page might reveal the users' Internet domain (extension such as .com or .edu), date of transaction, amount of time spent visiting the site, screens used, number of mouse clicks taken to get to a screen, any use of hot links, the exact material that was downloaded, and whether users encountered any problems in downloading material. Log analysis might also focus on the amount of access to the library's specific electronic databases.

OBTRUSIVE TESTING

With obtrusive testing subjects are aware that they are being tested, as opposed to unobtrusive testing (similar to the use of "mystery shoppers" in the retail industry). Obtrusive testing involves participants in a workshop or students who have received library instruction being given some test questions that are representative of that instruction and being given a time limit in which to develop and execute a successful search strategy. The success of that search strategy and perhaps students' ability to clarify a vague question would be evaluated. Unobtrusive testing is less relevant to outcomes assessment, as librarians are not likely to be in a situation in which they can test subjects who are unaware that they are being tested.

THINK-ALOUD PROTOCOL

With this method subjects articulate their thought processes and opinions while directly interacting with library resources to accomplish a given task. The protocol shows how users interpret and seek to accomplish each part of that task.

STANDARDIZED OR LOCALLY DEVELOPED TESTS

Included in this method might be the questionnaire that the library staff uses for a pretest and posttest. Even if standardized tests exist that do what the staff want, their usefulness should still be validated and shown to be relevant to the particular study population. Staff-developed tests should be checked for validity and reliability.

LOGS AND DIARIES

Participants might be asked to show through their logs or diaries how they developed and executed a search strategy on a given topic.

HISTORICAL RESEARCH

This method provides a contextual framework by placing the current investigation in the context of what was done before through an examination of relevant records and documents.

OBSERVATION

Some library staff members might observe the behaviors of subjects or workshop participants. When using this method it is critical that observers do not influence user behavior. Observation could document nonverbal behaviors.

SELF-ASSESSMENT

Participants might provide their own assessment of a program.

The literature review and theoretical framework disclose the various methods that others have tried and provide some guidance in the selection of the actual method(s) to use. The more that researchers rely on hypothesis testing, especially when it looks at statistical significance, the greater the reason that the method must be quantitative. Still, in some circumstances, the think-aloud protocol, logs and diaries, and observation are relevant.

If the researcher uses a questionnaire or a test, it is critical that the instrument be pretested to improve the instrument and to review the procedures for data collection. The pretest might be completed in three stages. First, the researcher validates that each study objective has a corresponding question(s) on the instrument. Second, that person shares the instrument with perhaps four to eight library colleagues and, in a group, they provide oral comments about the clarity of the wording of each question. Third, the researcher gathers some student workers or library volunteers and repeats the group interview. If necessary, there might be a fourth stage: repeat the process with some faculty members, some students in a class, or some participants in a library workshop. In fact, this final stage may be useful in gaining support for use of the instrument in a broader setting and in ensuring that the outcomes, indeed, match the assessment plan.

Criteria of Relevance

Relevance relates to both the research design and methodology. In the case of a quantitative research study, it refers to reliability and validity. Reliability seeks to determine the degree to which the data collected are consistent; consistency is the extent to which the same results are produced from different samples of the same population. Reliability means freedom from random error—unpredictable error that occurs in research. If a measure repeatedly produces the same response, it is considered reliable. As random error decreases, reliability increases. Error is introduced, for instance, through questions that are ambiguous (open to varied interpretation) or lack definitions for uncommon terms or through data entry errors (e.g., inconsistent coding).

Validity refers to the extent to which study findings are generalizable to a population (external validity) or to the extent to which a question or a data collection instrument accurately measures what it purports to measure (internal validity).[15]

Internal validity "is essentially a problem of control"—eliminating those variables that suggest alternative explanations or that prevent the identification of causal relationships. Eight factors pose threats to interval validity:

1. *History* refers to the length of time between the pretest and posttest. A factor other than the independent variable may account for the change in the dependent variable.

2. *Maturation* relates to any change due to biological or psychological factors that occur over time and not from the treatment itself. Maturation is more of a concern the longer the period between the conduct of the pretest and posttest.

3. Testing may affect the dependent variable if participants are alerted to (or educate themselves about) the topic under investigation. Students, for instance, might do better on a second test simply because they had already taken the test. If they received a posttest, their performance may reflect a marked improvement due to the fact that they were pretested. As a result, any improvement in performance may not be a result of the manipulation of the independent variable.

4. Measuring instruments or observational techniques, if they are not sufficiently compatible with the instruments or techniques, may account for change in the dependent variable. Furthermore, validity may be influenced by the fact that the researchers as observers, raters, graders, interviewers, or coders gained experience, became tired, obtained a more complete understanding of the project, or eased their expectations of test subjects.

5. *Statistical regression* refers to the tendency of extreme scores to move toward the common mean as repeated samples are drawn. The assignment of subjects to a particular group on the basis of extreme views may affect study findings. Any change may be attributed to the differential selection of subjects rather than to the actual treatment received.

6. A nonrandom assignment of subjects to groups might indicate that the groups were dissimilar from the beginning. As a consequence, any change may be attributed to the differential selection of subjects rather than to the actual treatment received.

7. *Mortality* refers to the possibility that some subjects may have dropped out of the study after completion of the pretest but before the administration of the posttest.

8. *Interaction* means that one or more of the previous threats may be active at once and may produce an interaction. This is especially likely in those cases in which subjects were not randomly assigned to groups and assessment was based on existing, intact groups.

Conclusions regarding causal relationships become possible when threats to validity have been rendered implausible. More simply, validity centers on removing systematic influences that move responses in another direction. When a systematic influence is present, the measure is biased. Bias, for instance, results through

poor sampling—the sample is not reflective of a known population

faulty wording of a question—the wording evokes a particular response

sloppy administration of data collection instrument—investigators bias responses

inappropriate interpretation of the results—investigators let their beliefs shape the interpretation of findings

In addition to internal and external validity, four other kinds of validity are relevant to outcomes assessment: *content*, *construct*, *criterion*, and *convergent* validity. Content validity is concerned with the representativeness of the measuring instrument in describing the content that it is intended to measure. The central question is "How well does the content of the instrument represent the entire universe of content that might be measured?" Face validity, which represents the investigator's appraisal that the content reflects what he or she is attempting to measure, is a form of content validity. Face validity is also judgmental and subject to interpretation.

Construct validity examines whether or not the theoretical construct or trait is actually measured. For example, does a study actually measure library anxiety? Criterion validity compares scores on the data collection instrument with certain criteria known or commonly believed to measure the attribute under study. The purpose is to determine the extent to which the instrument covers a criterion. Any criterion must display *relevance* (represents successful performance on the behavior in question), *reliability* (a consistent measure of the attribute over time or from situation to situation), and the *absence of bias* (the scoring of a criterion measure should not be influenced by any factors other than actual performance on the criterion). A problem in the application of criterion validity is that many types of behavior cannot be converted into an appropriate criterion.

The two forms of criterion validity are predictive and diagnostic. The purpose of the former is to estimate or predict a future outcome, whereas the latter diagnoses the existing or current state of a subject. The central difference between the two relates to the time when the data depicting the criterion are collected. To qualify as predictive validity, the correlation is between the test scores and observations of future behavior. Diagnostic validity requires that the correlation not be delayed but be made at approximately the same time.

Convergent validity focuses on how accurately a question reflects substantial concurrent differences or is correlated with known values of the underlying construct. A question has convergent validity if it displays scores similar to other questions measuring the same underlying construct.

Evaluator Mark S. Litwin, in his discussion of reliability and validity, adds an important (but brief) chapter on multiculture issues. He notes that "when designing new survey instruments or applying established ones in populations of different ethnicity, creed, or nationality, you must make sure that your items translate well into both the language and the culture of your target audience." He maintains that a well-validated survey instrument "may not measure the same dimension in that culture."[16] Cheryl A. Metoyer, who agrees with these concerns, offers the following example: among older Chinese people "it might be considered impolite to answer 'no' five times in succession, even if the true response is 'no.'" She then offers suggestions for researchers investigating cultural diversity.[17]

Both reliability and validity do not go hand in hand with *utility*. For example, researchers could develop a course evaluation form in which the questions are clearly worded and conform to face validity. However, if the administration, teaching faculty, and students do not agree on which questions have the greatest utility and best reflect the content, criteria, and constructs they regard as most important to ascertain, the instrument has little value. As this brief example illustrates, decisions about validity may be made within a political context.

Because the paramount purpose of outcomes assessment is to arrive at valid inferences about whether a program produced the desired change, such assessment should have reproducibility—"the ability of a research design to produce findings that are robust enough that another researcher using the same design in the same setting would achieve substantially the same result"—and some generalizability. At some point in time—once an institution or organization has conducted a vast number of investigations centered on outcomes assessment and the findings of these studies "yield convergent results"—reproducibility can be demonstrated through meta-analysis.[18] Meta-analysis examines different studies conducted at the same library or the parent institution or organization and determines if there were any variations among the outcomes and the hypotheses tested. Furthermore, such analysis looks at the type of research design and methodology used and at descriptive information about the programs or service itself.

STAGE 3
Data Collection, Analysis, and Interpretation

Stage 3 of the research process refers to data collection, processing, analysis, and interpretation within the context of the study's objectives, research questions, and hypotheses. Research and measurement are susceptible to error. With some surveys, measurement and classification error may be insignificant, whereas in other instances error might seriously limit the types of conclusions that can be drawn from the data set. Clearly, errors of measurement and classification are never totally eliminated; nonetheless, researchers try to minimize them and their impact on a study. Total error, which includes both sampling and nonsampling error, can be classified as

coverage errors, which result from inadequate sampling and low response rates

measurement errors, which are due to faulty data collection instruments, poor-quality interviewing, poor respondent recall, response errors, and mistakes in processing (editing, coding, data entry, and data analysis)

sampling errors, which are a function of the sample quality—whether a sample exactly represents a population[19]

Error also results from misrepresentation: falsification and exaggeration. Falsification should not be dismissed as unlikely to occur; there are numerous instances of it, especially in journalism and in research in the physical, medical, and behavioral sciences.[20] Some other possible sources of error include researcher or sponsorship bias or faulty interpretation by the investigator.

If statistical tests are used, they must be appropriate and the data displayed must be correctly interpreted. Investigators should not let a computer printout dictate the interpretation of statistical significance or conclude that there was statistical significance without the use of inferential statistics, which enable researchers to make projections from a sample to a population. The context of a study's objectives and hypotheses determines statistical significance.

STAGE 4
Presentation of Findings and
Use of the Data Collected

Whatever data are collected should be relevant for assessing library programs and services (in accordance with the assessment plan) and increasing the role of the library in meeting the goals of the parent institution or organization. Clearly, the intent is to align the library with that institution or organization, thereby ensuring that the library is a catalyst for change. As a result, the findings must be carefully and clearly presented especially to stakeholders—those who have an interest in the library, usually related to funding, but who are not necessarily library users. Some of the findings, most likely those related to outputs, other descriptive measures, and research questions, might be displayed graphically.[21] The purpose is to assist people in visualizing the findings and seeing how they support the assessment plan.

The presentation, however, will probably not be limited to a written report that incorporates graphics. Most likely, there will be oral presentations to library staff, stakeholders, and faculty or others who want to use the outcomes as part of their assessment plan. These presentations might be given using Microsoft's PowerPoint. In such instances, ample thought must be given to the layout of the presentation, and the presenter should not merely read each PowerPoint slide and stand in one place—right next to the mouse so that he or she can advance the slide show.

Reminder

A final caution is that experimentation, or any research for that matter, requires strict adherence to the highest ethical standards. Human subjects are involved, and they should be treated with respect. As well, the research data generated should protect the privacy rights of individuals, avoid the use of deceptive practices, and not place subjects in physical or mental peril.[22] To ensure proper protection, academic institutions have subjects' committees through which all proposed research must pass. Municipalities might also have an equivalent.

Conclusion

Any research study that evaluates performance, programs, and outcomes most likely contains inherent limitations and potential biases. By the use of random assignment to control and experimental groups, the employment of statistical analyses, and careful attention to issues of validity, these limitations and their possible impacts can be reduced (but never eliminated). Adapting from Rossi, Freeman, and Lipsey's discussion of evaluation, assessment should be "good enough" to provide "useful and credible results."[23] Library staff need to be knowledgeable about the research process to produce such results. Furthermore, the staff must set priorities about which programs and services will benefit the most from outcomes assessment.

Unless the results of research are properly communicated, all the efforts that went into the research are, to a great extent, for naught.[24]

Notes

1. Robert S. Kaplan and David P. Norton, *The Balanced Scorecard: Translating Strategy into Action* (Boston, Mass.: Harvard Business School Press, 1996), 21.

2. This chapter is partially adapted from chapter 5, "Evaluation Designs and Data Collection Techniques," of *Evaluation and Library Decision Making*, by Peter Hernon and Charles R. McClure. Copyright © 1990 by Ablex Publishing Corporation. Reproduced with permission of Greenwood Publishing Group, Inc., Westport, Conn.

3. Based on class notes of Dr. David C. Clark, who taught in the School of Education, Indiana University, Bloomington, Indiana, spring 1976. "Logical Structure: Theoretical Framework," 1, 2.

4. Peter H. Rossi, Howard E. Freeman, and Mark W. Lipsey, *Evaluation: A Systematic Approach*, 6th ed. (Thousand Oaks, Calif.: Sage, 1999), 239.

5. Ibid. Regrettably, accrediting bodies tend not to view customer satisfaction and service quality as relevant to outcomes assessment. This is unfortunate as both may have an impact on any change in user behavior.

6. For an excellent discussion of variables, see Bruce W. Tuckman, *Conducting Educational Research*, 2d ed. (New York: Harcourt Brace Jovanovich, 1978), chapter 4.

7. See Ronald R. Powell, *Basic Research Methods for Librarians*, 3d ed. (Greenwich, Conn.: Ablex, 1997), 27–37.

8. For a more-detailed explanation, see Peter Hernon, *Statistics: A Component of the Research Process* (Norwood, N.J.: Ablex, 1994), 103–4.

9. Powell, *Basic Research Methods for Librarians*, 126.

10. Ibid., 134–5.

11. Ibid., 139–40. These pages offer an excellent introduction to ex post facto designs.

12. See Robert Swisher and Charles R. McClure, *Research for Decision Making: Methods for Librarians* (Chicago: American Library Assn., 1984), 103–28; M. Carl Drott, "Random Sampling: A Tool for Library Research," *College & Research Libraries*, 30 (March 1969): 119–25; Philip M. Clark, "Sample Size Determination: A Comparison of Attribute, Continuous Variable and Cell Size Methods," *Library & Information Science Research*, 6 (1984), 407–24.

13. See also Peter Hernon and John R. Whitman, *Delivering Satisfaction and Service Quality: A Customer-Based Approach for Libraries* (Chicago: American Library Assn., 2001), 102 (questions 8–12).

14. See Robert P. Weber, *Basic Content Analysis* 2d ed. (London, Eng.: Sage, 1990).

15. For an identification of the major factors that injure the external validity or representativeness of a study, see Powell, *Basic Research Methods for Librarians*, 130–1.

16. Mark S. Litwin, *How to Measure Survey Reliability and Validity* (Thousand Oaks, Calif.: Sage, 1995), 69.

17. Cheryl A. Metoyer, "Issues in Conducting Research in Culturally Diverse Communities," *Library & Information Science Research*, 22 (2000), 235-42. See also Cheryl A. Metoyer, "Missing Links in Reaching Culturally Diverse Students in Academic Libraries," *Journal of Academic Librarianship*, 26 (May 2000), 157-8; and Cheryl Metoyer-Duran, "Cross-cultural Research in Ethno-Linguistic Communities: Methodological Considerations," *Public Libraries* 21, no. 1 (1993), 18–25.

18. Rossi, Freeman, and Lipsey, *Evaluation*, 273.

19. Hernon and Whitman, *Delivering Satisfaction and Service Quality*, 133.

20. See, for instance, Ellen Altman and Peter Hernon, *Research Misconduct: Issues, Implications, and Strategies* (Greenwich, Conn.: Ablex, 1997).

21. For in-depth information on developing a report and graphing results for a presentation, see Hernon and Whitman, *Developing Satisfaction and Service Quality*, 87–90, 136–9.

22. Altman and Hernon, *Research Misconduct*, 185–6.

23. Rossi, Freeman, and Lipsey, *Evaluation*, 239–40.

24. Powell, *Basic Research Methods for Librarians*, 232.

8

Evidence Demonstrating the Achievement of Outcomes

Outcomes assessment should primarily serve the learners'
needs, with the goal of improving learning.[1]

Chapter 6, which provided an overview of outcomes assessment, highlighted some ways libraries can collect data to determine whether their programs and services achieve the intended outcome. An outcome can be defined in terms of a behavioral change or view of productivity that encourages faculty-student cooperation and that enables the library to assist faculty in being productive. Outcomes should not be limited solely to students; they can also look at faculty and communities served by public libraries. Chapter 7 explained research as an inquiry process, which consists of interlocked steps; that chapter set the stage for this chapter and appendix J. This chapter illustrates how libraries can gather evidence to document their progress in achieving outcomes—at times an illusive concept that can be difficult to measure with any precision.

Some of the methods explored in this chapter require the conduct of research as outlined in chapter 7, whereas others do not. It is up to the individual library to determine which methods it wants to use and to understand the comparative advantages and disadvantages of each method. Clearly, the accomplishment of some outcomes might be shared with other educators, namely schoolteachers and the faculty of academic institutions. Appendix J reports on an actual research study, one involving the use of an experimental design, conducted by accounting faculty for inclusion in Suffolk University's assessment plan (described in chapter 3). Perhaps other institutions might be able to use that study as a model for what they might do.

The purpose of outcomes assessment is to assess programmatic and educational outcomes and to use these assessments to improve the quality of the programs and services offered. Outcomes data are pieces of information that become important in the determination of quality. Simply stated, outcomes assessment validates or invalidates what is happening with the current programs and services, and it can be used to guide and improve efforts toward achieving predetermined goals and objectives. In effect, learning outcomes might define what students should be able to do at the time of their graduation and ideally throughout their professional careers. Assessing the degree to which outcomes are achieved reflects how well the institution or organization meets its instructional mission.

Often-Used Measures (but Not Outcomes)

Libraries, and the broader institutions or organizations of which they are a part, collect and report numerous pieces of data to federal and state government, accrediting bodies, and others. For example, academic institutions report admissions and enrollments, the results of fund-raising efforts, the rate of discounting student tuition, retention rate, number of students transferring from other institutions, employment rate for graduating seniors, and so on. Academic libraries, like public libraries, gather assorted data showing fiscal expenditures (inputs) and the extent of their activities (outputs). Outcomes have been confused with outputs or performance measures, but in fact, they are quite different.[2] Outcomes align the library with the broader institution or organization, and they examine results that are oriented toward change.

Easy-to-Gather Indicators

Outcomes assessment involves gathering and evaluating quantitative and qualitative data that demonstrate congruence among the institution's mission and goals, the outcomes of its educational activities, and outcomes associated with faculty productivity. Michael F. Middaugh, assistant vice president for institutional research and planning at the University of Delaware, believes that "in addition to assessing academic achievements, institutions should seek ways to assess the degree to which students' attitudes, social and ethical values, interests, and commitment to scholarship and lifelong learning develop as the result of their education."[3]

Middaugh states that two credible student outcomes (but not student learning outcomes) are the *persistence rate* (the number of students who enter the college or university and endure through to graduation) and the *graduation rate* (number of incoming students in relationship to the number graduating), as long as the percentages are considered along with the following indicators of the institution's instructional activities:

  employment rate of the graduates

  feedback from employers relative to the adequacy of preparation
    of graduates

  success on certification, licensure, and other professional
    credentialing

  number of students pursuing postbaccalaureate education at good
    quality graduate or professional schools[4]

In addition, Middaugh notes:

> Variables measuring the quality of interaction with faculty should be expanded beyond instruction. Variables taking on increasing importance in higher education and reflecting indirectly on the quality of faculty activity include the following:
>
> > opportunities to work with faculty on substantive projects of undergraduate research
> >
> > opportunities for internships and practica that provide work-related experience prior to graduation
> >
> > the proportion of graduating students who author or coauthor an article or chapter with a faculty mentor
> >
> > the proportion of graduating students presenting or copresenting a paper at a professional meeting with a faculty mentor[5]

An outcome is the proportion of graduating students who received honors/awards resulting from their collaboration with faculty mentors. Naturally, for any of these process-oriented measures, librarians would want to determine the role that the library played in its achievement. Still, librarians could serve as faculty mentors, thereby producing data similar to what departments and programs compile.

Higher Order and Lower Order Outcomes

As pointed out in the *Information Literacy Competency Standards for Higher Education*, there are "different levels of thinking skills . . . associated with various learning outcomes—and, therefore, different instruments or methods are essential to assess those outcomes."[6] For instance, learning outcomes can be subdivided into "higher order" and "lower order" thinking competencies based on Bloom's *Taxonomy of Educational Objectives*.[7] An example of a lower order competency is to "identify keywords, synonyms and related terms for the information needed," whereas a higher order competency is to extend "initial synthesis, when possible to a higher level of abstraction to construct [a] new hypothesis that may require additional information."[8] Clearly, lower order competencies relate to information gathering and the types of resources that the information seeker draws on. Higher order competencies are more complex to measure; they involve more than skills. Furthermore, they relate to problem solving and critical thinking, both of which can be more difficult to assess than lower order competencies. An assessment plan should recognize the methods appropriate to achieve a particular learning outcome and should distinguish between lower order skills and higher order competencies.

Higher order competencies, including research outcomes, require direct evidence of achievement; therefore, the range of methods that apply are rather limited. The key is that their achievement be neither assumed nor inferred; rather, the connection or association must be established.

Data Collection

Taking the information literacy indicators and outcomes identified in appendix H, librarians could meet with classroom teachers and determine where there is a common interest. They could also decide on those indicators and outcomes they want to meet together or independently. The indicators and outcomes selected might be cast in terms of questions for placement on a questionnaire (e.g., for use on a survey or a test) or in an interview guide (e.g., focus-group interview) that either the classroom teachers or librarians could administer. Ideally, library-related outcomes form part of a broader investigation of the extent to which classroom outcomes are met.

The key is not to be too ambitious, especially at first. Thus, librarians should scrutinize appendix H and begin with a modest number of indicators and outcomes as they decide where to concentrate their efforts. Public libraries might focus on workshops or cooperate with schoolteachers, perhaps those in secondary schools such as English or literature teachers or social science teachers. Academic libraries might concentrate on those programs having capstone courses or those that require students to maintain portfolios of their work over time.

The following sections build from the discussion of methods in chapter 7 and are intended to assist readers in understanding different methods and in exploring their suitability to their local situation. Any method must examine the role of the library within the context of the assessment plan. Some methods, such as general surveys (to be discussed), may mention libraries but only within a much broader context.

Direct Evidence

Some methods provide direct evidence that outcomes have been achieved and that the desired change occurred. Other methods provide indirect evidence and any connection about change must, therefore, be inferred. Figure 6 briefly classifies these types of methods.

FIGURE 6
Basic Methods for Gathering Evidence

DIRECT EVIDENCE	INDIRECT EVIDENCE
Qualitative Methods	**Qualitative Methods**
▪ Developmental portfolios	▪ Focus-group interviews
▪ Think-aloud protocol	▪ Curriculum and syllabus evaluations
▪ Directed conversations	▪ Exit interviews
	▪ External reviewers
Quantitative Methods	▪ Observations
▪ Content analysis	▪ Open letters
▪ Thesis/dissertation/senior paper evaluation	▪ Self-assessments
▪ Tests (standardized or locally developed, perhaps administered as pretest/posttest)	
▪ Videotape or audiotape evaluation	**Quantitative Methods**
▪ Nationally developed surveys	▪ General surveys

Developmental Portfolios

A developmental portfolio is a collection of a student's work (tests, papers, research, or artistic output) that can be used to demonstrate his or her efforts, progress, and achievements over time. The portfolio, which can be assembled within a course or in a sequence of courses in the subject major, is more than just a group of work stored in a file folder. It includes other features such as the instructors' evaluations and student self-reflections. The student, however, participates in deciding on the content, the criteria for selection, the criteria for judging merit, and evidence of his or her self-reflection.[9]

Portfolios might be saved in electronic format, perhaps stored on a CD-ROM. There are several commercially available portfolio programs that instructors can use to track student achievement. For example, Aurbach and Associate's Grady Profile (http://www.aurbach.com) provides a template for teachers and students to enter work samples. Other programs, such as HyperStudio (http://www.hyperstudio.com/) and FileMaker Pro (http://www.filemaker.com/index.html), allow teachers to create their own templates for portfolio assessment. They can customize portfolios to suit the needs of their classes.

Washington State University (WSU, Pullman) uses portfolio evaluations to assess the writing of students from Columbia Basin College who transferred to the university.

> [The portfolio] acts as a diagnostic aid to assure that all students can be successful college writers. The evaluation is [also] required of all WSU students after they have completed English 101 and before they have completed 61 credits. [Each portfolio] contains three papers written as part of WSU courses as well as two timed essays written in an examination environment. Portfolios are evaluated in two tiers by several evaluators and are given a designation of pass with distinction, pass, and needs work.[10]

Critical to outcomes assessment is the timed essay that tests the extent to which the students have gained the desired knowledge and skills. Furthermore, there must be written instructions for evaluators to follow as they determine whether the students passed. There must also be pretesting to ensure that the evaluators grade in a similar fashion (scorer or interscorer reliability). It is important that evaluators not grade subjectively and insert their own values into portfolio evaluation.

WSU uses portfolio evaluation to ensure that students who major in writing receive sufficient support and guidance to be successful in the writing-intensive courses. It is also used to identify the top 10 percent of students "who will receive the designation 'pass with distinction' on their transcripts as a statement of the importance of writing itself and as an incentive for students to excel in this area." Finally, "the portfolio is . . . a graduation requirement; students may not graduate unless they have received at least a 'pass' on the university writing portfolio."[11]

Think-Aloud Protocols

As researchers Jill H. Larkin and Barbara Rainard explain, "a simple and powerful way to get . . . data is simply to ask a person to do the task and talk aloud about all thoughts that occur."[12] Talking aloud is a type of verbal protocol analysis that seeks information about a participant's cognitive thoughts using verbal reports. These reports occur during data collection and can (and should) be compared with verbal reports given after the task has been completed. These subsequent reports, known as "think afters," are important because some participants might not be able to articulate well while they are carrying out a task that involves complex cognitive processing. "Think afters" can produce pertinent insights in such a situation. Yet, as researcher Jennifer L. Branch notes, "Think afters may be influenced by forgetting and fabrication."[13]

Directed Conversation

Some students, perhaps over lunch, might meet with a faculty member or librarian once a semester or once a year over the course of their undergraduate or graduate studies to discuss "their experiences with the library, . . . course-work with writing assignments, . . . their knowledge of computers, . . . the Internet and the libraries' online catalog, and . . . any other topic that might arise."[14] Anyone using this method might combine it with content analysis so that the discussion is taped and subsequently analyzed. If this approach is too time-consuming, specific questions (related to outcomes) should guide the discussion.

Content Analysis

In a most interesting paper, D. R. Newman, Brian Webb, and Clive Cochrane of the Department of Information Management, Queen's University, Belfast, discuss the use of content analysis to measure critical thinking during group learning. "The content analysis relies on identifying . . . examples of indicators of obviously critical and obviously uncritical thinking, from which several critical thinking ratios can be calculated."[15] They then show how to calculate these ratios for "relevance," "importance," and so on.

Thesis/Dissertation/Senior Paper Evaluation

Theses, dissertations, and senior papers are structured by a department, graduate school, or undergraduate school to enable students to demonstrate a mastery of an array of skills and knowledge appropriate to the major. An assessment might involve the use of citation analysis.[16]

Tests

Tests include measures of performance on national, state, or regional certification or licensure examinations; standardized tests, either commercially produced or locally developed; and general essay tests taken at different stages of a program of study. According to the University of Wisconsin–Madison,

> [Tests serve as a means to] review student achievement with respect to a common body of knowledge associated with a discipline or program. Departments have traditionally used tests in assessment programming to measure whether students have acquired a certain process- and content-related knowledge.[17]

Tests developed for a specific curriculum focus on the mission, goals, and objectives of departments and measure student behavior and learning. Furthermore, "a well-constructed and carefully administered test that is graded by two or more judges for the specific purpose of determining program strengths and weaknesses remains one of the most popular instruments for assessing most majors."[18] National, state, or regional tests enable institutional assessors to compare programmatic strengths and weaknesses with similar programs elsewhere.

The Graduate Record Examination (http://www.gre.org/) has a separate writing assessment that might be required of seniors or others; however, it does not have a library or information literacy component. A similar test is the College Basic Academic Subjects Examination, which offers scores for skills and competencies and for interpretative, strategic, and adaptive reasoning.[19] An important Web site is that for Critical Thinking on the Web: A Directory of Quality Online Resources (http://www.philosophy.unimelb.edu.au/reason/critical/assessing.html). This site leads, for example, to the *Sourcebook of Assessment Information*, produced by the National Postsecondary Education Cooperative (http://nces.ed.gov/npec/evaltests/). For critical thinking, problem solving, and writing, the *Sourcebook* offers six options from which to choose: domain introduction, domain skills, test profile, test review, test skills, and scores. The *Sourcebook* also leads to additional tests that measure critical thinking skills.

PRETEST AND POSTTEST EVALUATION

Pretest and posttest evaluation involves using equivalent tests or a repetition of the same test administered at the beginning of a course or program of study and at the end of that course or program. The purpose is to monitor progression of student learning during a prescribed period of time. The results obtained are often useful for determining where skills and knowledge deficiencies exist and how skills and knowledge develop. For example, Cardinal Stritch University (Milwaukee) uses pretest and posttest evaluation to compare freshmen and senior scores on the Academic Profile (Abbreviated Form). (See the Educational Testing Service network at http://www.ets.org/hea/acpro/forms.html.) However, "some students were never tested, some took the test more than once, and others didn't take the test seriously."[20] Clearly, studies must address such limitations as well as the fact that the study did not engage in the random assignment of students.

Appendix J represents an example of experimentation that examines students' Internet-based skills, any changes in perceptions toward computer-based assignments, and whether improvements in self-perceptions affect actual use of the Internet. Readers will note that this experiment represents the most-complex means of assessment provided in this book. The other examples are easier to administer and enable the staff to draw inferences, but not with the same precision as do experimentation and statistical analyses. For now, readers should gain familiarity with these other means, but they need to realize that, over time, outcomes assessment is likely to move more to the adoption of experimentation. Accrediting bodies, for instance, want academic institutions to begin to think in terms of outcomes assessment, to develop assessment plans, and to gain familiarity in applying assessment tools. This climate of assessment represents a good opportunity for librarians to form partnerships with faculty and others who might have a better understanding of statistics and research design. (See chapter 7.) At the same time, the staff can seek ways to learn more about experimentation and statistics, as they ascertain the extent to which they have indeed achieved their educational mission and the program of study has produced the desired consequences. This book would be amiss if it did not provide one detailed example of more complex measurement (such as represented by appendix J). Again, that does not mean that at this time libraries must conduct similar complex statistical assessments. For now, librarians should gain familiarity with the arsenal of strategies proposed in this book, and adopt those most useful to their given situation.

Videotape and Audiotape Evaluations of Performance

Similar to pretest and posttest evaluation, departments and faculty might use videotapes and audiotapes to assess student skills and knowledge at the beginning of a course or program and at the conclusion of that course or program. As a result, the students collectively and individually can critique the information search behavior recorded on the tapes. Librarians and faculty can share in the critique.

Nationally Developed Surveys

Examples of frequently mentioned surveys that provide benchmark data relative to understanding persistence and graduation rates, as well as providing a context to the accomplishment of learning outcomes and the quality of student experiences with faculty are

- National Survey of Student Engagement (Pew Charitable Trusts)
- Student Opinion Survey (American College Testing Program)
- College Student Experiences Questionnaire (Indiana University)

The National Survey of Student Engagement is a good instrument to examine first, that is, if the investigators want to use a general survey. The Web site (http://www.indiana.edu/~nsse/iqs.html) contains a list of frequently asked questions that, for instance, address the cost of the survey, survey administration, sample size, and data reporting. It is possible for students to complete the survey on the World Wide Web; "students will receive the URL address of the survey with their introductory letter to participate and in all follow-up correspondence." Naturally, the investigators would have to select and invite the students to participate.[21]

Eight questions pertain to the student's experience in using the library and can be answered using the scale of "never," "occasionally," "often," and "very often." Since at least one of these questions ("Gone back to read a basic reference or document that other authors referred to") is too general and simplistic, librarians, most likely, would want to supplement the questions asked with a separate survey.

Unlike the National Survey of Student Engagement, the Student Opinion Survey (http://blue.ue.psu.edu/psu/ue/aap/CSP/cspsurvey.htm) does not contain any questions about the library. The first thirty-three statements relate to satisfaction, while the remaining questions address program and demographic variables.

The College Student Experiences Questionnaire (CSEQ) (http://www. indiana.edu/~cseq/colenv.html) rates student learning and personal development in the following categories:

development of academic, scholarly, and intellectual qualities

development of aesthetic, expressive, and creative qualities

being critical, evaluative, and analytical

development of vocational and occupational competence

personal relevance and practical value of courses

Furthermore, the scales describe the following relationships: with other students, student groups, and activities; with faculty members; and with administrative personnel and offices. However, some questions relate to library experiences. Among its features, the CSEQ "provides an index of student satisfaction with [the] college [and] student ratings of key characteristics of the college environment."[22]

Indirect Evidence

The following methods provide indirect evidence that outcomes have been achieved and complement the methods providing direct evidence. In other words, the connection between the evidence and the outcomes must be inferred. Although these methods may be easier and cheaper to employ than those of direct evidence, they should not be relied on exclusively.

Focus-Group Interviews

Instead of interviewing students individually or having them complete a survey, students (or others) could be brought together in focus groups and given the opportunity to interact with their peers. Such interviewing might also be conducted with area employers, program graduates, or workshop participants.[23]

Curriculum and Syllabus Evaluation

According to the University of Wisconsin–Madison, "Departmental personnel change over the years and the higher education tradition of freedom within the classroom often leaves course content almost totally to individual instructors."[24] Curriculum evaluation involves matching objectives and expected outcomes for courses with what they actually cover. Syllabus analysis ensures standardization of the components of syllabi (e.g., all include grading and attendance policies, the presence of course-embedded outcomes, and course goals and objectives). Where multiple sections of a course are present, such analysis also tries to ensure that similar points are covered in each section.

Exit Interviews

In their exit interviews, students reflect on what they have learned, how they experienced courses, what they liked and did not like about various instructional approaches, what was important about the classroom environment that facilitated or hindered learning, and the nature of assignments that fostered their learning. The results are then used to improve programs and to discover ways to improve the learning environment.

External Reviews

External reviews involve peer review of programs and can link student achievement to a program's mission, goals, and objectives. They can also identify program strengths and weaknesses as the reviewers review a sample of a student's work from a variety of courses and determine how well the student gained mastery of program knowledge and skills.

Observations

"[By] watching, listening, asking questions, and collecting things, [evaluators can] describe what goes on, who or what is involved, when and where things happen, [and] how they occur . . . [as they monitor human interaction].[25] Observation balances observing and participating, but also relies on judicious interviewing. Anyone engaged in observation should be objective and ensure that any recording of behavior is both reliable and valid, especially since researchers can compare what people actually do with what they say they do. In some situations, people might be videotaped and their behavior subjected to analysis—assuming objective criteria guide the assessment.

Open Letters

Margaret A. Wylde, president of a research company, is an advocate of using an open letter, in which users comment, for instance, about the role that the library played in their education. Graduating seniors, the general public, or faculty might be invited to write such letters and to express what is on their minds. She advised that those collecting these letters read approximately fifty of them to look for patterns and then to

> establish categories and how the information will be interpreted
>
> examine the letters and categorize the information[26]

Self-Assessment

Students and others might be asked to assess what they have learned and the extent to which they have mastered certain outcomes. Where they find themselves deficient, they might be asked if (and how) they plan to offset those deficiencies. Self-assessment is best used when the faculty or program directors offer their own assessment of the students, so that both sets of evaluation can be compared and discussed. According to researcher Anne Marie Delaney,

> [Some assessment of perceived learning might be based on] self-assessment of what . . . [students] learned, how well they have been able to apply their knowledge in practice, and the extent to which their . . . [academic] program enabled them to achieve professional competence. [Furthermore,] the capacity for self-reflection potentially increases students' awareness of what they are learning, enhances their ability to learn from their present experience and apply this knowledge to future tasks. . . . [In conclusion,] incorporating self-assessment into assessment studies of professional education programs is consistent with the perspective that developing the capacity for self-reflection should be an integral component of professional education. . . .
>
> [Key areas of self-reflection are] to further one's own intellectual development, [while at the same time] to become more competitive in the job market. [Individuals also want to obtain the prerequisite degree] to advance professionally [and] to increase their salary level.[27]

As Delaney notes, it is important to ascertain the level of intellectual challenge offered by the program and courses.

General Surveys

Surveys of graduating seniors, graduate students, and alumni might be used to track their experiences, perceptions, and successes within specific areas of knowledge and skills. Librarians might identify any such surveys being conducted on campus or in the community and see if there might be some inclusion of questions about the library. Questions might also probe students' satisfaction with the library. (See chapter 10.) Surveys of graduating students and alumni might inquire about their past educational experiences and their desire for further education. Other questions might be grouped under the following categories:

> satisfaction with courses, [including] perceived professional growth
>
> preparation for diversity, [including] . . . the program's intellectual challenge
>
> professional experience scales, [including] professional challenges in teachers' relationship with students
>
> professional challenges in teachers' relationship with others[28]

Clearly, the questionnaire could be adapted to include questions about the library and its perceived role in professional growth and learning.

Alumni surveys provide insights into "student preparation for professional work, program satisfaction, and curriculum relevancy. . . . In most cases alumni surveying is an inexpensive way to gather data and for reestablishing relationships with individuals . . . [who] want to help the program continually improve."[29]

Employer surveys, on the other hand, indicate the level of satisfaction with the skills, knowledge, and abilities of program graduates. "Employers also assess programmatic characteristics by addressing the success of students in a continuously evolving job market."[30]

Follow-up surveys of graduates are similar to student surveys and exit interviews, but the surveys enable the former students to reflect on their education and to factor in their satisfaction with the knowledge, skills, and abilities they learned. Studies might also examine the retention or transfer of students and why students leave or come to the campus. The results might indicate areas of program deficiencies and strengths. Clearly, surveys provide insights into both student outcomes and student learning outcomes. The latter looks at behavior changes.

Illustrations of the Choice of Methods

Building on the previous discussion of methods for collecting direct and indirect evidence, the following subsections consist of three examples that illustrate the choice of method. The first two examples identify those methods that apply to specific performance indicators. The decision about a method should address issues such as whether the library wants or needs direct or indirect evidence, wants to measure higher or lower ordered abilities, and/or believes that a qualitative or quantitative approach will provide the most useful perspective.

The third example is probably the most intriguing. It shows that libraries can have computer technology programmed to provide insights into student use of Boolean search operators. Assessing such a learning outcome requires no additional or concentrated data collection.

Example 1

Some of the previously mentioned methods could apply to a series of workshops. For example, participants could be observed and their comments within the workshop recorded. They might be encouraged to keep a portfolio, to complete a test, or to participate in pretest and posttest evaluation. At times, library staff might have to conduct formal research to monitor and isolate any change that occurred in student or workshop participant information gathering, evaluation, and use.

For example, as part of its assessment plan, St. Louis Community College identified eight areas for establishing outcomes: think critically; communicate effectively; interact productively with others; value and practice inquiry; access, analyze, understand, and use information; accept personal responsibility; accept social responsibility; and appreciate aesthetic expression. Each area was defined, and the abilities that students should possess were identified. For instance,

A. Think critically. Critical thinking is inherent in logical reasoning and problem solving. One must value critical thinking in order to reason logically and solve problems. To think critically, one must understand the context of an idea and how it relates to the whole.

1. Integrate ideas: The student . . .
   a. identifies, organizes, and defines ideas from various sources which are then analyzed and synthesized
   b. examines his or her own viewpoint while also interpreting and integrating the ideas and beliefs of people from various cultures
   c. presents ideas using correct vocabulary
   d. recognizes how small tasks can be combined to perform larger tasks

2. Reflect ethically: The student . . .
   a. identifies and analyzes his or her values
   b. questions and critiques personal, societal, and cultural assumptions
   c. generates decisions based on rational and ethical analysis
   d. evaluates unpopular decisions for their value to the whole
   e. explores values related to social, political, economic, scientific, and technological developments

3. Reason logically: The student . . .
   a. recognizes both formal and informal arguments, their premises and conclusions
   b. distinguishes inductive from deductive arguments
   c. determines the strength or weaknesses of logical arguments
   e. formulates strong arguments
   f. examines supporting evidence and determines its relevance to a particular issue
   g. considers all sides to an issue or argument, using past experience, logical analysis, and fairness in assessing other viewpoints

4. Solving problems: The student . . .

    a. identifies, researches, and analyzes a problem

    b. uses inductive and/or deductive reasoning to solve the problem

    c. develops appropriate hypotheses

    d. models situations from the real world and uses the models to make predictions and informed decisions

    e. uses research, brainstorming, and creativity to formulate and evaluate solutions

    f. revises solutions as needed

    g. uses past experience to solve problems, when appropriate

    h. uses, values, and evaluates mathematical and quantitative reasoning

    i. develops conceptual understanding, decision-making, and analytic skills dealing with quantities, their magnitudes, and interrelations

    j. uses technology as an aid to understanding and as a tool in the solution of problems[31]

The twenty-five components for critical thinking could be regrouped into lower order and higher order competencies.[32] The faculty and librarians could then decide which ones they want to measure and how they plan to accomplish the assessment. Choices for direct evidence might be a portfolio and the assessment of written work, think-aloud protocol, directed conversation, or a test (for higher order abilities, an experimental design using a pretest and posttest) might be considered. Choices for indirect evidence might be observation and the use of external reviewers.

Example 2

Another example from the St. Louis Community College list is to access, analyze, understand, and use information. The assessment plan elaborates on and defines this task:

> Information is stored in a variety of formats and locations. One must understand the need for information and have the ability to identify what type of information is needed before one can access, evaluate and effectively use information for life-long learning. [As a consequence] the student . . .
>
>   a. understands how information and information sources are identified, defined, and structured
>
>   b. evaluates sources and information in terms of quality, currency, usefulness, and truthfulness
>
>   c. understands the variety of ways information sources are physically organized and accessed
>
>   d. incorporates a variety of tools for necessary information
>
>   e. uses technology to access, retrieve, and communicate information
>
>   f. uses gathered information for planned purposes.[33]

Only *b* involves a higher order competency, and it might require the use of a test (perhaps administered on a pretest and posttest basis), the think-aloud protocol, a portfolio, videotaping or audiotaping students, directed conversation, or the assessment of written work. The lower order competencies might be accessed using the same methods or a survey, self-assessment, observation, or external reviewers.

Example 3

A library might have the following objective and rationale for it:

Objective: To reduce the number of retrievals (hits) per search on aggregate and specialized databases

Rationale: The higher the number of retrievals per search, the more abstracts a student will have to peruse before finding what he or she needs or wants; the higher the number of retrievals, the longer the time it will take the student to find what he or she needs or wants; the higher the number of retrievals received, the more likely a student will feel "information overload"; and the longer a person spends looking at retrievals that do not meet his or her needs, the more frustrated that person becomes with the search.

Given the objective and rationale, assume that the library instructs students in the application of Boolean search operators (AND, OR, and NOT) to reduce the number of retrievals (hits) per search. This instruction is considered an intermediate, information-access-and-retrieval skill as part of the library's information literacy instruction program. The librarians teach other information-access-and-retrieval skills before they instruct students on the benefits and application of Boolean search operators.

Boolean search operators can be used on almost every database. The differences in syntax of using Boolean search operators among databases can be taught or discovered by using the databases' help screens. The librarians demonstrate this in a lecture/presentation mode, and then have the students conduct a search at the computer workstations.

The librarians teach the Boolean searching skill and tell students that the skill, once learned and applied, will save them time by quickly reducing the number of retrievals per search. Their retrievals will be "more on target," resulting in less information overload and less time reading through abstracts of articles or sources that do not meet their needs. Again, they demonstrate this in a lecture or presentation mode, doing a broad search and noting the number of retrievals. The librarians then conduct the search using a Boolean operator (usually AND) and they note the difference in the number of retrievals. They relate the number of retrievals found to the time it would take to review the abstracts. Next, they use an interactive mode in which students search for a broad topic, note the number of retrievals, apply the Boolean search operator AND, and note the reduction of retrievals.

During a demonstration the librarians also inform students that the Boolean search process will be useful in other courses and projects and will be something they can use when they leave college—lifelong skill. Library staff also instruct students on the application of Boolean search skills on an as-needed basis. For example, when reference librarians assist students in finding information, they instruct the students on the appropriate application of Boolean search operators to improve their search results.

Measurement

The library staff could use two measurements to gauge whether they were successful in instructing students on this skill:

> The librarian conducting a formal instruction will work with each student to ensure a reduction in the number of retrievals in a pre-Boolean and post-Boolean search using the Boolean search operator AND.

> Using statistics from the information vendors from which the library licenses access to databases, librarians could track the number of retrievals per search each month of the academic semester.

The expectation is that, by the last month of each academic semester, the number of retrievals per search will be reduced from the number retrieved during the second month of the academic semester. The library uses the second month because the formal instruction related to Boolean (as an intermediate skill) usually does not start until five to six weeks into each semester.

As one example, EBSCOhost's Academic Search Elite, one of the library's aggregate databases, allows the staff to gather statistics each month. They might retrieve the statistics for "number of searches" and "number of hits" for October and December, or April and May, and then calculate the number of hits per search:

Month	No. of Searches	No. of Hits	No. of Hits per Search
October 2000	4,755	10,453,645	2,198.5
December 2000	2,268	4,226,079	1,863.4

The number of hits per search dropped 15.2 percent from October to December. As a result, the library might claim that its efforts in instructing students on the application of Boolean search operators have reduced the number of retrievals per search. To strengthen its argument, the library collected data from the past year that showed no decrease. Since this is an indirect measure (one based on numeric inference), the library might conduct formal pretesting and posttesting of students in a class taught about Boolean searching methods. Thus, one would expect to see evidence of increased reliance on Boolean searching in the posttest.

Because the library offers EBSCOhost for specific databases that, let us assume, sociology, education, and psychology majors use, it can also track the same statistics for each of those databases. For example, if library staff make an effort to instruct all or most education majors in applying Boolean searching skills, staff can determine whether the number of retrievals per search has been reduced on the EBSCOhost's ERIC database.

Preparing to Use the Data Collected

Once data have been collected, the major findings might be summarized on a form such as the one depicted in figure 7. The purpose of that form and the one shown in figure 8 is to provide feedback, on a recurring basis, to the assessment plan. The intent, therefore, is to use the data collected for continuous quality improvement. Perhaps faculty and librarians might jointly discuss the findings and pursue ways to improve student learning. Even if faculty are unwilling to meet, librarians could do so; they should ensure that findings once gathered are acted on.

FIGURE 7
Use of Assessment Data by Discipline,
Program, or Department

Date _____

Discipline _____
Program _____
Department _____

1. Summarize the assessment results:

2. Indicate areas where these results suggest
   improvements:

   a. classroom:

   b. program of study:

   c. library services:

3. Suggestions for revision of the assessment plan:

FIGURE 8
Classroom Assessment

Date _____

Name_____
Course name/number _____
Department _____
Number of students _____

1. Identify the assessment methods used:

2. Summarize the major results you discovered:

3. What effect will those results have on your teaching?

4. How could the library be helpful in improving
   your teaching and student learning?

Conclusion

Librarians and faculty might employ different assessment methods in tandem. They will have to determine if they want to concentrate their efforts on capstone courses or on assessment either embedded in courses or in a program of study. When the librarians are not the course instructors, they might still be involved in shaping the outcomes for the portion of the course or program related to information literacy. When the assessment is the responsibility of someone other than the classroom instructor, librarians might become part of the review or assessment panel or committee.

As educator Marianne T. Bock observes, the interpretation resulting from outcomes assessment, even when the research process has been applied and hypothesis testing used, may be tentative. Some important variables (e.g., campus environment, alcohol abuse, and racism) may be present and should not necessarily be ignored as they could influence the attainment of outcomes or the interpretation of an outcome. Bock adds that "another variable affecting learning outcomes is students' willingness to take responsibility for their own learning."[34] Student learning styles and diversity might also have an impact on outcomes assessment. As a consequence, outcomes assessment is not an exact science. At times, the findings may merely be impressionistic. However, is not such assessment better than having no assessment data and making no attempt to improve learning and better meet the information needs and information-gathering behavior of the user community?

No single measure tells the entire story, but multiple measures do yield useful information.[35]

Notes

1. Cesarina Thompson and Jean E. Bartels, "Outcomes Assessment: Implications for Nursing Education," *Journal of Professional Nursing* 15, no. 3 (May–June 1999), 172.
2. Bonnie Gratch Lindauer, "Defining and Measuring the Library's Impact on Campuswide Outcomes," *College & Research Libraries* 59, no. 6 (Nov. 1998), 546–70.
3. Michael F. Middaugh, *Understanding Faculty Productivity: Standards and Benchmarks for Colleges and Universities* (San Francisco: Jossey-Bass, 2001), 150.
4. Ibid., 29.
5. Ibid., 84.
6. ACRL, *Information Literacy Competency Standards for Higher Education* (Chicago: American Library Assn., 2000), 6.
7. Benjamin S. Bloom, ed., *Taxonomy of Educational Objectives: The Classification of Educational Goals, Handbook I: Cognitive Domain* (New York: David McKay, 1956).
8. ACRL, *Information Literacy Competency Standards for Higher Education* 6.
9. L. F. Paulson, P. R. Paulson, and C. Meyer, "What Makes a Portfolio a Portfolio?" *Educational Leadership* 48, no. 5 (Feb. 1991), 60–3.
10. Washington State University, Office of Institutional Research and Writing, "Columbia Basin College Student Performance on the Washington State University Writing Portfolio, 1993–1998" (1998), ERIC, ED 433889.
11. Ibid., 4.
12. Jill H. Larkin and Barbara Rainard, "A Research Methodology for Studying How People Think," *Journal of Research in Science Teaching* 21, no. 3 (1984), 236.
13. Jennifer L. Branch, "Investigating the Information-Seeking Processes of Adolescents: The Value of Using Think Alouds and Think Afters," *Library & Information Science*

Research 22, no. 4 (2000), 389. See also John S. Carol and Eric J. Johnson, *Decision Research: A Field Guide* (Newbury Park, Calif.: Sage, 1990).

14. Ronald F. Dow, "Using Assessment Criteria to Determine Library Quality," *Journal of Academic Librarianship* 24, no. 4 (July 1998), 279–80.

15. D. R. Newman, Brian Webb, and Clive Cochrane, A Content Analysis Method to Measure Critical Thinking in Face-to-Face and Computer Supported Group Learning, 1. Available: http://www.qub.ac.uk/mgt/papers/methods/contpap.html. Accessed 8 Dec. 2000.

16. See Blaise Cronin, *The Citation Process: The Role and Significance of Citations in Scientific Communication* (London, Eng.: Taylor Graham, 1984).

17. University of Wisconsin–Madison, Office of the Provost, Outcomes Assessment: VI. Assessment Instruments and Methods Available to Assess Student Learning in the Major, 3. Available: http://www.wisc.edu/provost/assess/manual/manual2.html. Accessed 30 Oct. 2000.

18. Ibid.

19. *College Basic Academic Subjects Examination* (Itasca, Ill.: The Riverside Publishing Co., n.d.). Available www.riverpub.com. Accessed 27 July 2001.

20. Don Weimer, "Dealing with Messy Data: Analyzing Pre- and Post-test Assessment Results in the Real World," paper presented at the 1999 Annual Forum of the Association for Institutional Research (1999), ERIC, ED 433756.

21. To view the paper or Web version of the National Survey of Student Engagement, see http://www.indiana.edu/~nsse/sample.html. Note that this survey is also discussed in chapter 9.

22. Indiana University, *College Student Experiences Questionnaire.* Available: http://www.Indiana.edu/~cseq/colenv.html. Accessed 20 Oct. 2001.

23. See Peter Hernon and Ellen Altman, *Assessing Service Quality: Satisfying the Expectations of Library Customers* (Chicago: American Library Assn., 1998), 137–46.

24. University of Wisconsin–Madison, Outcomes Assessment, 7.

25. Margaret LeCompte, Judith Preissle, and Tesch Renata, *Ethnography and Qualitative Design in Educational Research*, 2d ed. (New York: Academic Press, 1993), 196.

26. Margaret A. Wylde, "How to Read an Open Letter," *American Demographics* 16, no. 9 (Sept. 1994), 48–52.

27. Anne Marie Delaney, "Quality Assessment of Professional Degree Programs," *Research in Higher Education* 38, no. 2 (1997), 243, 244, 247, 248.

28. Ibid., 261–3.

29. University of Wisconsin–Madison, Outcomes Assessment, 7.

30. Ibid., 8.

31. The Assessment Plan and a Five-Year Plan for Full Implementation of Assessment at St. Louis Community College (1999), 78–9, ERIC, ED 433065.

32. Patricia Davitt Maughan, the user research coordinator at the University of California–Berkeley, reports that the library measured "the 'lower-order' information literacy skills of graduating seniors. The most fundamental conclusion that can be drawn . . . is that students think they know more about accessing information and conducting library research than they are able to demonstrate when put to the test." See Patricia Davitt Maughan, "Assessing Information Literacy among Undergraduates: A Discussion of the Literature and the University of California–Berkeley Assessment Experience," *College & Research Libraries* 62 (Jan. 2001), 71.

33. The Assessment Plan, 81.

34. Marianne T. Bock, "The Measure of Professional Productivity: Using Student Learning Outcomes Criteria," paper presented at the 1997 Annual Meeting of the Association for the Study of Higher Education (n.m. 1997), ERIC, ED 415811.

35. Middaugh, *Understanding Faculty Productivity*, 29.

9

Service Quality and Satisfaction

A measure of library quality based solely
on collections has become obsolete.[1]

Outcomes—be they learning or research outcomes—by themselves do not convey the whole story. As figure 9 suggests, other factors can influence an assessment plan and probably have an impact on the learning environment and on the extent to which libraries can realize stated outcomes. Clearly, the entire institution must embrace learning, knowledge production, scholarship, and

Figure 9
Factors Having an Impact on the Achievement of Learning Outcomes

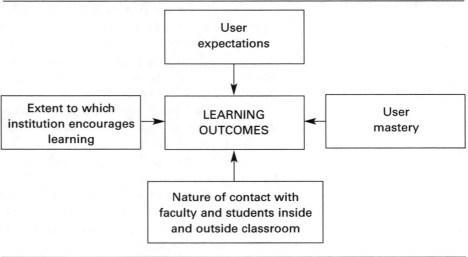

research as central to its mission and must ensure that each unit within that institution contributes to the quality of the learning achieved and the research and scholarship produced, whether that quality is defined in terms of program graduates or the work produced by the faculty and students. One indication that institutions should not concentrate solely on outcomes assessment is the emergence of a National Survey of Student Engagement developed by the Pew Charitable Trusts. (See nationally developed surveys in chapter 8 for more information.)

> [It] gauges the extent to which colleges encourage actual learning [and contains questions] clustered into five "national benchmarks of effective educational practices":
>
> > level of academic challenge
> >
> > the amount of active and collaborative learning (e.g., how often students made class presentations, worked on group and community projects, and tutored others)
> >
> > student interaction with faculty members
> >
> > access to enriching educational experiences (e.g., internships and study-abroad programs)
> >
> > level of campus support (gauged by factors like how much the college helps students cope with nonacademic responsibilities and supports social life)[2]

Some of the items in the survey include the following:

> campus environment emphasizes spending significant amounts of time studying and on academic work
>
> number of written papers or reports of 20 pages or more
>
> discussion of ideas from reading or classes with faculty members outside class
>
> number of hours per week spent preparing for class (studying, reading, writing, rehearsing and other activities related to your academic program[3]

Items such as these get at the environmental context of assessment, but libraries should still examine faculty, student, and administrators' perceptions of service quality and satisfaction. Both concepts contribute to one's receptivity to learning and how satisfied one is with a particular learning environment. Either service quality or satisfaction can be an end in itself; each is worthy of examination as a framework for evaluating library services from a customer's or user's perspective. By paying proper attention to assessment, service quality, and satisfaction, libraries are, in effect, promoting continuous quality improvement. Improvement leads to change, and library leaders must manage that change and ensure that the library's assessment plan is realistic and realized. Both service quality and satisfaction should be part of any culture of assessment and evaluation.

To complicate matters, libraries have so many evaluation choices. As Peter Hernon and educator Ellen Altman showed, there are at least eleven evaluation questions for libraries to consider. Librarian Danuta A. Nitecki grouped these questions (how much?, how many?, how economical?, how prompt?, how accurate?, how responsive?, how well?, how valuable?, how reliable?, how courteous?, and how satisfied?) under four headings: expectations, efficient management, reliability, and value.[4] This grouping illustrates the importance of evaluation to libraries and suggests that each question has value in different contexts. Thus, prior to data collection, librarians should review the questions and ensure that those selected produce insights relevant to their assessment plan.

Service Quality

Over time, libraries have used various indicators to assess and convey quality. Historically, quality has served as a surrogate for the size and content of collections: bigger collections of the right materials equal quality. However, quality can also

> reflect how good a service is (value, on the other hand, reflects how much good the service does)
>
> be interpreted in terms of standards, goal attainment, performance measures, and user satisfaction and, thus, comprise a means toward meeting a library's service goals
>
> be related to [customer-oriented] outputs in terms of meeting user expectations
>
> be viewed as the properties and characteristic traits of a service that enable it to satisfy specific or implied needs
>
> [be reflected through] a long-term, overall evaluation that examines users' perceptions of service
>
> [show] the difference between users' expectations for excellence and their perceptions of the service delivered[5]

Quality might even be viewed in terms of technical quality and customer quality. The former relates to the mechanical and procedural aspects that ensure that services function effectively and efficiently. Any measure of technical quality is an internal indicator of service performance as driven by operational specifications. Customer quality, on the other hand, relates to user perceptions of service delivery, and it includes those factors that users judge to be important. In other words, customer quality, or the customer's view of quality, equals service quality.

Service Quality

Service quality, which focuses on the interaction between the customer and the service provider, involves an evaluation of specific attributes, and this judgment is cognitive. Moreover, it views expectations from the perspective of the Gaps Model of Service Quality, developed by the three authors to characterize the planning gaps that could arise between an organization and its customers if appropriate information were not collected and converted into action by the organization. The model posits five gaps that reflect a discrepancy between

1. customers' expectations and management's perceptions of these expectations
2. management's perceptions of customers' expectations and service quality specifications

3. service quality specifications and actual service delivery
4. actual service delivery and what is communicated to customers about it
5. customers' service expectations and the perceived quality of service delivered[6]

Although all five gaps may hinder an organization in providing high quality service, the fifth gap is the basis of a customer-oriented definition of service quality that examines the discrepancy between customers' expectations for excellence and their perceptions of the actual service delivered. Expectations are *desired* wants—the extent to which customers believe a particular attribute is *essential* for an excellent service provider.[7] Perceptions are a judgment of service performance.

The definition of service quality presented in the gaps model recognizes that expectations are subjective and are neither static nor predictable. Confirmation/disconfirmation theory, which compares expectations with performance, influences the model. After having some experience with a service, a customer can compare any expectations with actual performance and his or her perception is confirmed (if they match), negatively disconfirmed (if expectations exceed perceptions), or positively disconfirmed (if perceptions exceed expectations). Terry G. Vavra, an educator and president of a customer satisfaction firm, in a discussion of satisfaction, notes that the term *positive disconfirmation* is confusing. As a consequence, he substitutes the words *affirmed, confirmed*, and *disconfirmed* to describe the three situations:

- Expectations are *confirmed* when perceived performance *meets* them
- Expectations are *affirmed* when perceived performance *exceeds* them
- Expectations are *disconfirmed* when perceived performance *falls short* of them[8]

As Nitecki emphasizes:

Service quality is not a number on a scale. It is not a ranking. It is not something produced to specifications or replicated identically across different libraries. Rather, service quality refers to the relationships between library customers and the library organization, between expectations for excellent services and perceptions of services delivered.[9]

She regards service quality as "an important activity toward creating a high quality library that exceeds customer expectations, is strategically managed, performs reliable service, and delivers value."[10]

Sample Service Quality Survey

Nitecki and Hernon took the SERVQUAL questionnaire, which has been used in various service industries to measure and compare service quality, and replaced its statements with ones more meaningful to a particular library, thereby producing an instrument useful for local planning and diagnostic purposes. Their study took place at Yale University libraries, and the success of the project suggests that it can be replicated at other institutions.[11] Nonetheless, the statements will likely require modification from setting to setting because each library has different priorities for service improvement.

Nitecki and Hernon targeted a sample of library users; they did not examine the perceptions of nonusers because these individuals would not have an opinion on service quality. Nonusers, on the other hand, might offer insights into the library's service image and reputation or the role and value of the library in resolving their information needs.

Figure 10 reprints parts A and C of the Yale questionnaire. Questions 31 and 32 in section C would need to be rewritten for a public library.[12] Apparently, a number of libraries do not want to make comparisons with other service industries, preferring instead to compare the service expectations of their users with those of users at other libraries. With this in mind, section B of figure 10 was recast to emphasize the following dimensions:

affect of service (a combined measure of the following dimensions)

- empathy (caring, individualized attention the library provides to its users)

- responsiveness (willingness to help users and provide prompt service)

- assurance (knowledge and courtesy of employees and their ability to inspire trust)

ubiquity and ease of access (timely, ready, and easy access to relevant material; convenient hours of operations; and improved remote access to collections)

reliability (ability to perform the promised service dependably and accurately)

library as a place (the physical building as a place of information gathering, study, and reflection and an affirming symbol of the life of the mind)

adequacy or comprehensiveness of collections (deep collections of relevant print and electronic resources to meet immediate needs)

self-sufficiency or self-reliance (users can be self-reliant within the information-gathering process)[13]

An additional dimension is about tangibles such as the appearance and functionality of the physical facilities and equipment. Section B has value not only for making general comparisons with other libraries but also for providing insights into users' views of the library, their service priorities, and what users believe necessary for them to be successful in the information gathering.

FIGURE 10
Service Quality Survey

SECTION A
Ideal Library

Directions: Based on your experiences as a user of library services, please think about the ideal kind of library that would deliver an *excellent service quality.* Please indicate the extent to which you think such a library should possess the feature described by each of the statements listed below.

If you feel a feature is **"of no importance"** for excellent libraries, circle the number **"1"** for **"strongly disagree."**

If you feel a feature is **"of highest importance"** for excellent libraries, circle **"10"** for **"strongly agree."**

If your feelings are less strong, circle one of the numbers in the middle.

If you have **"no opinion,"** however, please skip the statement.

XXX Library

Directions: The same set of statements relate to your feelings about the services offered by XXX Library. For each statement, please show the extent to which you believe the library has the feature described by the statement.

Circling a **"1"** means that you **"strongly disagree"** that the library has that feature.

Circling a **"10"** means that you **"strongly agree."**

You may circle any of the numbers in the middle that reflect your feelings.

If you have **"no opinion,"** however, please skip the statement.

There are no right or wrong answers. All we are interested in is a number that truly conveys your feelings regarding excellent service quality in libraries. Your individual response will be kept confidential but will help us try to ensure that library services meet your expectations.

SD = strongly disagree   SA = strongly agree

	IN IDEAL LIBRARY	IN XXX LIBRARY
	SD → ↓ SA ↑↓	SD ↑↓ SA ↑↓
1. The online catalog		
a. Displays information that is clear and easy to understand	1 2 3 4 5 6 7 8 9 10	1 2 3 4 5 6 7 8 9 10
b. Has easy-to-follow instructions	1 2 3 4 5 6 7 8 9 10	1 2 3 4 5 6 7 8 9 10
c. Indicates the number of copies available	1 2 3 4 5 6 7 8 9 10	1 2 3 4 5 6 7 8 9 10
d. Is an accurate source of information about *all* materials held by the library	1 2 3 4 5 6 7 8 9 10	1 2 3 4 5 6 7 8 9 10
e. Is easily accessible from outside the library building	1 2 3 4 5 6 7 8 9 10	1 2 3 4 5 6 7 8 9 10
2. The library Web site		
a. Is attractive	1 2 3 4 5 6 7 8 9 10	1 2 3 4 5 6 7 8 9 10
b. Is easy to navigate	1 2 3 4 5 6 7 8 9 10	1 2 3 4 5 6 7 8 9 10
c. Enables me to		
(1) Access a variety of electronic resources	1 2 3 4 5 6 7 8 9 10	1 2 3 4 5 6 7 8 9 10
(2) Interact with library staff	1 2 3 4 5 6 7 8 9 10	1 2 3 4 5 6 7 8 9 10
(3) Log on easily	1 2 3 4 5 6 7 8 9 10	1 2 3 4 5 6 7 8 9 10
(4) Log on whenever I want	1 2 3 4 5 6 7 8 9 10	1 2 3 4 5 6 7 8 9 10
d. Includes online request forms (reference and interlibrary loan)	1 2 3 4 5 6 7 8 9 10	1 2 3 4 5 6 7 8 9 10

	IN IDEAL LIBRARY	IN XXX LIBRARY
	SD → ↓ ... SA ↓	SD → ↓ ... SA ↓

3. Equipment in good working order is available when I need it. The library provides

a. Computer dedicated only for online catalog use

IN IDEAL LIBRARY	IN XXX LIBRARY
1 2 3 4 5 6 7 8 9 10	1 2 3 4 5 6 7 8 9 10

b. Computer printers

| 1 2 3 4 5 6 7 8 9 10 | 1 2 3 4 5 6 7 8 9 10 |

c. Computer workstations (e.g., for access to the Web, electronic texts, and journals)

| 1 2 3 4 5 6 7 8 9 10 | 1 2 3 4 5 6 7 8 9 10 |

d. Microform/fiche printers

| 1 2 3 4 5 6 7 8 9 10 | 1 2 3 4 5 6 7 8 9 10 |

e. Microform/fiche readers

| 1 2 3 4 5 6 7 8 9 10 | 1 2 3 4 5 6 7 8 9 10 |

f. Photocopiers

| 1 2 3 4 5 6 7 8 9 10 | 1 2 3 4 5 6 7 8 9 10 |

4. The staff are

a. Approachable and welcoming

| 1 2 3 4 5 6 7 8 9 10 | 1 2 3 4 5 6 7 8 9 10 |

b. Available when I need them

| 1 2 3 4 5 6 7 8 9 10 | 1 2 3 4 5 6 7 8 9 10 |

c. Courteous and polite

| 1 2 3 4 5 6 7 8 9 10 | 1 2 3 4 5 6 7 8 9 10 |

d. Expert in

(1) Finding general information

| 1 2 3 4 5 6 7 8 9 10 | 1 2 3 4 5 6 7 8 9 10 |

(2) The literature of my discipline

| 1 2 3 4 5 6 7 8 9 10 | 1 2 3 4 5 6 7 8 9 10 |

e. Friendly and easy to talk to

| 1 2 3 4 5 6 7 8 9 10 | 1 2 3 4 5 6 7 8 9 10 |

5. The staff provide assistance to help me

a. Identify resources I need

| 1 2 3 4 5 6 7 8 9 10 | 1 2 3 4 5 6 7 8 9 10 |

b. Retrieve resources I need

| 1 2 3 4 5 6 7 8 9 10 | 1 2 3 4 5 6 7 8 9 10 |

c. Evaluate information I find

| 1 2 3 4 5 6 7 8 9 10 | 1 2 3 4 5 6 7 8 9 10 |

d. Learn how to find information

| 1 2 3 4 5 6 7 8 9 10 | 1 2 3 4 5 6 7 8 9 10 |

6. Library materials

a. Encompass curriculum-supporting videos and films

| 1 2 3 4 5 6 7 8 9 10 | 1 2 3 4 5 6 7 8 9 10 |

b. Meet my course/research needs

| 1 2 3 4 5 6 7 8 9 10 | 1 2 3 4 5 6 7 8 9 10 |

7. Materials I requested from closed stacks come within the time frame quoted by the library staff

| 1 2 3 4 5 6 7 8 9 10 | 1 2 3 4 5 6 7 8 9 10 |

8. When I request materials, I am told how long they will take to arrive

a. From restricted collections

| 1 2 3 4 5 6 7 8 9 10 | 1 2 3 4 5 6 7 8 9 10 |

b. Through interlibrary loan

| 1 2 3 4 5 6 7 8 9 10 | 1 2 3 4 5 6 7 8 9 10 |

9. Materials are

a. In their proper places on the shelves

| 1 2 3 4 5 6 7 8 9 10 | 1 2 3 4 5 6 7 8 9 10 |

b. Reshelved promptly

| 1 2 3 4 5 6 7 8 9 10 | 1 2 3 4 5 6 7 8 9 10 |

10. It is easy to

a. Browse print collections

| 1 2 3 4 5 6 7 8 9 10 | 1 2 3 4 5 6 7 8 9 10 |

b. Find where materials are located in the building

| 1 2 3 4 5 6 7 8 9 10 | 1 2 3 4 5 6 7 8 9 10 |

Service Quality **125**

FIGURE 10
Service Quality Survey (Continued)

	IN IDEAL LIBRARY	IN XXX LIBRARY
	SD SA	SD SA

11. Directional signs are clear and helpful   1 2 3 4 5 6 7 8 9 10   1 2 3 4 5 6 7 8 9 10

12. It is easy to find out, in advance, when the library is open   1 2 3 4 5 6 7 8 9 10   1 2 3 4 5 6 7 8 9 10

13. The library fine policy is clearly stated   1 2 3 4 5 6 7 8 9 10   1 2 3 4 5 6 7 8 9 10

14. Any other expectations which you consider important:

    a. _____   1 2 3 4 5 6 7 8 9 10   1 2 3 4 5 6 7 8 9 10

    b. _____   1 2 3 4 5 6 7 8 9 10   1 2 3 4 5 6 7 8 9 10

SECTION B

Directions: Listed below are eleven features pertaining to libraries and the services they offer. We would like to know how important each of these features is to you when you evaluate a library's quality of service. Please allocate a **total of 100 points** among the eleven features according to how important each feature is to you. The more important a feature is to you, the more points you should allocate to it. Please be sure that the points you allocate to the eleven features add up to 100.

15. The appearance and functionality of the library's physical facilities and equipment   _____ points

16. The library's ability to perform promised services dependably and accurately   _____ points

17. The library's willingness to help users and provide prompt services   _____ points

18. The knowledge and courtesy of the library staff and their ability to inspire trust and confidence   _____ points

19. The caring, individualized attention the library provides to its users   _____ points

20. Timely, ready, and easy access to relevant material   _____ points

21. Convenient hours of operation   _____ points

22. Improved access to electronic collections   _____ points

23. A physical building that serves as a place of information-gathering, study, and reflection   _____ points

24. Deep collections of relevant material—print and electronic—to meet my immediate needs   _____ points

25. Self-reliant in finding information/sources held by the library   _____ points

TOTAL points allocated __100__ points

26. Which *one* feature among items 15–25 is *most*
    important to you? (Circle your choice.)   1 2 3 4 5 6 7 8 9 10 11

27. Which *one* feature among items 15–25 is *least*
    important to you? (Circle your choice.)   1 2 3 4 5 6 7 8 9 10 11

28. Is there anything else not included in the features of items
    15–25 that you find important in evaluating the quality of
    service you receive?

    _____ Yes (please specify:_____

    _____ No

SECTION C

Directions: Please answer a few more questions for us.

29. Overall, to what extent does the service that XXX Library provides
    meet your expectations for an excellent library?

Falls Short	**Meets**	**Surpasses**

    −3   −2   −1   0   +1   +2   +3

30. Please estimate how many times you have used the library during
    this school term.

    a. _____ Daily   d. _____ Less than once a week

    b. _____ Several times a week   e. _____ Other (please specify):_____

    c. _____ Once a week   _____

31. What best describes you?

    a. _____ Undergraduate student   d. _____ Staff

    b. _____ Graduate student   e. _____ Other (please specify):_____

    c. _____ Faculty   _____

32. What general category best describes your discipline?

    a. _____ Behavioral sciences   e. _____ Social sciences

    b. _____ Humanities   f. _____ Undecided

    c. _____ Medical sciences   g. _____ Other (please specify):_____

    d. _____ Physical sciences   _____

Thank you very much for participating in this study.

Adaptation of Yale University survey reported in Danuta A. Nitecki and Peter Hernon,
"Measuring Service Quality at Yale University's Libraries," *Journal of Academic
Librarianship* 26, no. 4 (July 2000), 259–73.

Satisfaction

Satisfaction focuses on a specific transaction, or in the case of *overall satisfaction*, it is a cumulative judgment based on collective encounters with a service provider over time. Satisfaction judgments are more affective and emotional reactions to an experience or collection of experiences than are quality judgments. "Simply put, satisfaction is a sense of contentment that arises from an *actual* experience in relation to an expected experience."[14]

Because service quality probes are precise statements on which the library seeks customer input, they serve as a planning tool. Judgments about satisfaction, on the other hand, tend to be global in the type of questions asked. Unlike service quality, satisfaction focuses less on specific statements and relies more on open-ended questions. In satisfaction surveys, there can be a probing of how customers rate the library in a few specific areas; the list is much shorter and more general than found in a service quality questionnaire. The intention of satisfaction surveys is to identify if some general areas require scrutiny, whereas service quality studies examine specific expectations that might be targeted for improvement. Satisfaction surveys offer organizations the opportunity to gauge the temperament of customers regarding an array of services they use or have used. A service quality questionnaire, such as the one used at Yale University, might ask about any other expectations respondents might consider important, let them insert whatever they want, and rate it. (See figure 10, section A, item 14.) In such an instance, the study of service quality assumes a diagnostic function as respondents are encouraged to comment on whatever they choose.

Figure 11 reproduces a satisfaction survey intended for use with graduating college seniors. Naturally, the instrument would be revised for other audiences. For additional guidance in developing a satisfaction survey, see *Assessing Service Quality* and *Delivering Satisfaction and Service Quality*.[15]

Conducting a Service Quality or Satisfaction Study

Library managers and staff need to decide whether they want to examine either service quality or satisfaction and how any data gathered will be useful for outcomes assessment. It is possible that they might attach some satisfaction questions to a service quality instrument. At any rate, upon reviewing the questionnaires contained in this chapter's figures, they could select the same questions or statements if they feel these reflect their service priorities. On the other hand, they could substitute other questions or statements, perhaps after examining figures 7.4, "Sample Statements on Service Quality Expectations," and 7.5, "Aspects of Service Quality," in *Assessing Service Quality*.[16] As an alternative, libraries might limit their investigation to a particular area or service (e.g., reference or interlibrary loan).[17]

Of course, in either a service quality or a satisfaction survey, libraries should not ignore the networked environment and the use of electronic resources and Web services that users can gain access to from home, the office, library, or other locations. Before conducting the survey, some library customers should be invited to review (and comment on) the list of candidate

Figure 11
Satisfaction Survey for Graduating Seniors

Date _____

Please take a moment to complete this questionnaire and tell us how we are doing. Your candid responses will help us provide high quality service. Thank you. *(Director's name)*

SECTION A

1. Overall, how satisfied were you with the education you received? (Circle the appropriate number)

Completely dissatisfied									Completely satisfied
1	2	3	4	5	6	7	8	9	10

2. If you did not circle *10,* why not?

SECTION B

3. Please rate the college/university on the following items.

	Poor									Excellent
a. Adequately prepared me for a professional career	1	2	3	4	5	6	7	8	9	10
b. Has a good academic reputation	1	2	3	4	5	6	7	8	9	10
c. Has knowledgeable faculty	1	2	3	4	5	6	7	8	9	10
d. Offered an extensive array of relevant courses	1	2	3	4	5	6	7	8	9	10
e. Offered courses that I wanted to take at convenient times	1	2	3	4	5	6	7	8	9	10
f. Provided a high quality education	1	2	3	4	5	6	7	8	9	10
h. Provided a sense of student community	1	2	3	4	5	6	7	8	9	10
i. Provided courses on topics that address the most significant developments in the field	1	2	3	4	5	6	7	8	9	10
j. Provided me with a sufficient understanding about program content and expectations prior to enrollment	1	2	3	4	5	6	7	8	9	10
k. Provided me with an education that will facilitate career growth and development	1	2	3	4	5	6	7	8	9	10
l. Valued diversity	1	2	3	4	5	6	7	8	9	10

4. When I had a problem, a department/program advisor showed a sincere interest in helping to solve it.

    1   2   3   4   5   6   7   8   9   10

5. The administration and staff were helpful.

    1   2   3   4   5   6   7   8   9   10

6. The library had the resources that met my course needs.

    1   2   3   4   5   6   7   8   9   10

(Continued)

Figure 11
Satisfaction Survey for Graduating Seniors (Continued)

SECTION C

7. What did you like the **most** about your program of study?

8. What did you like the **least** about your program of study?

9. If the college/university could have done **one** thing to improve things for you, what would it be?

10. Overall, please rate how much the library contributed to your learning.

11. If you did not circle 7, why not?

12. If the library could have done **one** thing to improve things for you, what would it be?

SECTION D

13. How frequently did you use the library?

    a. _____ Never   c. _____ Frequently

    b. _____ Occasionally   d. _____ Other (please specify) _____

                                                           _____

14. Would you recommended the college/university to someone else?

    a. _____Yes   b. _____ No

15. While taking courses, were you primarily a

    a. _____ Full-time student   b. _____ Part-time student

Thank you for your participation.

statements, and library managers should verify that the statements, indeed, reflect local service priorities.

Assessing Service Quality lays out the procedures for conducting a study of service quality and satisfaction. *Delivering Satisfaction and Service Quality*, however, provides some additional insights into conducting a study—especially if it is to be Web-based—and analyzing and presenting the findings.[18]

Conclusion

The purpose of data collection instruments presented in this chaper is to keep the library attuned to the expectations of its customers—to value their comments and participation. Instead of (or in addition to) conducting a survey, librarians might receive feedback from users by means of comment cards, such as those used by restaurants and hotels, tracking complaints and offering users toll-free hotlines. They might also employ focus-group interviews and advisory panels to try out new ideas and approaches. Regardless of the method employed, it is important to ascertain user expectations and to contrast those expectations with users' perception of how well the library delivers its service.

Outcomes assessment should not ignore user perceptions of service quality and satisfaction because these perceptions may influence the extent to which outcomes can be realized. Service quality and satisfaction focus on creating a supportive, nurturing environment conducive to learning and the conduct of research.

> *If your customers think . . . [there] is a problem, then there is a service quality problem whether or not you think it is real. To improve the service quality, you need to have a way to systematically find out about it.*[19]

Notes

1. Danuta A. Nitecki, "Changing the Concept and Measure of Service Quality in Academic Libraries," *Journal of Academic Librarianship* 22, no. 3 (May 1996), 181.

2. Leo Reisberg, "Are Students Actually Learning?" *Chronicle of Higher Education* (17 Nov. 2000), A67.

3. Ibid., A70.

4. Peter Hernon and Ellen Altman, *Assessing Service Quality: Satisfying the Expectations of Library Customers* (Chicago: American Library Assn., 1998), 51–5; Danuta A. Nitecki, Measuring Library Service Quality: Assignment: Focus on Your Library's Services, Online Lyceum of the Assn. of Research Libraries. Available (with password): http://mccoy.lib.siu.edu/OLMS6/module2/m02a02measuring.html.

5. Danuta A. Nitecki, Measuring Library Service Quality: Service Quality: Background and Theory, Online Lyceum of the Assn. of Research Libraries. Available (with password): http://mccoy.lib.siu.edu/OLMS6/module1/m01p01.shtml.

6. Valarie Zeithaml, A. Parasuraman, and Leonard Berry, *Delivering Quality Services* (New York: The Free Press, 1990).

7. A. Parasuraman, Leonard L. Berry, and Valarie A. Zeithaml, "Refinement and Reassessment of the SERVQUAL Scale," *Journal of Retailing* 67, no. 4 (1991), 420–50.

8. Terry G. Vavra, *Improving Your Measurement of Customer Satisfaction: A Guide to Creating, Conducting, Analyzing, and Reporting Customer Satisfaction Measurement Programs* (Milwaukee, Wisc.: ASQ Quality Press, 1997), 42.

9. Danuta A. Nitecki, Measuring Library Service Quality: Strategically Managing an Organization, Online Lyceum of the Assn. of Research Libraries. Available (with password): http://mccoy.lib.siu.edu/OLMS6/module1/m01p05.shtml.

10. Danuta A. Nitecki, Measuring Library Service Quality: Service Quality Course Conclusion, Online Lyceum of the Assn. of Research Libraries. Available (with password): http://mccoy.lib.siu.edu/OLMS6/module3/m03p18.shtml.

11. Danuta A. Nitecki and Peter Hernon, "Measuring Service Quality at Yale University's Libraries," *Journal of Academic Librarianship* 26, no. 4 (July 2000), 259–73.

12. For guidance, see Peter Hernon and John R. Whitman, *Delivering Satisfaction and Service Quality: A Customer-Based Approach for Libraries* (Chicago: American Library Assn., 2001).

13. Colleen Cook and Fred Heath, "Users' Perceptions of Library Service Quality: A LIBQUAL+ Qualitative Study" (presented at the Assn. of Research Libraries Symposium on the New Culture of Assessment: Measuring Service Quality, Washington, D.C., 20–21 Oct. 2000).

14. Peter Hernon and John R. Whitman, *Delivering Satisfaction and Service Quality: A Customer-Based Approach for Libraries* (Chicago: American Library Assn., 2001), 32.

15. Peter Hernon and Ellen Altman, *Assessing Service Quality: Satisfying the Expectations of Library Customers* (Chicago: American Library Assn., 1998), 180–8; Hernon and Whitman, *Delivering Satisfaction and Service Quality*, 99–108.

16. Hernon and Altman, *Assessing Service Quality*, 108–12.

17. See Danuta A. Nitecki, "An Assessment of the Applicability of SERVQUAL Dimensions as Customer-Based Criteria for Evaluating Quality of Services in an Academic Library" (Ph.D. diss. University of Maryland, 1995); Danuta A. Nitecki, "Assessment of Service Quality in Academic Libraries: Focus on the Applicability of the SERVQUAL," in *Proceedings of the 2nd Northumbria International Conference on Performance Measurement in Libraries and Information Services* (Newcastle upon Tyne, Eng.: Department of Information and Library Management, University of Northumbria at Newcastle, 1998), 181–96.

18. Hernon and Altman, *Assessing Service Quality*; Hernon and Whitman, *Delivering Satisfaction and Service Quality*.

19. Danuta A. Nitecki, Measuring Library Service Quality: Three Points about Measurement, Online Lyceum of the Assn. of Research Libraries. Available (with password): http://mccoy.lib.siu.edu/OLMS6/module2/m02p03.shtml.

10

Making a Commitment to Accountability and Learning Outcomes Assessment

Whether we like it or not, accountability—the enforcement of quality—requires external minimum standards.[1]

Accountability implies an obligation to plan—to know what a program or institution intends to accomplish, determine how well it has accomplished its promises, make improvement when those promises are unfulfilled, and review those promises and set new ones as needed. Accountability focuses on changes and the effectiveness of instruction, programs, and institutions in an atmosphere of continuous quality improvement. Some questions central to accountability are

> How well have students or participants mastered the knowledge, skills, and competencies taught?
>
> How has their performance improved over time (throughout a program of study)?
>
> How well do the courses, programs, and institution achieve their goals and objectives?

Most critical to outcomes assessment is that the answers to these questions reflect more than the perceptions of those enrolled in those courses and programs and more than the grades given by the instructors. There should be an independent assessment, one that places courses within the context of a program of study and looks at the progress that the participants made from the time of their entry into the program until their graduation. That assessment might even look at how well the foundation of lifelong learning has been laid.

Complicating matters, accountability should not be confined to student learning outcomes. It should also extend to outcomes related to research and scholarship and, in the case of public libraries, to the accomplishment of the service responses that the library selected as its priorities. What impact has the library made on its community through those service responses?

Planning is central to accountability and to outcomes assessment. The assessment plan is a document that announces what changes in user skills, values, and perceptions the library wants to produce (defined in terms of outcomes). It also reflects and measures the extent to which the outcomes have been achieved and what additional actions are necessary to improve the effort to produce change. It might be that outcomes merit modification or reconceptualization; clearly, the assessment plan is not static but is an evolving document that will guide the library over time. The intent of outcomes assessment is not to blame librarians and other instructors for failure to achieve the intended results but to focus on program improvement.

Implicit in accountability is that stakeholders have the right to know about the quality of the program of study and that libraries (and other units of an organization or institution) must report to the stakeholders about the effectiveness of their actions and the achievement of their promises—stated as outcomes. An important question is "Which stakeholders have the right to know?" The answer is taxpayers, government bodies and representatives providing oversight and financial support, parents or students paying tuition, accrediting bodies, and undoubtedly others.

Outcomes assessment is a collection of activities organized around the measurement of formally stated outcomes that enable programs and institutions to demonstrate the extent to which the assessment plan has been realized. Libraries involve representatives of the larger community served (e.g., faculty and staff) in the development of the assessment plan (see chapter 3) and in the alignment of that plan with any plan that the institution produced. Clearly, programs and institutions have choices about which outcomes they will focus on and how they will measure them. However, those measures should be clearly worded so that they are not ambiguous or open to varied interpretation.

Accountability is more than a precise specification of results. It also addresses values and judgments and requires leadership to accomplish. By viewing information literacy as one foundation of the library's approach to assessment, there is a need for a philosophical discourse on information and digital literacy in a global context. That discourse is beyond the scope of this book, but it does frame the discussion of information literacy in the context of lifelong learning.

Accountability through learning outcomes assessment is a creative process tailored to the needs and preferences of each program or institution. Engaging in benchmarking or comparisons with "peer" institutions may reveal "best practices" and suggest some innovations that a library might pursue. However, the goal of assessment is not to compare one's programs or institutions with other programs and institutions; rather, it is to challenge each program and institution to improve its performance and to align the rhetoric about program success with *audit evidence*. That evidence, as past chapters have shown, need not always be direct or rigorously collected.

Higher education is beginning to realize that outcomes differ from outputs and performance measures. This book has documented some of the confusion between outcome measures (directed at learning and research) and output and performance measures. At this time, most attention has focused on student learning outcomes, but chapter 6 shows how research outcomes could be developed. As well, other chapters have stressed that outcomes need not be confined to students.

Learning Assessment— an Imperfect Science

Educator Jane V. Wellman regards the assessment of learning as "an imperfect science, one that has not yet evolved into measures that . . . [are] commonly understood and [that are] easily transferred to different types of institutions."[2] In fact, the assessment of learning is not a science but, rather, a tool of the social sciences in which those conducting the assessment draw inferences and make interpretations. They may not always be able to rely on more rigorous research procedures such as the types of experimentation discussed in chapter 7 and appendix J. Librarians and teaching faculty may be unwilling (and, in some instances, unable) to invest their time and resources in the assessment of educational outcomes. Quite frankly, such assessment may not relate to their scholarly interests, they may not want to treat their students as research "subjects," and the rewards may be intrinsic and local. In other words, institutions may not regard such assessment as important for those involved in it. How do the reward structures (e.g., promotion, tenure, and salary raises) support outcomes assessment?

Nonetheless, as discussed in several chapters, the tool chest of methodologies for assessing outcomes is identifiable. Some tools (e.g., the use of capstone courses and portfolios) have received the most attention. However, as shown at The Citadel, pre/posttesting seems promising, especially since the approach adopted there does not involve the more sophisticated experimental design documented in appendix J, in which the assessment team employs inferential statistics. However, simpler approaches always increase the margin of error associated with the interpretation of the findings, thus reinforcing that assessment is not an exact or perfect "science."

What Will Be Good Enough?

Libraries should develop an assessment plan and set outcomes realistically. They should not be overtly ambitious and make more promises than they can honor. There is no magical number of outcomes measures to adopt or evidence to gather. It is impossible to speak in absolute terms, showing that the desired change that occurred can be attributed directly (and solely) to the program of study. Only with the use of repeated measures (use of an experimental design over time) can more solid evidence be gathered. At some point, the pool of evidence from the use of different data-collection efforts may be large enough and sufficiently rigorous in its data collection to permit the results of the various studies to be analyzed by means of meta-analysis. As Ronald R. Powell notes, "There is a growing interest in meta-analysis, which generally refers to a set of statistical procedures used to summarize and integrate many studies that focused on the same issue. It represents a numerical rather than narrative method of relating findings and is considered to be more objective, reliable, and rigorous."[3] Clearly, each program and institution will have to determine what will be good enough. However, the answer should not mean that all future data collection will be terminated or done sporadically. Rather, the focus is more on the types and frequency of data collection.

The intent now is to get librarians and others involved in assessment and to encourage them, over time, to build on the foundation. The purpose of outcomes assessment is to align the library better with its parent institution and to ensure that the library produces evidence supporting its impact on the communities it serves. No longer should libraries merely collect data related to inputs, outputs, and performance measures. It is time, so argue some accrediting bodies and advocates of accountability, for libraries to join the larger institution in documenting change in user behavior and in producing lifelong learners who are knowledgeable about information literacy (both digital and nondigital).

The Need to Clarify Terminology

As is evident from previous chapters, there has been some confusion about outcomes, outputs, institutional effectiveness, and educational quality. Two of the purposes of this book are to draw attention to the terminology and to offer a consistent view of outcomes assessment and the need for libraries to develop assessment plans. We concur with university librarian Sarah Pritchard, who has stated that:

> More research is needed that will lead to agreed-upon measures of library- and information-related outcomes in higher education. As noted, such outcomes might include library literacy, success in graduate school, success in job seeking, faculty research productivity (as shown by grants and publications), and the library's success as a department in attracting gifts and external funding to the campus. With targeted research initiatives where subjective opinion indicates that the library and the university are vital and effective . . . , it might be possible gradually to establish progressive correlations among measures of inputs, processes, outputs, and performance or satisfaction. There might emerge several multidimensional models of effectiveness or an expanded index like that of the ARL, reflecting this more complete view of mission attainment.[4]

ACRL is responding to this challenge with a program to give librarians the skills to create baseline data that support the merits of information literacy programs. ACRL received a National Leadership Grant from the federal Institute of Museum and Library Services for its project, Assessing Student Learning Outcomes in Information Literacy Programs: Training Academic Librarians. The grant "will fund the training of academic librarians to work with faculty to design, implement, and evaluate tools for assessing student learning outcomes resulting from information literacy courses taught by librarians and faculty. Ultimately, such training will not only enhance the status of librarians as educators but also highlight the importance of campus information literacy programs."[5] In today's vernacular, ACRL is "walking the talk."

Setting Priorities

Obviously, librarians could become full-time data collectors and accomplish little else. The intent of outcomes assessment is not to produce such data collectors. Rather, the focus is on setting priorities and ensuring that the rhetoric about program successes matches reality. In other words, libraries and the larger institutions are accountable for their promises and claims. Academic libraries should involve faculty, staff, and administrators in developing the assessment plan. Public libraries should also involve their larger community, especially those individuals who helped a library shape and decide on its service responses. After all, these individuals will probably be interested in determining the extent to which a service response has been achieved and had an impact on the community.

A Taxonomy of Faculty and Library Relationships

Outcomes assessment, managing and shaping change in a time of fiscal retrenchment, dealing with the explosion of electronic resources, and the need to review and often expand services are all indicators of a changing relationship between libraries and members of the communities they serve. University librarian James G. Neal outlines a taxonomy that covers seven faculty and library relationships. These relationships are not mutually exclusive and include the following types of relationships:

> *servant relationship*, in which the library responds "to faculty demands without an opportunity to influence expectations and without mutual respect"
>
> *stranger relationship*, in which the faculty and library "do not work together, but coexist independently in the academy"
>
> *parallel relationship*, in which "faculty and library activities do not intersect, where library collections and services are underutilized, and where faculty's information needs are satisfied from other sources"
>
> *friend relationship*, in which the faculty and library are "cooperative and mutually supportive more out of tradition than intense dependence"
>
> *partner relationship*, in which there is "mutual dependence" between the two and "a shared commitment to improving the quality of both the library and the university"
>
> *customer relationship*, in which there is "a market relationship, with a recognition of the consumer and broker nature of the interaction"
>
> *team or knowledge management relationship*, in which there is a "fuller integration of interests and activities and high levels of personal investment in collaboration"[6]

Neal notes that other relationships within a university focus on interaction with numerous units on and beyond campus for the advancement of research and development, business development through financial planning and human resources, and so on.

Outcomes assessment draws on the customer and on the partner relationships. The former relationship provides a climate that makes the communities served more receptive to what the library is trying to do, whereas the partner relationship realizes that no group can accomplish change without support and cooperation from other groups. Faculty and librarians must work together and have the support of the administration and of stakeholders. Library directors and other managers must engage in personnel recruitment and retention to strengthen the team so it is able and willing to engage in outcomes assessment. There must also be staff development to gain the necessary skills and expertise and to produce a culture and infrastructure of assessment. Some resources may have to be diverted to the accomplishment of the assessment plan. Clearly, as Neal states, "organizational flexibility and agility are essential, and structural and personnel policy development may be valuable" to the accomplishment of assessment and behavioral changes.[7]

Undoubtedly, a partnership relationship will yield a higher quality assessment plan, one that can become an action plan around which libraries, departments, and institutions marshal their resources for a common goal. Furthermore, the evidence will be more varied and directly relevant if a true partnership emerges.

Public Libraries and Assessment

Assessment, including outcomes assessment, should not be viewed as an activity limited to colleges and universities and their libraries. Public libraries would benefit from engaging in assessment and from continuing to develop partnership roles with public education and other segments of the community, including the business community.

The discussion in chapter 6 on the government information service response applies to all service responses. For example, the information literacy service response focuses on outputs. A section on how well the service met the needs of users looks at outputs and respondents' self-reports of satisfaction; however, it does not involve the library's setting of objectives for outcomes assessment. In other words, how has commitment to the service response *changed* the participants' behavior over time?

Lifelong learning, another service response, might contain the following components:

> electronic and print pathfinders
>
> how-to programs on topics of general public interest
>
> special topical displays of materials and resources
>
> artist-in-residence programs
>
> demonstrations and exhibits
>
> history and biography resources.[8]

The manual advises librarians to look at indicators such as "people served," "how well the service met the needs of people served," and "total units of service delivered."[9]

For both of these service responses, the measures tend to be outputs (number of . . .) and only the discussion of "how well the service meets the needs of people served" goes beyond these. Measures of the latter type, based on survey results, provide indirect evidence about satisfaction, perceptions of excellence, and so on. They do not take advantage of the discussion of outcomes assessment and the impact of the library's efforts in contributing to lifelong leaning and information literacy. Have these programs or efforts resulted in a change of behavior? What evidence is offered to support the answer? These answers should not be based merely on self-reporting or self-assessments. Finally, state libraries such as Florida's expect libraries submitting grant proposals to use outcomes assessment as a measure of accountability.

A Challenge

Academic librarians have preferred prescriptive standards because they can use them to seek institutional support when library programs are undersupported—fall below a minimal number. Regardless of their preferences, the movement is toward less-prescriptive measures. As a result, these librarians should leverage information literacy requirements in new standards as part of the library's role and responsibilities to fulfill its educational mission. Some of the accrediting bodies are giving libraries entry into instruction via information literacy. Thus, librarians should embrace the accountability movement and adopt a partner relationship that will result in a broadly supported assessment plan and outcomes assessment. Whatever outcomes measures are adopted must be relevant to the larger institution and not focus solely on the uniqueness of the library. For example, the measures for each service response in public libraries might be rewritten to appeal to educators in primary, middle, and high schools and to reflect student progress in achieving the objectives underlying the service responses.

Now that ACRL has produced information literacy standards, performance indicators, and outcomes (see appendix H), and now that there are creative applications of direct learning measures such as those developed by The Citadel, libraries can become proactive players in their institution or organization by adopting and measuring learning outcomes. Therefore, readers of this book are encouraged to

identify goals and objectives related to learning and research outcomes (achieved through a partnership relationship)

develop modules covering what the library can offer

measure the results

report the results

use the results to improve the delivery of the instructional methodologies employed and the assessment applications, as well as to revise the goals and objectives

Conclusion

The need for accountability has led to demands for evidence of institutional effectiveness. The need for such effectiveness has served as a springboard for a call for evidence that portrays educational quality and effectiveness, and the demand for educational quality has led to a focus on student learning outcomes. Outcomes assessment has often relied on the gathering of indirect rather than direct evidence. Furthermore, outcomes assessment is a natural progression from the use of input measures (e.g., those relating to staff, time, equipment, space, and public relations) and output measures (e.g., those relating to the number of instructions held, students participating, reference questions asked, and interlibrary loan requests received and filled). Some libraries, such as at The Citadel, have been creative in their adoption of outcomes assessment and have been doing such assessment for years. Thus, it cannot be said that outcomes assessment is merely a result of pressure from accrediting bodies and stakeholders; nor should outcomes assessment be seen as a fad that will soon wane. Such assessment looks at impacts and might be regarded as a type of "impact assessment": change in behavior directly attributed to contact with the library. Such assessment becomes more important as the place of the physical library in a digital age is questioned and as some proponents of distance education argue that a library is no longer needed. Outcomes assessment relies on a plan that offers a realistic and accomplishable vision of the role that the library plays in educating and serving its communities.

We all benefit from the successes that libraries achieve as they contribute to information literacy and lifelong learning: The public will, most likely, become library supporters throughout their lives and more effective and efficient library users. They will be better able to retrieve, evaluate, and use information.

> *Because libraries engage in many activities that can be easily counted, librarians have tended to focus on quantities of use as indicators of the goodness of the service.*[10]

Notes

1. Jane V. Wellman, "Accreditors Have to See Past 'Learning Outcomes,'" *The Chronicle of Higher Education* (20 Sept. 2000), B20.
2. Ibid.
3. Ronald R. Powell, *Basic Research Methods for Librarians*, 3d ed. (Greenwich, Conn.: Ablex, 1997), 198. He also notes some cautions in the use of meta-analysis, 199.
4. Sarah M. Pritchard, "Determining Quality in Academic Libraries," *Library Trends* 44, no. 3 (winter 1996), 591.
5. "ACRL Awarded Prestigious IMLS Grant," *College & Research Libraries News* 61, no. 10 (Nov. 2000), 885.
6. James G. Neal, "The Entrepreneurial Imperative Advancing from Incremental to Radical Change in the Academic Library," *Portal: Libraries and the Academy* 1 (Jan. 2001), 9.
7. Ibid., 10.
8. Sandra Nelson, *The New Planning for Results: A Streamlined Approach* (Chicago: American Library Assn., 2001), 212.
9. Ibid., 213–14.
10. Peter Hernon and Ellen Altman, *Assessing Service Quality: Satisfying the Expectations of Library Customers* (Chicago: American Library Assn., 1998), 55.

Southern Association of Colleges and Schools
1998 Criteria for Accreditation, Section V: Educational Support Services

STANDARD 5.1
Library and Other Learning Resources

5.1.1. *Purpose and Scope* Because adequate library and other learning resources and services *are essential* to teaching and learning, each institution *must* ensure that they are available to all faculty members and enrolled students wherever the programs or courses are located and however they are delivered. Each institution *must* develop a purpose statement for its library and other learning resource services. The library and other learning resources *must* be evaluated regularly and systematically to ensure that they are meeting the needs of their users and are supporting the programs and purpose of the institution.

The scope of library and other learning resources, the types of services, and the variety of print and nonprint and electronic media depend on the purpose of the institution. Learning resources and services *must* be adequate to support the needs of users. The size of collections and the amount of money spent on resources and services do not ensure adequacy. Of more importance are the quality, relevance, accessibility, availability, and delivery of resources and services and their actual use by students regardless of location. These considerations *must* be taken into account in evaluating the effectiveness of library and learning resource support. Priorities for acquiring materials and establishing services *must* be determined with the needs of the users in mind.

5.1.2. *Services* Each institution *must* ensure that all students and faculty members have access to a broad range of learning resources to support its purpose and programs at both primary and distance learning sites. Basic library services *must* include an orientation program designed to teach new users how to access bibliographic information and other learning

resources. Any one of a variety of methods, or a combination of them, may be used for this purpose: formal instruction, lectures, library guides and user aids, self-paced instruction, and computer-assisted instruction. Emphasis should be placed on the variety of contemporary technologies used for accessing learning resources. Libraries and learning resource centers *must* provide students with opportunities to learn how to access information in different formats so that they can continue lifelong learning. Librarians must work cooperatively with faculty members and other information providers in assisting students to use resource materials effectively.

Libraries and learning resource centers should provide point-of-use instruction, personal assistance in conducting library research, and traditional reference services. This should be consistent with the goal of helping students develop information literacy—the ability to locate, evaluate, and use information to become independent lifelong learners. Adequate hours *must* be maintained to ensure accessibility to users. Professional assistance should be available at convenient locations during library hours.

Library collections *must* be cataloged and organized in an orderly, easily accessible arrangement following national bibliographical standards and conventions. Students and faculty *must* be provided convenient, effective access to library resources needed in their programs. Convenient, effective access to electronic bibliographic databases, whether onsite or remote, *must* be provided when necessary to support the academic programs.

Libraries and other learning resource centers *must* have adequate physical facilities to house, service, and make library collections easily available; modern equipment in good condition for using print and nonprint materials; provision for interlibrary loan services designed to ensure timely delivery of materials; and an efficient and appropriate

Source: Southern Association of Colleges and Schools, 1998 Criteria for Accreditation, Section V: Educational Support Services.

Available: http://www.sacscoc.org/COC/SectV.htm. Accessed 7 Dec. 2000.

circulation system. Libraries should provide electronic access to materials available within their own system and electronic bibliographic access to materials available elsewhere.

5.1.3. *Library Collections* Institutions *must* provide access to essential references and specialized program resources for each instructional location. Access to the library collection *must* be sufficient to support the educational, research, and public service programs of the institution. The collections of print and nonprint materials *must* be well organized. Institutions offering graduate work *must* provide library resources substantially beyond those required for baccalaureate programs. Librarians, teaching faculty, and researchers *must* share in the development of collections, and the institution *must* establish policies defining their involvement.

Each library or learning resource center *must* have a policy governing resource material selection and elimination and should have a procedure providing for the preservation, replacement, or removal of deteriorating materials in the collection.

5.1.4. *Information Technology* Although access to learning resources is traditionally gained through a library or learning resource center, a wide variety of contemporary technologies can be used to access learning resource materials. Institutions should supplement their traditional library with access to electronic information. Where appropriate, institutions should use technology to expand access to information for users at remote sites, such as extension centers, branch campuses, laboratories, clinical sites, or students' homes. The institution *must* provide evidence that it is incorporating technological advances into its library and other learning resource operations.

5.1.5. *Cooperative Agreements* Cooperative agreements with other libraries and agencies should be considered to enhance the resources and services available to an institution's students and faculty members. However, these agreements *must* not be used by institutions to avoid responsibility for providing adequate and readily accessible library resources and services. Cooperative agreements *must* be formalized and regularly evaluated.

5.1.6. *Staff* Libraries and other learning resources *must* be adequately staffed by professionals who hold graduate degrees in library science or in related fields such as learning resources or information technology. In exceptional cases, outstanding professional experience and demonstrated competence may substitute for this academic preparation; however, in such cases, the institution *must* justify the exceptions on an individual basis. Because professional or technical training in specialized areas is increasingly important in meeting user needs, professionals with specialized nonlibrary degrees may be employed, where appropriate, to supervise these areas.

The number of library support staff members *must* be adequate. Qualifications or skills needed for these support positions should be defined by the institution. Organizational relationships, both external and internal to the library, should be clearly specified. Institutional policies concerning faculty status, salary and contractual security for library personnel *must* be clearly defined and made known to all personnel at the time of employment.

5.1.7 *Library/Learning Resources for Distance Learning Activities* For distance learning activities, an institution *must* ensure the provision of and ready access to adequate library/learning resources and services to support the courses, programs, and degrees offered. The institution *must* own the library/learning resources, provide access to electronic information available through existing technologies, or provide them through formal agreements. Such agreements should include the use of books and other materials. The institution *must* assign responsibility for providing library/learning resources and services and for ensuring continued access to them at each site.

When formal agreements are established for the provision of library resources and services, they *must* ensure access to library resources pertinent to the programs offered by the institution and include provision for services and resources which support the institution's specific programs in the field of study and at the degree level offered.

APPENDIX B — Mildred F. Sawyer Library
Student Learning Outcomes Assessment Plan for Information Literacy

Suffolk University's Mission Statement places students at the center of its efforts and value structure, and emphasizes academic excellence through teaching, based on the application of theory and research to practice and public service. The Mildred F. Sawyer Library's Mission Statement identifies three education goals: students should be able to find and evaluate information, learn rather than amass information, and turn information into knowledge. Additionally, students are expected to become independent, self-sufficient, self-directed lifelong information users.

Conducting student learning outcomes assessments is intended and designed to improve library services. *Outcomes*, as viewed by the Association of College and Research Libraries' Task Force on Academic Library Outcomes Assessment Report (available: http://www.ala.org/acrl/outcome.html), are "the ways in which library users are changed as a result of their contact with the library's resources and programs." The results from our outcomes assessment efforts may not be able to stand up to scientific scrutiny, but they should be able to give the staff of the Mildred F. Sawyer Library a basis for informed judgment on which instructional methodologies work and which do not work.

As stated in the Association of College and Research Libraries' *Information Literacy Competency Standards for Higher Education* ([Chicago: Assn. of College and Research Libraries, 2000] Available: http://www.ala.org/acrl/ilintro. html), *information literacy* is "a set of abilities requiring individuals to recognize when information is needed and have the ability to be able to locate, evaluate, and use effectively the needed information." Information literacy forms the basis for lifelong learning. It is common to all disciplines, to all learning environments, and to all levels of education. It enables learners to master content and extend their investigations, become more self-directed, and assume greater control over their own learning.

Student information literacy performance indicators (outcomes) are the abilities to

identify a variety of types of information and formats of potential sources of information

construct and implement effectively designed search strategies

retrieve information online or in person using a variety of methods

evaluate the availability of needed information and make decisions on broadening the information-seeking process beyond institutionally held resources

apply initial criteria for evaluating both the information and its sources

recognize many of the ethical, legal, and socioeconomic issues concerning the use of information and information technology

Identified learning objectives may be grouped by content, skills and abilities, and attitudes and values. Each of these groups may, in turn, be evaluated by level of achievement.

BASIC LEVEL
Find Information "Owned" by the Mildred F. Sawyer Library

Content

locating information in, or provided by, the Sawyer Library in various physical and virtual formats

distinguishing among and between material formats (how a book can be distinguished from an article, etc.)

using information technology such as computer workstations and World Wide Web browsers to locate, determine the availability, and access information sources

recognizing that information is available in a multiplicity of formats and from a multiplicity of sources; not everything is in electronic format via the World Wide Web

constructing a search strategy using appropriate commands for the information retrieval system selected (e.g., Boolean operators, truncation, and proximity for search engines; internal organizers such as indexes for books)

effectively using time spent when conducting research and enhancing search results

recognizing how librarians and faculty "develop" print and nonprint collections using selection criteria. In addition, the Sawyer Library recommends dozens of Web sites and includes links to them on electronic help guides. Students learn that high quality resources can be found by using our collections and guides.

Skills and Abilities

identify information needs for a course(s)
- identify key concepts and terms that describe the information need

find and locate information in, or provided by, the Sawyer Library
- list terms that may be useful for locating information on a topic
- identify keywords or phrases that represent a topic in general sources (e.g., library catalog, periodical index, online source) and in subject-specific sources
- use a specialized dictionary, encyclopedia, bibliography, or other common reference tool in print format for a given topic
- identify alternate terminology, including synonyms, broader or narrower words, and phrases that describe a topic
- effectively search the library's online catalog to identify relevant books, print and e-journals, microforms, and databases
- apply language and protocols (e.g., Boolean, adjacency, and others) appropriate to the online catalog
- locate materials in the library
- use library-developed help guides

effectively search in the library's licensed databases
- identify which database(s) would be an appropriate tool for a particular topic
    use subject-specific databases
- apply fields such as author, title, subject, and keyword to search for information sources in one database
- use search language and protocols (e.g., Boolean, adjacency, and others) appropriate to the licensed database
- find and use abstracts (understand how to use the online catalog to find information sources identified in abstracts)
- identify and retrieve appropriate full-text articles
- distinguish between full-text and bibliographic databases
- apply the same searching strategies in additional subscription databases to determine database-specific syntax
- apply advanced searching strategies in subscription databases

- identify the source of help within a database and use it effectively
- employ e-mail to send articles in addition to printing articles in the library

access the library's subscription databases on and off campus
- identify various formats in which information is available (e.g., book, journal, multimedia, database, Web site, data set, audio/visual)
- recognize when to use a book and when to use a journal article
- differentiate between scholarly and nonscholarly journals
- differentiate between sources that are primary and secondary
- differentiate between sources that are abstracts and full-text
- use background information sources effectively to gain an initial understanding of the topic
- consult with the course instructor and librarians to develop a manageable focus for the topic
- narrow a broad topic and broaden a narrow one by modifying the scope or direction of the question being investigated
- select appropriate tools (e.g., indexes, online databases) for research on a particular topic
- expand the research by using appropriate general or subject-specific sources to discover terminology related to the topic
- examine footnotes and bibliographies from retrieved items to locate additional relevant sources
- follow, retrieve, and evaluate relevant online links for additional sources
- recognize that the library pays for access to databases, information tools, full-text resources, etc., and may use the Web to deliver them to its clientele
- present and communicate information to others using academic citations styles such as those of the Modern Language Association and the American Psychological Association
- locate information about documentation styles either in print or electronically, e.g., through the library's Web site

Attitudes and Values

students become confident and skillful information users

students effectively take advantage of access to information and use technology available in the Sawyer Library on and off campus

INTERMEDIATE LEVEL
Find Information Other Libraries and Information Providers "Own"

Content

locate and organize information from various libraries and sources

understand and use the information-search process in a variety of Web-based resources such as directories

Skills and Abilities

find print/microform resources in other libraries

- use other libraries' online catalogs
- use other Boston libraries, especially members of the Fenway Library Consortium

create an effective Web search

- identify the differences between freely available Internet search tools and subscription or fee-based databases
- effectively use Web search engines/directories such as Google
- effectively use Web-based academic search directories such as Argus
- apply Boolean, truncation, proximity, and phrase search strategies; search within domains
- differentiate between the results of a search using a general Web search engine (e.g., Google) and a library-provided tool (e.g., Web-based article index, full-text electronic journal, Web-based library catalog)

Attitudes and Values

students become confident and skillful information users

students become independent information users

ADVANCED LEVEL
Evaluate Information Resources from Any Source

Content

locate, organize, and evaluate information from any source

examine and compare information from various sources in order to evaluate reliability, validity, accuracy, authority, timeliness, and point of view or bias

distinguish between fair use and plagiarism, and understand the appropriate and legal use of information and information technology

Skills and Abilities

assess and evaluate information

- understand how to identify and evaluate bias and the credibility of information
- evaluate the quality of the information retrieved using criteria such as authorship, point of view/bias, date written, citations
- assess the relevance of information found by examining elements of the citation such as title, abstract, subject headings, source, and date of publication

critically evaluate Web pages

recognize intellectual property rights and copyright

- recognize the social/ethical/political/economic implications of information and intellectual property

Attitudes and Values

students become confident and skillful information users

students develop critical thinking skills

students become ethical users of the intellectual property of others

TEACHING OUTCOMES

Staff of the Mildred F. Sawyer teach the outcomes through application of these methods:

individual encounters at the reference desk, in working with students at computer workstations, and in responding to e-mail or telephone calls

in-depth research consultations

bibliographic instruction classes held in the library or in another part of the university

printed help guides, also accessible through our Web site

Staff of the Mildred F. Sawyer offer these specific curriculum modules/sessions through bibliographic instruction as part of the effort to achieve the outcomes:

select information resources in the Sawyer Library

select types and formats of information resources (primary versus secondary, books versus journals, and others)

differentiate between scholarly and nonscholarly sources

design efficient and enhanced searching by utilizing basic, intermediate, and advanced searching in the library's online catalog, licensed databases, and Web directories/ engines using search fields, Boolean, proximity, phrases, and domains

identify relevant print, microform, nonprint, and electronic information sources using abstracts, bibliographies, and the online catalog to ascertain the location of the identified sources

design search strategies that include the effective and appropriate use of subscription, full-text databases

apply the correct mechanisms to access the library's subscription databases on and off campus

evaluate Web pages

apply intellectual property rights and copyright to the resources cited in class papers, theses, and dissertations

USE OF ASSESSMENT RESULTS

Staff of the Mildred F. Sawyer have identified the following measures to collect/compile data and determine how well outcomes are being achieved.

Direct Measures

provide bibliographic instruction
- specific: number of classes conducted by course.

answer reference questions
- specific: Do reference questions asked change as the semester progresses from directional and "basic" to content and "advanced"?

collect and analyze collections and document delivery statistics
- specific: changes in the Fenway Library Consortium's Walk-in InterLibrary Loan statistics

collect and analyze servers (Web and proxy) statistics
- specific: Collect information on the use of the proxy server in September and October. Conduct "basic" instruction on connecting to the proxy server. Then, collect information on the use of the proxy server in October, November, and December. As a result of the instruction, use of the proxy server should increase during each academic semester.

collect and analyze vendor statistics
- specific: Collect information concerning the number of searches conducted, and the number of hits per search in October from EBSCO Academic Search Premier. Conduct "basic" instruction concerning the application of Boolean search techniques on this database. Then, collect information concerning the number of searches conducted and the number of hits per search in November and December from EBSCO Academic Search Premier. As a result of the instructions, the number of hits per search should decline as

students appropriately apply Boolean search strategies to more effectively find information.

recognize primary versus secondary sources
- specific: pre/posttesting

use online catalogs of other libraries
- specific: Fenway Library Consortium's Walk-in InterLibrary Loan statistics
- specific: pre/posttesting

apply search strategies including Boolean, proximity, phrases, domain, etc.
- specific: pre/posttesting

use Web search directories; for example, Google versus Argus
- specific: pre/posttesting

evaluate Web sites
- specific: pre/posttesting

recognize issues associated with intellectual property and copyright
- specific: pre/posttesting

Indirect Measures

determine how the library influences students' information-seeking behavior (based on faculty perceptions)
- specific: faculty surveys

examine student bibliographies for selected courses such as Science 301
- review students' citations to scholarly/nonscholarly articles
- review students' citations to Web sites
- review students' citations to nonelectronic sources

use other libraries' collections and resources
- specific: student surveys
- specific: faculty surveys

degree of satisfaction with Mildred F. Sawyer Library
- specific: student (surveys and meeting with groups of students and with individuals)
- specific: faculty (surveys and meeting with groups of faculty members and individuals)

The staff of the Mildred F. Sawyer Library use assessment results to improve academic programs by

incorporating results and analysis into progress reports

incorporating results and analysis into modifying/revising educational goals and objectives, instructional methods employed, and learning modules offered

APPENDIX C

Mildred F. Sawyer Library
Faculty Support Outcomes Assessment Plan

Suffolk University's Mission Statement places students at the center of its efforts and value structure and emphasizes academic excellence through teaching based on the application of theory and research to practice and public service. The Mildred F. Sawyer Library's Mission Statement supports the teaching, learning, and research needs of faculty and provides a place for students and faculty to read and study, to gather and deliberate, and to question, challenge, and support one another.

Faculty are central in all higher education endeavors. From the library's perspective, the focus to date has been on acquiring requested information resources and making information more accessible rather than addressing specifically how and why the faculty uses the library. The Sawyer Library needs to measure the ways in which the library supports the faculty.

Conducting faculty support outcomes assessments is intended and designed to improve library services. *Outcomes*, as viewed by the Association of College and Research Libraries' Task Force on Academic Library Outcomes Assessment Report (available: http://www.ala.org/acrl/outcome.html), are "the ways in which library users are changed as a result of their contact with the library's resources and programs." The results from our outcomes assessment efforts may not be able to stand up to scientific scrutiny, but they should be able to give the staff of the Mildred F. Sawyer Library a basis for informed judgment about which support mechanisms work and which do not work.

Specifically, we want to identify the ways in which the Sawyer Library is supporting the faculty's research and contributing to their teaching efforts. For example, what library resources do faculty need to conduct research and to teach? Is the library providing those resources? Has faculty research improved/benefited from the growth of library resources, such as office and off-campus access to electronic resources? Have library resources aided in teaching? Do faculty members collaborate with library staff concerning classroom support and/or professional responsibilities? How may the library improve our efforts to support the faculty?

Faculty support performance indicators (outcomes) focus on the ability and willingness of the faculty to use the library

as a resource supporting their course requirements, such as reserves, collections, reference staff, facility

to instruct students on general and specific basic, intermediate, and advanced information literacy skills

to instruct students on course-specific, topic-based research processes

as a resource to support the information needs as a result of faculty research, publication, and other professional responsibilities and endeavors

to update and maintain faculty information seeking, retrieval, and evaluation skills so that they can transfer these skills to students, as well as applying them to their professional responsibilities effectively and efficiently

SUPPORT OBJECTIVES

Content

knowledge of available library resources and services

use of library resources to support course requirements and assignments

use of library instructional sessions for teaching information literacy skills and course-specific research

use of library resources for research and other professional endeavors (e.g., collection development, document delivery, and interlibrary loan)

use of the library to update information-seeking, retrieval, and evaluation skills

Skills and Abilities

effectively and efficiently access, search, and retrieve information from any electronic resource

critically evaluate Web-based sources

incorporate article-level persistent URLs on syllabi from library-licensed databases

Attitudes and Values

library resources are available and supportive

147

students should learn how to use the library because of the information literacy skills acquired

the library is an active partner in instructional and classroom endeavors

the library is an active partner in professional endeavors

[Library Staff Responsibilities]

Staff of the Mildred F. Sawyer Library support the outcomes through application of these methods:

promotion of library resources and services through a variety of means (e.g., the library's Web site, newsletters, e-mails, and presentations)

faculty development in one-on-one collaboration and in meetings/presentations in offices, programs/ departmental meetings, or general faculty meetings

assisting faculty by presenting instructional sessions to students concerning library services, resources, and skills

assisting faculty in developing learning modules concerning library resources, services, and skills that they can employ themselves in their classroom

maintaining the library's services infrastructure of collections, staff, technology, and facilities

USE OF ASSESSMENT RESULTS

Staff of the Mildred F. Sawyer Library have identified the following measures to collect/compile data and determine how well the objectives support the identified outcomes:

Direct Measures

Faculty require student use of library resources (collection, staff, facility, and technology) for course assignments. (Report number, type, and extent of library usage as required by course assignments.)

Coverage of information literacy skills development in course content and assignments is measured. (Report number, type, and extent of library usage as required by course assignments.)

Instruction by librarians in all courses is measured. (Report number, type, and for which courses instruction sessions have been conducted.)

Document delivery and interlibrary loan usage by faculty are measured. (Report documents or interlibrary loans requested and filled.)

Indirect Measures

Has use of the library affected teaching and course assignments? (faculty surveys)

Does the library provide adequate resources to support courses? (faculty surveys)

Does the library provide adequate training/instruction for students and faculty? (faculty surveys)

Has use of the library affected faculty application of research methods and techniques? (faculty surveys)

Has use of the library had a positive impact on faculty publications? (faculty surveys)

The staff of the Mildred F. Sawyer Library use the assessment results to improve our faculty support efforts by incorporating results and analysis into

progress reports

modifying/revising objectives and methods employed

assessment plans

Information Literacy

In October 1998, the Wisconsin Association of Academic Librarians (WAAL) adopted standards for information literacy and competencies for statewide implementation that outline specific information competency skills.

The student who is information literate is able to

1. Identify and articulate needs [that] require information solutions

    1.1 Recognize a specific information need
    1.2 Focus and articulate the information need into a researchable question
    1.3 Understand that the type and amount of information selected is determined in part by the parameters of the need as well as by the information available

2. Identify and select appropriate information sources

    2.1 Recognize the availability of a variety of sources and of assistance with using them
    2.2 Identify types of information resources in a variety of formats (e.g., primary or secondary, books or periodicals, print or electronic) and understand their characteristics
    2.3 Select types of information resources appropriate to a specific information need

3. Formulate and efficiently execute search queries appropriate for the information resource

    3.1 Understand that different information sources and formats require different searching techniques, including browsing
    3.2 Select the search strategies appropriate to the topic and resource
    3.3 Understand that various resources may use different controlled vocabularies to refer to the same topic
    3.4 Use search language appropriate to the source, such as a controlled vocabulary, key words, natural language, [and] author and title searches to locate relevant items in print and electronic resources

    3.5 Use online search techniques and tools (e.g., Boolean operators and symbols, limiters, and truncation) to locate relevant citations and to further refine the search

4. Interpret and analyze search results and select relevant sources

    4.1 Understand that search results may be presented according to various ordering principles (e.g., relevance ranking, author, title, date, or publisher)
    4.2 Assess the number and relevance of sources cited to determine whether the search strategy must be refined
    4.3 Recognize the components of a citation and differentiate between types of resources cited, such as a book, periodical, or government document as well as the format (e.g., electronic or physical)
    4.4 Use the components of a citation (e.g., currency, reputation of author or source, format, or elements of a URL) to choose those most suitable for the information need
    4.5 Perceive gaps in information retrieved and determine whether the search should be refined

5. Locate and retrieve relevant sources in a variety of formats from the global information environment

    5.1 Understand the organization of materials in libraries and use locally produced location guides
    5.2 Understand how to use classification systems and their rationale
    5.3 Use location information in the bibliographic record to retrieve locally owned resources
    5.4 Use local resources to locate information sources in the global information environment
    5.5 Understand that libraries have developed methods for locating and sharing resources not owned locally and use the appropriate resource sharing system, such as interlibrary loan or document delivery, to retrieve information

Source: Information Literacy Committee of the Wisconsin Association of Academic Librarians, Information Literacy Competencies and Criteria for Academic Libraries in Wisconsin, October 1998. Available: http://facstaff.uww.edu/WAAL/infolit/ilcc.html. Accessed 8 Feb. 2001.

5.6 Understand that the Internet may be a useful resource for locating, retrieving, and transferring information electronically

6. Critically evaluate the information retrieved

6.1 Use a variety of criteria, such as author's credentials, peer review, and reputation of the publisher, to assess the authority of the source

6.2 Assess the relevancy of a source to an information need by examining publication date, purpose, and intended audience

6.3 Recognize omission in the coverage of a topic

6.4 Recognize and evaluate documentation for the information source, such as research methodology, bibliography, or footnotes

6.5 Distinguish between primary and secondary sources in different disciplines and evaluate their appropriateness to the information need

6.6 Apply evaluation criteria to all information formats

7. Organize, synthesize, integrate, and apply the information

7.1 Use appropriate documentation style to cite sources used

7.2 Summarize the information retrieved (e.g., write an abstract or construct an outline)

7.3 Recognize and accept the ambiguity of multiple points of view

7.4 Organize the information in a logical and useful manner

7.5 Synthesize the ideas and concepts from the information sources collected

7.6 Determine the extent to which the information can be applied to the information need

7.7 Integrate the new information into existing body of knowledge

7.8 Create a logical argument based on information retrieved

8. Self-assess the information-seeking processes used

8.1 Understand that information-seeking consists of evolving, nonlinear processes that include making multiple decisions and choices

8.2 Describe the criteria used to make decisions and choices at each step of the particular process used

8.3 Assess effectiveness of each step of the process and refine the search process in order to make it more effective

8.4 Understand that many of the components of an information-seeking process are transferable and, therefore, are applicable to a variety of information needs

9. Understand the structure of the information environment and the process by which both scholarly and popular information is produced, organized, and disseminated

9.1 Understand that information structure (e.g., how information is produced, organized, and disseminated) can vary from discipline to discipline

9.2 Understand that the value of a particular type of information resource (e.g., book, article, conference proceeding) may vary from discipline to discipline

9.3 Understand that the information structure in a particular discipline can change and modify search strategies to accommodate these changes

10. Understand public policy and the ethical issues affecting the access and use of information

10.1 Understand the ethics of information use, such as knowing how and when to give credit to information and ideas gleaned from others by appropriately citing sources in order to avoid plagiarism

10.2 Respect intellectual property rights by respecting copyright

10.3 Understand concepts and issues relating to censorship, intellectual freedom, and respect for differing points of view

10.4 Understand the social/political issues affecting information, such as
   a. privacy
   b. privatization and access to government information
   c. electronic access to information
   d. the exponential growth of information
   e. equal access to information

1999–2000 Freshmen Pre/Posttest
from the Daniel Library, The Citadel

PRETEST

Company _____

Student number _____-_____-_____   Date____/____/_____

Clearly list all of the steps you would go through in order to perform the following tasks:

1. Find a book in The Citadel Library on the subject of *earthquakes*.

2. Find a journal or magazine article on the subject of *earthquakes*.

3. How many times *last semester* did you
   a. visit your high school library?   _____
   b. check out books from that library?   _____
   c. use a computer database in that library?   _____
   d. obtain a copy of an article from that library?   _____
   e. attend library instruction with a class?   _____
   f. complete assignments that require library research? _____

Indicate how much each of the following statements is true for you.

		NOT TRUE ↓				VERY TRUE ↓
4.	I feel comfortable in libraries	1	2	3	4	5
5.	I am good with computers	1	2	3	4	5
6.	I enjoy reading	1	2	3	4	5
7.	I can usually find what I need at the library	1	2	3	4	5
8.	I like puzzles and brain teasers	1	2	3	4	5
9.	I prefer Macintosh computers	1	2	3	4	5
10.	I probably don't spend much time at the library	1	2	3	4	5
11.	I like to do my studying at the library	1	2	3	4	5
12.	I usually get the help I need at the library	1	2	3	4	5
13.	I have learned a lot about research from libraries	1	2	3	4	5

POSTTEST

Company _____

Student number _____-_____-_____   Date_____/_____/_____

_____

Clearly list all of the steps you would go through in order to perform the following tasks:

1. Find a book in The Citadel Library on the subject of *earthquakes*.

2. Find a journal or magazine article on the subject of *earthquakes*.

3. How many times *this school year* (1999–2000) did you.
    a. visit the Daniel Library?   _____
    b. check out books from the Daniel Library?   _____
    c. use a computer database in the Daniel Library
       (or from your computer or a lab)?   _____
    d. obtain a copy of an article from the library?   _____
    e. attend library instruction with a class?   _____
    f. complete assignments that require library research?   _____

Indicate how much each of the following statements is true for you.

	NOT TRUE ↓			VERY TRUE ↓
4. I feel comfortable in libraries	1	2	3	4	5
5. I am good with computers	1	2	3	4	5
6. I enjoy reading	1	2	3	4	5
7. I can usually find what I need at the library	1	2	3	4	5
8. I like puzzles and brain teasers	1	2	3	4	5
9. I prefer Macintosh computers	1	2	3	4	5
10. I probably don't spend much time at the library	1	2	3	4	5
11. I like to do my studying at the library	1	2	3	4	5
12. I usually get the help I need at the library	1	2	3	4	5
13. I have learned a lot about research from libraries	1	2	3	4	5

2000–2001 Freshmen Pre/Posttest
from the Daniel Library, The Citadel

PRETEST

Company _____

Student number _____-_____-_____   Date_____/_____/_____

Clearly list all of the steps you would go through in order to perform the following tasks:

1. Find a book in The Citadel Library on the subject of *earthquakes.*

2. Find a journal or magazine article on the subject of *earthquakes.*

Circle the correct response.

During the previous year:

3. Did you receive instruction on how to use your local library or your school's library/media resources center?	Never	Once	2–5 times	More than 5 times
4. Did you use a local library or your school's library/media resources center to use or check out books, articles, or other material for your classes?	Never	Once	2–5 times	More than 5 times
5. Did you use resources from a local library or your school's library/media resources center to prepare a research paper or bibliography?	Never	Once	2–5 times	More than 5 times
6. Did you use the Internet or World Wide Web to prepare a research paper or bibliography?	Never	Once	2–5 times	More than 5 times
7. Did you use the library as a quiet place to read or study?	Never	Once	2–5 times	More than 5 times
8. Did you ask a librarian, a school media specialist, or a staff member for help in finding information on a topic?	Never	Once	2–5 times	More than 5 times
9. Did you use a computerized index or database (of journal articles or books) to find information on a topic?	Never	Once	2–5 times	More than 5 times

Do you agree?

10. Do you agree with the statement, "Everything is on the Web"?	Strongly Agree	Agree	Disagree	Strongly Disagree	Don't Know
11. A step in using Web-based materials for research is to examine the Web page for information about its author's qualifications and affiliation.	Strongly Agree	Agree	Disagree	Strongly Disagree	Don't Know
12. You must always document information found on the Internet.	Strongly Agree	Agree	Disagree	Strongly Disagree	Don't Know

POSTTEST

Company _____

Student number _____-_____-_____   Date_____/_____/_____

Clearly list all of the steps you would go through in order to perform the following tasks:

1. Find a book in The Citadel Library on the subject of _earthquakes._

2. Find a journal or magazine article on the subject of _earthquakes._

Circle the correct response.

During the fall 2000 semester:

3. Did you receive instruction on how to use the Daniel Library?	Never	Once	2–5 times	More than 5 times
4. Did you use the Daniel Library to use or check out books, articles, or other material for your classes?	Never	Once	2–5 times	More than 5 times
5. Did you use resources from the Daniel Library to prepare a research paper or bibliography?	Never	Once	2–5 times	More than 5 times
6. Did you use the Internet or World Wide Web to prepare a research paper or bibliography?	Never	Once	2–5 times	More than 5 times
7. Did you use the library as a quiet place to read or study?	Never	Once	2–5 times	More than 5 times
8. Did you ask a librarian or a staff member for help in finding information on a topic?	Never	Once	2–5 times	More than 5 times
9. Did you use a computerized index or database (of journal articles or books) to find information on a topic?	Never	Once	2–5 times	More than 5 times

Do you agree?

10. Do you agree with the statement, "Everything is on the Web"?	Strongly Agree	Agree	Disagree	Strongly Disagree	Don't Know
11. A step in using Web-based materials for research is to examine the Web page for information about its author's qualifications and affiliation.	Strongly Agree	Agree	Disagree	Strongly Disagree	Don't Know
12. You must always document information found on the Internet.	Strongly Agree	Agree	Disagree	Strongly Disagree	Don't Know

APPENDIX

G

History 203, Student Research Survey
from the Daniel Library, The Citadel
April 24, 2000

1. What did you learn in the library research instruction classes that you did not previously know?

2. What was not covered in the library research instruction classes that you wish had been covered?

3. What was most helpful about the library research instruction classes?

4. What was least helpful?

5. What sources did you use to find research material (books, journal articles, etc.) for your paper? Check all that apply.

Historical Abstracts	_____
America: History & Life	_____
Expanded Academic Index	_____
WorldCat	_____
Daniel Library catalog	_____
C of C catalog	_____
bibliographies in books	_____
bibliographies in articles	_____
Internet Web sites	_____
other (please expain):_____	

(Continued)

6. Did you use material (books, journal articles, etc.) from the Daniel Library?

7. Did you get material (books, journal articles, etc.) from interlibrary loan?

8. If you answered *yes* to number 7, approximately how many items did you get?

9. Assuming you did not wait until the last minute, did the interlibrary loan material arrive in time to use in your paper?

10. Where did you do most of your research?

    Daniel Library   _____
    ITS labs   _____
    your own computer   _____
    other (please explain): _____

11. Two class periods were devoted to library research instruction. Was this adequate training?

12. If you answered *no* to number 11, was it too much or too little instruction?

13. When/if you sought individual research help in the Daniel Library, did you receive adequate assistance? Please explain.

14. What we most want to know is if the Daniel Library is meeting your research needs in terms of research instruction, reference help, and library materials. Please tell us about your research experience—what worked, what didn't, successes, problems, or anything else that may help us to help you.

Note: After completing the survey the students were invited to informally discuss their research experience with the library instructors. While that discussion is not reported here, the most significant point made by a majority of the students was their wish for the library to subscribe to J-STOR. Over one-third of the students said they had gone to the C of C library to use it and that it was the most useful source they found. Oddly, their use of J-STOR is not reflected in their survey answers.

APPENDIX H

Information Literacy Standards, Performance Indicators, and Outcomes

STANDARD ONE

The information literate student determines the nature and extent of the information needed

Performance Indicators

1. The information literate student defines and articulates the need for information. Outcomes include:

    confers with instructors and participates in class discussions, peer workgroups, and electronic discussions to identify a research topic or other information need

    develops a thesis statement and formulates questions based on the information need*

    explores general information sources to increase familiarity with the topic

    defines or modifies the information need to achieve a manageable focus*

    identifies key concepts and terms that describe the information need*

    recognizes that existing information can be combined with original thought, experimentation, and/or analysis to produce new information*

2. The information literate student identifies a variety of types and formats of potential sources for information. Outcomes include:

    knows how information is formally and informally produced, organized, and disseminated

    recognizes that knowledge can be organized into disciplines that influence the way information is accessed

identifies the value and differences of potential resources in a variety of formats (e.g., multimedia, database, Web site, data set, audio/visual, book)

identifies the purpose and audience of potential resources (e.g., popular vs. scholarly, current vs. historical)

differentiates between primary and secondary sources, recognizing how their use and importance vary with each discipline

Realizes that information may need to be constructed with raw data from primary sources

3. The information literate student considers the costs and benefits of acquiring the needed information. Outcomes include:

    determines the availability of needed information and makes decisions on broadening the information-seeking process beyond local resources (e.g., interlibrary loan; using resources at other locations; obtaining images, videos, text, or sound)

    considers the feasibility of acquiring a new language or skill (e.g., foreign or discipline-based) in order to gather needed information and to understand its context

    defines a realistic overall plan and time line to acquire the needed information*

4. The information literate student reevaluates the nature and extent of the information needed. Outcomes include:

    reviews the initial information need to clarify, revise, or refine the question*

    describes criteria used to make information decisions and choices*

Source: American Library Assn., Assn. of College and Research Libraries, *Information Literacy Competency Standards for Higher Education* (Chicago: Assn. of College and Research Libraries, 2000), 8–14. Another source revisits learning outcomes and offers a somewhat different characterization of the outcomes discussed in this appendix; see American Library Assn., Assn. of College and Research Libraries, Instruction Section, "Objectives for Informa-

tion Literacy Instruction: A Model Statement for Academic Libraries," *College & Research Libraries News* 62, no. 4 (April 2001), 416–28.

Note: *Indicates a learning outcome that might be converted into a research outcome.

STANDARD TWO

The information literate student accesses needed information effectively and efficiently

Performance Indicators

1. The information literate student selects the most appropriate investigative methods or information retrieval systems for accessing the needed information. Outcomes include:

   identifies appropriate investigative methods (e.g., laboratory experiment, simulation, fieldwork)*

   investigates benefits and applicability of various investigative methods*

   investigates the scope, content, and organization of information retrieval systems

   selects efficient and effective approaches for accessing the information needed from the investigative method or information retrieval system

2. The information literate student constructs and implements effectively designed search strategies. Outcomes include:

   develops a research plan appropriate to the investigative method*

   identifies keywords, synonyms, and related terms for the information needed

   selects controlled vocabulary specific to the discipline or information retrieval source

   constructs a search strategy using appropriate commands for the information retrieval system selected (e.g., Boolean operators, truncation, and proximity for search engines; internal organizers such as indexes for books)

   implements the search strategy in various information retrieval systems using different user interfaces and search engines with different command languages, protocols, and search parameters

   implements the search using investigative protocols appropriate to the discipline*

3. The information literate student retrieves information online or in person using a variety of formats. Outcomes include:

   uses various search systems to retrieve information in a variety of formats

   uses various classification schemes and other systems (e.g., call number systems or indexes) to locate information resources within the library

or to identify specific sites for physical exploration

   uses specialized online or in-person services available at the institution to retrieve information needed (e.g., interlibrary loan/document delivery, professional associations, institutional research offices, community resources, experts, and practitioners)

   uses surveys, letters, interviews, and other forms of inquiry to retrieve primary information*

4. The information literate student refines the search strategy if necessary. Outcomes include:

   assesses the quantity, quality, and relevance of the search results to determine whether alternative information retrieval systems or investigative methods should be utilized*

   identifies gaps in the information retrieved and determines if the search strategy should be revised

   repeats the search using the revised strategy as necessary

5. The information literate student extracts, records, and manages the information and its sources. Outcomes include:

   selects among various technologies the most appropriate one for the task of extracting the needed information (e.g., copy/paste software functions, photocopier, scanner, audio/visual equipment, or exploratory instruments)

   creates a system for organizing the information

   differentiates between the types of sources cited and understands the elements and correct syntax of a citation for a wide range of resources

   records all pertinent citation information for future reference

   uses various technologies to manage the information selected and organized

STANDARD THREE

The information literate student evaluates information and its sources critically and incorporates selected information into his or her knowledge base and value system

Performance Indicators

1. The information literate student summarizes the main ideas to be extracted from the information gathered. Outcomes include:

---

*Note: *Indicates a learning outcome that might be converted into a research outcome.*

reads the text and selects main ideas

restates textual concepts in his/her own words and selects data accurately

identifies verbatim material that can be then appropriately quoted

2. The information literate student articulates and applies initial criteria for evaluating both the information and its sources. Outcomes include:

examines and compares information from various sources in order to evaluate reliability, validity, accuracy, authority, timeliness, and point of view or bias*

analyzes the structure and logic of supporting arguments or methods

recognizes prejudice, deception, or manipulation*

recognizes the cultural, physical, or other context within which the information was created and understands the impact of context on interpreting the information

3. The information literate student synthesizes main ideas to construct new concepts. Outcomes include:

recognizes interrelationships among concepts and combines them into potentially useful primary statements with supporting evidence*

extends initial synthesis, when possible, at a higher level of abstraction to construct new hypotheses that may require additional information*

utilizes computer and other technologies (e.g., spreadsheets, databases, multimedia, and audio and visual equipment) for studying the interaction of ideas and other phenomena

4. The information literate student compares new knowledge with prior knowledge to determine the value added, contradictions, or other unique characteristics of the information. Outcomes include:

determines whether information satisfies the research or other information need*

uses consciously selected criteria to determine whether the information contradicts or verifies information used from other sources*

draws conclusions based upon information gathered*

tests theories with discipline-appropriate techniques (e.g., simulators, experiments)*

determines probable accuracy by questioning the source of the data, the limitations of the information-gathering tools or strategies, and the reasonableness of the conclusions*

integrates new information with previous information or knowledge

selects information that provides evidence for the topic*

5. The information literate student determines whether the new knowledge has an impact on the individual's value system and takes steps to reconcile differences. Outcomes include:

investigates differing viewpoints encountered in the literature

determines whether to incorporate or reject viewpoints encountered

6. The information literate student validates understanding and interpretation of the information through discourse with other individuals, subject-area experts, and/or practitioners. Outcomes include:

participates in classroom and other discussion

participates in class-sponsored electronic communication forms designed to encourage discourse on the topic (e.g., e-mail, bulletin boards, and chat rooms)

seeks expert opinion through a variety of mechanisms (e.g., interviews, e-mail, and discussion lists)

7. The information literate student determines whether the initial query should be revised. Outcomes include:

determines if original information needs have been satisfied or if additional information is needed

reviews search strategy and incorporates additional concepts as necessary

reviews information retrieval sources used and expands to include others as needed

---

Note: *Indicates a learning outcome that might be converted into a research outcome.

STANDARD FOUR

The information literate student, individually or as a member of a group, uses information effectively to accomplish a specific purpose

Performance Indicators

1. The information literate student applies new and prior information to the planning and creation of a particular product or performance. Outcomes include:

   organizes the content in a manner that supports the purposes and format of the product or performance (e.g., outlines, drafts, [or] storyboards)

   articulates knowledge and skills transferred from prior experiences to planning and creating the product or performance

   integrates the new and prior information, including quotations and paraphrasing, in a manner that supports the purposes of the product or performance

   manipulates digital text, images, and data as needed, transferring them from their original locations and formats to a new context

2. The information literate student revises the development process for the product or performance. Outcomes include:

   maintains a journal or log of activities related to the information seeking, evaluating, and communicating process

   reflects on past successes, failures, and alternative strategies

3. The information literate student communicates the product or performance effectively to others. Outcomes include:

   chooses a communication medium and format that best supports the purposes of the product or performance and the intended audience

   uses a range of information technology applications in creating the product or performance

   incorporates principles of design and communication

   communicates clearly and with a style that supports the purposes of the intended audience

STANDARD FIVE

The information literate student understands many of the economic, legal, and social issues surrounding the use of information and accesses and uses information ethically and legally

Performance Indicators

1. The information literate student understands many of the ethical, legal, and socioeconomic issues surrounding information and information technology. Outcomes include:

   identifies and discusses issues related to privacy and security in both the print and electronic environments

   identifies and discusses issues related to free vs. fee-based access to information

   identifies and discusses issues related to censorship and freedom of speech

   demonstrates an understanding of intellectual property, copyright, and fair use of copyrighted material*

2. The information literate student follows laws, regulations, institutional policies, and etiquette related to the access and use of information resources. Outcomes include:

   participates in electronic discussions following accepted practices (e.g., "Netiquette")

   uses approved passwords and other forms of ID for access to information resources

   complies with institutional policies on access to information resources

   preserves the integrity of information resources, equipment, systems, and facilities

   legally obtains, stores, and disseminates text, data, images, or searches

   demonstrates an understanding of what constitutes plagiarism and does not represent work attributable to others as his/her own*

   demonstrates an understanding of institutional policies related to human subjects research*

3. The information literate student acknowledges the use of information sources in communicating the product or performance. Outcomes include:

   selects appropriate documentation style and uses it consistently to cite sources*

   posts permission-granted notices, as needed, for copyrighted material*

Note: *Indicates a learning outcome that might be converted into a research outcome.

APPENDIX
I

Example of Research Components

TOPICAL AREA

Faculty use of library resources in teaching and research

Explore ways to improve library services and collections

What do faculty think should be changed to accommodate their professorial needs?

REFLECTIVE INQUIRY

Problem Statement

The academic library has been characterized as a *crossroads community*, meaning that it is relevant to every department and program on campus and that the "library has an internal community of library resources and services . . . and an external community of teachers, researchers, and students, as well as campus telecommunications and computing resources and services. The common cultural and historical heritage aspect of community is also relevant to the academic library and the university, particularly given the important symbolic role held by the academic library in many universities."[1]

Such a community is important for the university and its library to strive to achieve as they prepare for reaccreditation and for ensuring that the library plays a critical role in the research and teaching needs of the faculty. In recent years at this university no study has been conducted to measure faculty use of library resources in teaching and research or ways to improve library collections and services for faculty. Furthermore, what changes do faculty think should be made in library collections and services as the new century unfolds?

The findings of this study will be relevant to the library in its review of existing services and resources and as the library, in its self-study, shows the extent to which the faculty perceive its services and collections to be *adequate*. The findings will be used not only to document the present but also to plan future services that address changes in scholarly communication and information needs of the faculty.

Literature Review

The review will be conducted in library literature to identify studies done elsewhere that might be relevant to this library in conducting the study.

Theoretical Framework

A search will be conducted across disciplines and will focus on "scholarly communication" and "information needs." The concepts will be fully understood before the reflective inquiry is finalized and the results are applied to the "procedures."

Logical Structure

The diagram charts areas that the study must address. First, the decision has been made to limit the problem to one university, but the evaluators must decide when to conduct the study and what method(s) of data collection will be used. Second, the direction of the problem statement has been diagrammed and, third, so has the "who" component—faculty.

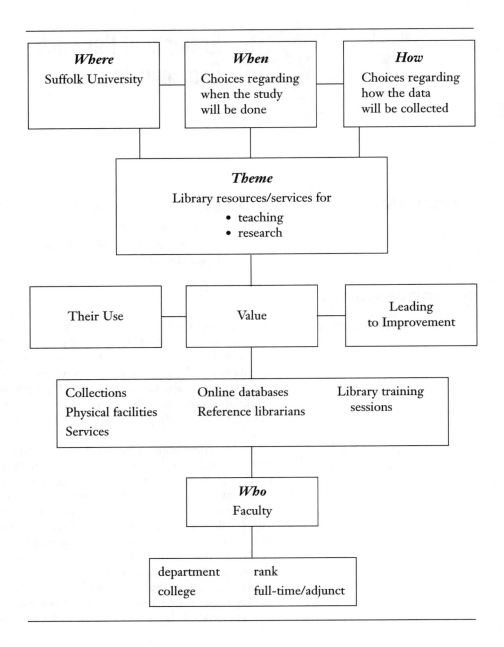

| **Where**
Suffolk University | **When**
Choices regarding when the study will be done | **How**
Choices regarding how the data will be collected |

Theme
Library resources/services for
- teaching
- research

| Their Use | Value | Leading to Improvement |

| Collections
Physical facilities
Services | Online databases
Reference librarians | Library training sessions |

Who
Faculty

| department
college | rank
full-time/adjunct |

Objectives

- To determine the frequency of use of the library per month for teaching (classroom assignments)

- To determine the frequency of use of the library per month for research

- To identify any recommendations for improving library collections and services

- To compare the frequency of use of the library for teaching purposes per month by faculty rank

- To compare the frequency of use of the library per month for research purposes by faculty rank

- To compare the use of the library per month for teaching purposes and research purposes

- To compare the current use of library collections/physical facilities in research activities by faculty rank (taken from "means of data analysis" [at the end of this appendix])

Research Questions

- How often do faculty use the library for research per month?

- How frequently do they use the online catalog for research?

Hypothesis

There is no statistically significant difference ($p = .05$) between the current use of library collections/physical facilities (in research activities) by faculty rank (taken from objective and applied to the "means of data analysis" [at the end of this appendix]).

PROCEDURES

Research Design

The decision will be made to survey all teaching faculty at the university. The evaluators will gather the list of those currently teaching and prepare the questionnaire for delivery to them by campus mail. A decision to be made here is when the survey will be conducted and what steps will be taken to ensure a high rate of completion.

Methodology

The decision has been made to conduct the survey by means of a mailed questionnaire.

CRITERIA OF RELEVANCE

The use of a pretest will determine if the questions are clearly worded so that respondents will not be confused. Thus, there might be a pretest of the library staff whereby they gather together and are asked to comment on the questions and their sequencing. As well, five to eight faculty members might be brought together for the same purpose. (reliability)

How will the open-ended questions be analyzed? If different people summarize those results, is there interscore reliability? To ensure interscore reliability, the scorers must be trained.

Are the questionnaire and the data collection process consistent with the literature on scholarly communication and information needs? (internal validity)

QUESTIONNAIRE

The following questionnaire matches the reflective inquiry and was used at Suffolk University to gain faculty input on the library's assessment plan. Additional means of gathering data might be used. Other libraries could modify the instrument to meet their needs. For instance, item 5a, collections/physical facilities, could be separated into two options.

LIBRARY SERVICES SURVEY

Date

Dear Faculty Member,

The purpose of this survey is to measure the faculty use of library resources in teaching and research. We are in the process of preparing for reaccreditation, and we would like feedback on your use of library resources and ways to improve its services and enhance its resources. We need to know how you use the library now and what you think should be changed in the future to better suit your professional needs. Therefore, we would appreciate very much if you would help us by answering the questions on the enclosed survey.

This questionnaire contains twenty-eight questions that are divided into five parts for your convenience. Answering the survey should take only a few minutes. Please circle the correct answer or write in the space provided. Your opinion and comments are very important to us. We will use them to evaluate our compliance with our mission as it relates to the NEASC accreditation guidelines and to improve the library services and facilities.

Thank you in advance for answering this questionnaire. We greatly appreciate your opinion and welcome all your comments.

Sincerely,

The Committee for NEASC Self-Study:
Standard 7, Library and Information Services

> Please return the completed questionnaire
> via interoffice mail or e-mail to:

SECTION A. Demographic Information

1. What is your faculty rank?
    a. ___ instructor   d. ___ professor
    b. ___ assistant professor   e. ___ other (please specify):_____
    c. ___ associate professor   _____

2. Are you a member of
    a. ___ CASB   b. ___ SSOM

3. Your department: _____

4. How many years have you been with Suffolk University? ___ years

5. Do you currently use the following elements of Sawyer Library
    in your research activities?
    a. collections/physical facilities   ___ Yes   ___ No
    b. electronic databases   ___ Yes   ___ No
    c. reference librarians   ___ Yes   ___ No
    d. library training sessions   ___ Yes   ___ No

6. Do you currently use the following aspects of Sawyer Library
    in classroom assignments?
    a. collections/physical facilities   ___ Yes   ___ No
    b. projects designed to require reference
       librarian assistance   ___ Yes   ___ No
    c. Instruction sessions on specific topics   ___ Yes   ___ No

7. How many times per month do you use the services of the Sawyer Library
    for research?
    a. ___ less than 3   c. ___ 8–11
    b. ___ 4–7   d. ___ 12 or more

8. How many times per month do you use the services of the Sawyer Library
    for classroom assignments?
    a. ___ less than 3   c. ___ 8–11
    b. ___ 4–7   d. ___ 12 or more

Developed by Lewis Shaw, Andrea Arrago, Melissa Haussman, and Rebecca Fulweiler, Suffolk University, Boston, Mass.
Permission granted to adapt and reproduce for nonprofit educational purposes.

SECTION B. Library Use in Research and Teaching

9. How frequently do you use the following resources
   of the library for *research:*

	VERY FREQUENTLY		SOMETIMES		NEVER
a. collections/physical facilities	1	2	3	4	5
b. online catalog	1	2	3	4	5
c. online databases	1	2	3	4	5
d. reference librarians	1	2	3	4	5
e. training by library staff	1	2	3	4	5

10. How frequently do you use the following resources
    of the library for classroom assignments:

a. collections/physical facilities	1	2	3	4	5
b. online catalog	1	2	3	4	5
c. online databases	1	2	3	4	5
d. reference librarians	1	2	3	4	5
e. training by library staff	1	2	3	4	5

11. How would you rate the following aspects of the
    library collection?

	EXCELLENT		ADEQUATE		POOR
a. book collection for undergraduate teaching	1	2	3	4	5
b. book collection for graduate teaching	1	2	3	4	5
c. book collection for research	1	2	3	4	5
d. journal and periodical collection for undergraduate teaching	1	2	3	4	5
e. journal and periodical collection for graduate teaching	1	2	3	4	5
f. journal and periodical collection for research	1	2	3	4	5
g. microfilm/microfiche collection	1	2	3	4	5
h. microfilm/microfiche readers and printers	1	2	3	4	5
i. electronic periodical databases	1	2	3	4	5

12. How would you rate the online catalog for

a. usefulness	1	2	3	4	5
b. currency and ease of use	1	2	3	4	5
c. adequacy	1	2	3	4	5

Developed by Lewis Shaw, Andrea Arrago, Melissa Haussman, and Rebecca Fulweiler, Suffolk University, Boston, Mass.
Permission granted to adapt and reproduce for nonprofit educational purposes.

	EXCELLENT		ADEQUATE		POOR

13. How would you rate the online databases for

a. usefulness of online databases	1	2	3	4	5
b. access to the online databases (e.g., are the research stations working, and are there enough workstations)	1	2	3	4	5
c. promptness of ordering full-text articles from interlibrary loan	1	2	3	4	5
d. use of online databases off campus	1	2	3	4	5
e. use of online databases on-campus (i.e., from your office)	1	2	3	4	5
f. use of online databases in library	1	2	3	4	5

14. Approximately how many articles/publications have you written in the past five years using the following Sawyer Library resources?*

    a. ___ interlibrary loan   c. ___ online resources

    b. ___ reference staff   d. ___ physical collections

SECTION C. Training by Library Staff

15. How would you rate the adequacy of the training provided by the staff of the library for

	EXCELLENT		ADEQUATE		POOR
a. yourself	1	2	3	4	5
b. students	1	2	3	4	5

16. How often have you utilized training on how to use the resources of the library?

	VERY FREQUENTLY		SOMETIMES		NEVER
a. yourself	1	2	3	4	5
b. students	1	2	3	4	5

17. Do you feel you need more training in using the library resources?

    a. yourself   ___ Yes   ___ No

    b. students   ___ Yes   ___ No

---

* Question 14 provides a crude estimate, one that libraries may want to follow up with selective in-person interviews or with group interviews.

Developed by Lewis Shaw, Andrea Arrago, Melissa Haussman, and Rebecca Fulweiler, Suffolk University, Boston, Mass.
Permission granted to adapt and reproduce for nonprofit educational purposes.

18. If you answered *yes* to the previous question, how often?

a. ___ every 3 months   c. ___ every year

b. ___ every 6 months   d. ___ every time a new feature is added

SECTION D. Library Staff and Physical Facilities

	EXCELLENT		ADEQUATE		POOR
19. How would you rate the helpfulness of the library staff?	1	2	3	4	5
20. How would you rate library staff availability when needed?	1	2	3	4	5
21. In what condition is the computer equipment?	1	2	3	4	5
22. How would you rate the copy service?	1	2	3	4	5
23. How do you like the overall appearance and atmosphere in the library?	1	2	3	4	5

SECTION E. Feedback and Comments

24. Have advances in library technology (e.g., online databases and online catalog) helped you in research?   a. ___ Yes   b. ___ No

If yes, please comment:

25. Have advances in library technology (e.g., online databases and online catalog) helped you in teaching?   a. ___ Yes   b. ___ No

If yes, please comment:

26. Has the knowledge of the library staff helped you in research?   a. ___ Yes   b. ___ No

If yes, please comment:

27. Has the knowledge of the library staff helped you in teaching?   a. ___ Yes   b. ___ No

If yes, please comment:

28. Please provide your additional comments in the space below.

Thank you.

Developed by Lewis Shaw, Andrea Arrago, Melissa Haussman, and Rebecca Fulweiler, Suffolk University, Boston, Mass.
Permission granted to adapt and reproduce for nonprofit educational purposes.

MEANS OF DATA ANALYSIS

Analyze each open-ended response and place the responses into categories. Make a frequency count of each question involving yes/no or scale of 1 to 5. The summary findings then could be placed into a graph or table. From "Section A. Demographic Information," questions 1, 2, 3, 6, and 7 might be compared with each other or with some other questions using cross-tabulation and the chi-square test of independence. For example, question 1 might be compared with the first item in question 5.

Cross tabulation of current use of library collections/physical facilities (item 5a) with faculty rank (item 1)

FACULTY RANK	YES	NO
instructor		
assistant professor		
associate professor		
professor		
other		

Note

1. Deborah J. Grimes, *Academic Library Centrality: User Success through Service, Access, and Tradition* (Chicago: Assn. of College and Research Libraries, 1998), 120.

Enhancing Skills through Technology
A Project for Advanced Accounting Students

SUDIP BHATTACHARJEE and LEWIS SHAW

Advances in information technology require accountants to access and assimilate timely information, analyze relevant input, and solve unstructured problems commonly found in various consulting and strategic decision-making situations. Educationally, these developments suggest that accounting students should use technology to obtain information from various sources. Less obvious, but equally crucial, are students' perceptions of their abilities to use computers effectively. Positive perceptions of one's technological ability are essential to the successful utilization of computers.[1] Negative perceptions may prevent an individual from gaining access to or effectively using computers in the workplace.[2]

In today's global economy and higher education's ever-increasing reliance on technology, it is critical that a study examine whether or not simple enhancements of existing teaching tools (e.g., a financial analysis of a company project) can further develop students' skills in accessing information and improve their perceived ability to work on computer-based projects. Do gender-related technology differences exist among accounting students given that women are entering the profession in equal numbers to men, and the use of computers is now an important aspect of most accounting tasks?[3] The purpose of this study is to look at this question and at gender differences in accounting students' perceptions of computer-based tasks. (Although variables such as ethnicity, race, and socioeconomic differences may also impact perceptions toward computers, this study restricts itself to analyzing gender differences.)

The type of project that students worked on for this study may show that, even if female students start the assignment with lower perceived computer-related abilities, participation in the project could eliminate any gender differences. Given the widespread use of technology, assignments designed to produce higher perceived computer abilities for all accounting students, regardless of gender, would be valuable for their careers.

In an area such as technology, where measuring utilization of the latest resources is difficult, an effective measure-ment tool to evaluate success is through self-assessment instruments. At the same time, efforts to develop students' skills and positive perceptions of technology should take into account any gender differences in perceptions and attitudes toward computers. Substantial research shows that female students indicate lower self-efficacy (personal judgments of one's capability to organize and execute courses of action to achieve goals) and confidence with the use of computer technology than do male students.[4] These gender differences appear to be the result of less computer exposure for females rather than to differences in opinion between the genders on the functionality of computers.[5] In fact, greater exposure to technology appears to narrow differences in perceptions between male and female students in business and other programs.[6] Most of this research, however, has been conducted on nonaccounting students.

LITERATURE REVIEW

The ability to obtain and analyze information from various sources and the skills to solve unstructured problems are some of the attributes that have been specifically identified as requirements for future accounting graduates.[7] With greater focus on the analysis, interpretation, and evaluation of information that enters into decision processes, accountants need to become more knowledgeable of the data needs of end users.[8] For instance, management asks accountants to use technology to develop and present up-to-the-minute predictive data used for various strategic decisions.[9] Furthermore, accountants are expected to add value to an organization's decision making by understanding the complex interrelationships involved in information systems and by using their critical thinking skills to apply the knowledge to new situations.[10] In fact, an ability to use technical knowledge and problem-solving skills tends to characterize auditors with superior performance evaluations as they move up the firm hierarchy.[11]

These developments require accountants to possess both the skills to access information and the perceived and

Sudip Bhattacharjee is assistant professor, Department of Accounting and Information Systems, Virginia Polytechnic Institute and State University, and Lewis Shaw is assistant profes-sors in the Accounting Department, Suffolk University (Boston, Mass.). An alternative version of this paper appears in *Accounting Education: An International Journal* (2001).

actual ability to use computers and to work independently on unstructured tasks. Enhancing self-confidence with technology is crucial since computer anxiety and self-efficacy are important predictors of attitudes toward computers and willingness to learn about computer systems.[12] Research has shown a relationship between individuals' perceptions of the importance of technology and their proficiency in using technology.[13] It appears that attitudes toward computers have a significant influence on the effective use of computers, with these attitudes being molded by individuals' positive or negative experiences with computers.[14] Negative attitudes toward computers may prevent individuals from gaining access to, or effectively using, computers in their workplaces and may even limit their chances of getting or holding employment.[15] Given the importance of information technology in the accounting profession, enhancing perceptions of confidence toward technology is vital to ensure successful utilization of technology, including computers and related software.[16]

Enhancing Skills and Perceptions through Technology

Enhancing existing teaching tools through the use of technology in the classroom can facilitate the development of computer-related competencies. A technology such as the Internet conveniently allows individuals to seek out relevant items of information and go back and review sections of the information they wish to examine. This enables students to build upon existing knowledge structures and permits them to interact freely with information.[17] Moreover, technology allows students to be self-directed and have control over their learning environment, promoting more active learning.[18] In fact, in a recent study ranking students' preferences for research sources, World Wide Web (Web) sources of information were ranked highest in terms of enjoyment, trustworthiness, currency, and relevancy.[19]

Research also suggests that, when used as a supplement to traditional methods of teaching, technology can improve certain skills and perceptions that are otherwise difficult to acquire.[20] Moreover, it can free up class time for other learning experiences.[21] The use of technology gives students some control over the pace of work and the flexibility to choose information sources. As they work independently and access information from many sources, technology allows them to develop skills for obtaining data from multiple sources. This format also provides students with an opportunity to develop their perceived ability to use computers to complete complex unstructured projects as well as to assimilate and use relevant information from many sources.

Technology and Gender

A substantial body of research identifies gender differences in the usage of computers, comfort with technology, and attitudes toward the importance of computers. For example, one study compared the amount of computer usage and the psychological characteristics of accounting students.[22] The researchers found that males were more positive and less resistant toward increased computer usage in accounting classes than were females. These results are significant given that females have been graduating with accounting degrees in equal numbers to men since 1986.[23] Furthermore, the use of technology has now been integrated into all aspects of accounting and assurance service functions.[24]

These results about gender differences are consistent with earlier studies of nonaccounting undergraduate and graduate students, indicating that female students have greater computer anxiety than male students.[25] Studies also show that females are less likely to enter computer-related courses due to greater computer anxiety, which can result in lower levels of satisfaction from tasks that involve technology.[26] One researcher assigned students a financial analysis assignment using a spreadsheet program.[27] Self-reported perceptions indicated that, relative to male students, female students had significantly lower self-efficacy in computing as a result of less previous computer experience and less encouragement to work with computers. Studies have also shown lower self-efficacy for women in the area of computers and technology. For example, two researchers found that women have lower self-efficacy and outcome expectations and higher anxiety about computer usage.[28] These findings strongly confirm that both self-efficacy and outcome expectations impact one's reactions and interactions with information technology. Other studies show lower self-efficacy in females in regard to technology, math skills, and areas of strategic management.[29]

Additional research suggests that lack of exposure to technology may be the reason for females' attitudinal differences toward computer tasks.[30] Recent surveys show that men use computer technology such as the Internet much more than do women, and women report less experience and higher levels of trait anxiety for such tasks.[31] Using nonaccounting business majors, one investigator showed that males enjoy learning about computers and working with computers more so than females.[32] This may be the result of more computer exposure and greater encouragement to study computers for men from an early age. Even though females had less exposure to and comfort with computers, those surveyed agreed on its overall value to society. Furthermore, after taking a one-semester computer course, female students' attitudes toward the importance of computer skills and their confidence with computers improved consistently. In fact, females' computer literacy was equal to that of males by the end of the course.

Similarly, another investigator reported that male high school students had more technology experience and confidence than females at the start of a computer-related course.[33] However, testing students before and after the course confirmed that female students' attitudes and abilities with computers were at par with the attitudes and abilities of male students by the end of the study.

It appears that less computer exposure and lower computer self-efficacy in female students may account for differences in attitudes toward computers between the genders. In fact, assignments designed to incorporate technology in the classroom appear to narrow such gender difference in perceptions toward computers.

PROCEDURES

Similar to traditional assignments involving the financial analysis of a business, students were required to access and analyze financial and nonfinancial information. However, they were also required to look beyond traditional sources of information used in many company-analysis projects and seek out more timely information from the Internet to provide a more complete analysis of the company. The project format was kept simple and flexible to ensure that students could work independently with limited faculty support. (See figure J.1.)

FIGURE J.1
Company Analysis Project Activities

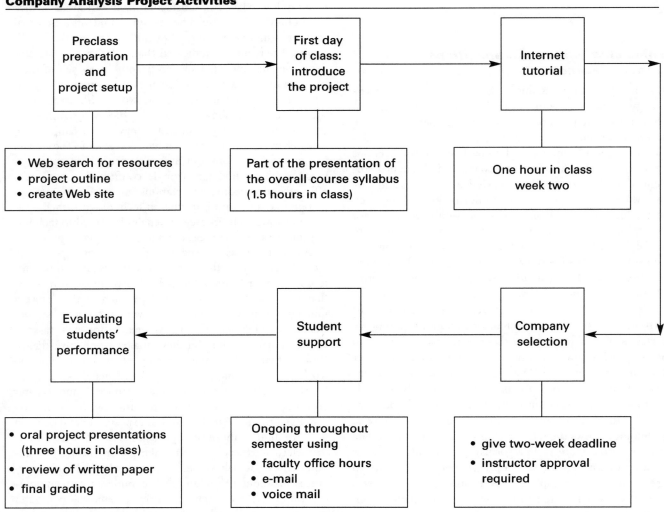

Before the semester began, the instructor prepared a project outline containing a detailed description of the goals of the project, company-selection instructions, suggestions for the types of information to be included in the analysis, timelines for completion, and the evaluation criteria. (See figure J.2.) The description of the project clarified the requirements of the written paper and the oral report that each student needed to complete by the end of the semester to receive a satisfactory project grade. The project grade counted for 20 percent of the overall course grade.

In addition, since students required technical familiarity with the Internet for their company research, a one-hour training session was presented on basic Internet usage in the second week of class. The instructor gave a brief overview of the Internet, including its history and some of its key technological features. The lecture covered Internet terminology, ways to navigate the Web, and a demonstration of resources specifically relevant for the accounting field. An Internet assignment was also provided that included exploring the course and project Web pages, visiting several accounting-related sites, and using search engines.

After receiving the training, students responded to various preproject questions about their Internet skills and

---

FIGURE J.2
Excerpts from Company Analysis Project Description

Your report must be based on the *most recent information available* on your company, its industry, and the economic environment. In order to access this information, you must rely only on sources that are up-to-date and accurate. Keep in mind that you will be evaluated based on how effectively you are able to incorporate the most "cutting edge" information on your company into your report. *This type of information is readily available over the Internet.*

You could use the following information to gather information on your company:

> The company's annual report
> The company's 10-K Report to the SEC
> The company's last few quarterly reports
> Recent articles in *The Wall St. Journal,* other newspapers and business publications
> The company's Web site
> Fortune 500 (from *Fortune* magazine)
> Fortune 500 (a listing of companies with annual reports online)

Your project should include, but is not limited to, the following information:

> The name of the company
> The year of the annual report and other sources
> What comparative years are given?
> Is this a consolidated financial report?
> Who is the auditor?
> What type of opinion is given?

What method of inventory valuation is used?

What method of depreciation is used?

What are the primary products or services provided?

What is interesting about the management letter?

Describe a footnote disclosure you found interesting

Where is the company located?

How are the company's securities currently performing?

Is there anything noteworthy about the company since its most recent financial report?

Is there any recent event that might impact the future of the company?

Provide some information about the company that is not presented in the financial statements or the annual report

What do financial analysts think about your company, its performance, and its future prospects?

Ratio analysis:
> Compare to prior years and to industry standards
> Include at least two ratios from each category
> Explain what the ratios indicate about your company

Conclusion:
> Is this company positioned well? Why?
> Is this company a good investment? Why?

Other comments

Note: Underlining denotes hyperlink.

perceptions. Thereafter, they worked independently on their projects throughout the semester. This involved virtually no class time, other than an occasional reminder of the project. The instructor periodically generated in-class excitement about the project by interjecting current events related to students' selected companies. Students utilized the instructor's office hours or e-mail to get help or direction on their information gathering, analysis, and project write up.

Project presentations were scheduled for the last week of class at which time students also responded to various postproject questions. Students were evaluated on their knowledge of the company, their presentation skills, and their ability to evaluate their companies intelligently. Written reports were graded based on a number of criteria, including substantial analysis of and conclusions about the company, grammatical correctness, appropriate format and writing style, and proper bibliography and citations.

Study Design

The 56 students (26 males and 30 females) from two different sections of an advanced accounting [class] taught by the same instructor participated in the project.[34] Since no significant differences were observed between the two classes for any of the variables in the study, the combined results of the two sections are reported. Table J.1 compares the demographic information of male and female students who participated in the study. The results show no differences in the overall GPA between the male (mean = 3.00;

TABLE J.1
Analysis of Students' Demographic Details by Gender

	Males (n = 26)	Females (n = 30)	p Values
GPA	Mean 3.00	3.03	.796
	SD 0.56	0.50	
Accounting GPA	Mean 2.98	3.14	.259
	SD 0.61	0.47	
Age*	Mean 24.6	24.3	.797
	SD 4.72	2.68	

* The participants consisted of traditional (full-time) undergraduate students and part-time evening students, who tend to be older than full-time students (t-test was used).

SD = 0.56) and female (mean = 3.03; SD = 0.50) students ($t = -.259$; $p = .796$). Furthermore, there were no gender differences in the age and the accounting GPA of the students.

The project was evaluated by testing students' Internet-based skills and by apparent changes in perceptions toward computer-based assignments. A comparison was also done to see if improvements in self-perceptions affected actual use of the Internet. Additionally, gender effects were analyzed for each variable. The variables were measured at both pre- and postproject stages. The preproject scores were obtained after students went through the one-hour training session on basic Internet usage. The postproject measures were obtained at the end of the semester. Therefore, any changes in scores from the pre- to the postproject stage reflect the impact of the project on the variables.[35]

Students' technical skills were determined by evaluating improvements in their Internet knowledge at the pre- and postproject stage. Written assignments were evaluated to see if they acquired the skills to access information from multiple sources. Additionally, several self-reported measures tested their perceptions before and after the project. Students reported on their perceived ability to use computers to solve complex problems, their ability to work independently to complete problems, their knowledge of searching the Internet for information, and the perceived usefulness of the Internet for analysis. Finally, a comparison was made between students' perceptions and actual Web usage.[36]

Students' Internet Skills

Separate multiple-choice tests were conducted before and after the project to evaluate students' Internet skills and understanding of the Internet. Students responded to ten questions concerning World Wide Web address formats, definitions of Web terminology, ways of maneuvering around the Web, and types of search engines available. (See figure J.3.) The responses were recorded (on a scale of 1 to 10) to obtain separate pre- and postproject scores. Students were not graded based on these results. Before the start of the project, the Internet knowledge questions were tested to determine if the preproject questions were similar in difficulty to the postproject questions. The pre- and postproject questions were combined into another questionnaire, in random order, and administered to 22 additional accounting students who did not participate in the study. Each student's responses were graded to obtain a separate score (again, the scale was 1 to 10) of their performance in the preproject and the postproject questions. The results indicate no differences in the students' performance in the preproject (mean = 7.18; SD = 1.96) and the postproject (mean = 6.73; SD = 1.80) questions ($p = .429$). This indicates that the pre- and postproject Internet knowledge test questions were of similar difficulty level.

Name: _____   e-mail address: _____

Knowledge of the Internet has become a hot commodity in the job market. Based on our discussions in class, test your Internet knowledge by answering the following questions. Your responses will not be graded. I am only interested in assessing whether the class as a whole has understood basic Internet usage.

1. To access the Internet, one needs all of the following, except:
   a. a server
   b. a modem
   c. a provider
   d. a browser

2. Which of the following is a valid e-mail address?
   a. dean@nc.edu
   b. joe@johnson@NBX.COM
   c. DAVE.IRS. GOV
   d. ELU123@TESTING.jojo.Gov

3. Web site addresses begin with what?
   a. http://www
   b. ://www
   c. //http://
   d. www

4. Which of the following is *not* a valid domain extension (suffix of a Web address)?
   a. com
   b. exe
   c. edu
   d. org

5. If I am "surfing the net" with a Web browser such as Netscape Navigator and I come to a page that I want to come back to later on, I:
   a. move to a different machine
   b. send an e-mail
   c. set a bookmark
   d. none of the above

6. Which one of the following is a search engine?
   a. Internet Explorer
   b. Java
   c. Yahoo!
   d. Internet

7. What is the name of the language you use to write a Web page?
   a. HTTP
   b. FTP
   c. URL
   d. HTML

8. Which of the following terms is a "browser"?
   a. Internet Explorer
   b. World Wide Web
   c. Launcher
   d. E-mail

9. A word that looks underlined on a Web page is usually what?
   a. an important word
   b. the Web address
   c. "link" to another Web page
   d. a mistake

10. What does "URL" stand for?
    a. Universal Research Laboratory
    b. United Record Libraries
    c. Uniform Resource Locator
    d. Uniform Record Language

FINDINGS

Table J.2 presents the Internet knowledge scores for all 56 students combined, and separately for male and female students. Panel A of that table indicates that the postproject Internet knowledge scores (mean = 7.82; SD = 1.73) were significantly higher than the preproject (mean = 7.12; SD = 1.92) scores ($Z = -2.98$; Wilcoxon Matched-Paired Signed-Rank test $p = .003$).[37] These results indicate that this project improved students' Internet skills.

TABLE J.2
Students' Pre- and Postproject Internet Knowledge Scores—All Students (N = 56)

PANEL A   Internet Knowledge Scores

Variable		Preproject	Postproject	Z Statistic	p Value*
Internet Knowledge Scores (out of 10)	Mean	7.12	7.82	–2.98	.003
	SD	1.92	1.73		

PANEL B   Internet Knowledge Scores Split by Gender

Variable	Male (n = 26)	Female (n = 30)	p Values†
Internet Knowledge Scores (out of ten)			
Preproject			
Mean	7.42	6.86	.183
SD	1.90	1.84	
Postproject			
Mean	8.19	7.50	.252
SD	1.32	1.99	

* Wilcoxon Matched-Paired Signed-Rank test was used to analyze differences in the pre-
and postproject scores.

† Mann-Whitney tests were used to analyze differences in male and female scores.

The scores were computed separately for male and female students to get a finer measure of Internet knowledge (panel B of table J.2). There were no significant differences between the scores of male and female students at the preproject and the postproject stage ($p > .05$). The postproject Internet knowledge scores of male students were significantly higher than their preproject scores (mean = 8.19 versus 7.42; $p = .025$). Similarly, female students also had significantly higher postproject scores than preproject scores (mean = 7.50 versus 6.86; $p = .045$). It appears that students of both genders have similar Internet knowledge coming into the study and both improved these skills as a result of working on the assignment.

Skills to Access Information from Multiple Sources

Two independent coders evaluated the text and bibliography of each student's written assignment to determine the number of Web-based information sources (e.g., analysts' projections from the Internet) and text-based information sources (e.g., annual report) used in the analysis. The coders evaluated each student's written assignment and counted only those sources that were used substantially in the analysis. Since they demonstrated a high degree of agreement with each other (correlation = .928; $p < .001$), the average of the two coders was used in the analysis.

Panel A of table J.3 shows that students, on average, cited approximately the same number of text-based sources (4.11) as Web-based sources (4.16) in their written report ($p = .884$). It appears that students did look beyond the traditional information sources used in many company-analysis projects, demonstrating they access information from multiple sources. In addition, there was a gender difference in the types of information sources cited (panel B of the table). Specifically, there is no difference by gender in the use of text-based sources ($p = .460$); however, female students used significantly more Web-based sources than did male students (5.26 versus 2.87, respectively; $p = .008$).[38]

TABLE J.3
Number of Web-Based and Text-Based Sources Used in Written Analysis

PANEL A   Number of Web-Based and Text-Based Sources—All Students ($N = 56$)

	Text Sources	Web Sources	z Statistic	p Value
Mean	4.11	4.16	–.146	.884
SD	3.11	3.48		

PANEL B   Number of Web-Based and Text-Based Sources by Gender

Variable	Male ($n = 26$)	Female ($n = 30$)	p Values*
Text Sources			
Mean	3.66	4.50	.460
SD	2.79	3.36	
Web Sources			
Mean	2.87	5.26	.008
SD	2.87	4.08	

* Mann-Whitney tests were used to analyze differences in male and female scores.

Perceptions of Computer-Related Tasks

A questionnaire was administered both pre- and postproject-type scale. Table J.4 contains the means and standard deviations of students' preproject and postproject responses to each question. In addition, Wilcoxon Matched-Paired Signed-Rank test compared the preproject and postproject scores for each question.[39] Panel A of the table reports three questions that measure the assignment's influence on students' perceptions of technology applications and information search skills. The internal consistency of these three questions was calculated to determine if they were testing similar constructs (Cronbach's α: 0.72). One common method for evaluating internal validity is that the Cronbach's α should exceed 0.50.[40] Since the internal consistency measure exceeds this threshold, the three questions, taken together, provide a valid indication of perceived project completion and information search skills. Panel A of the same table reports that students claim to have improved their ability to complete an unfamiliar project (question 1) successfully, their perceived ability to use the computer and analyze a technical problem (question 2),

and their perceived knowledge of searching the Internet for information (question 3). As students worked independently (with guidance from the instructor) on this type of assignment and accessed information from various sources, they appear to have improved their perceptions of working with computers to solve complex assignments. Given the importance of information technology in the accounting profession, enhancing of students' attitudes toward computers and their willingness to learn about computer systems is crucial for their professional development.[41]

Panel B of table J.4 reports other perceptions of the general usefulness of the Internet in providing information that students may use for various types of tasks. The variables in panel B are independent of one another. The results indicate that students report an improved understanding of the utility of the Internet (questions 4 and 5), and felt that using the Internet should be an important aim of an upper-level accounting class (question 6). This suggests that, in addition to improving students' perceptions of working on computer-related projects, such an assignment

TABLE J.4
Students' Pre- and Postproject Perceptions—All Students (N = 56)

PANEL A   Project Completion and Information Search Skills

Question		Preproject	Postproject	p Value[*]
1. Ability to use technology to work independently and complete unfamiliar projects	Mean SD	3.59 0.72	4.11 0.62	.000
2. Ability to use computers to analyze information and evaluate technical issues	Mean SD	3.67 0.91	4.20 0.64	.000
3. Knowledge of searching the Internet for information	Mean SD	3.44 1.06	4.52 0.57	.000

Cronbach's α: 0.72

PANEL B   Other Perceptions of Students

Question		Preproject	Postproject	p Values[*]
4. Internet provides an easy way to find out company information	Mean SD	4.28 0.90	4.61 0.67	.032
5. Internet search for company information is more time-consuming than going to the library	Mean SD	2.21 1.24	1.89 1.1)	.042
6. Learning to use the Internet to access information should be an aim of an advanced accounting class	Mean SD	4.23 0.93	4.49 0.85	.044

[*] Wilcoxon Matched-Paired Signed-Rank test was used to analyze differences in the pre- and postproject scores.

can increase their perceived familiarity with the Internet and improve the understanding of the medium's functionality.[42]

Additional analysis tested gender differences in perceptions of the project and information search skills. Table J.5 shows that at the preproject stage female students had lower perceived ability to use technology to work independently (question 1) than did male students (mean = 3.41 versus 3.80; p = .046). This is consistent with prior research showing that females have greater anxiety and less confidence in completing computer-related tasks.[43] However, the assignment narrowed the gap between female and male students with no significant differences in perceptions between the genders at the postproject stage (mean = 4.00 versus 4.23; p = .157).

Similarly, females' perceptions of their ability to use computers to solve complex issues (question 2) were lower than those of male students at the start of the assignment (3.46 versus 3.92; p = .038), but this gap was narrowed by the end of the study (4.20 versus 4.19; p = .941). Additional analysis indicates that the change in perceptions from the preproject to the postproject stage was greater for female students than for male students (0.74. versus 0.27; p = .046). Finally, students' understanding of the Internet as an information source (question 3) was not significantly different at the preproject stage between female and male students (3.26 versus 3.65; p = .145). However, female students' perceptions were marginally higher than those of male students at the postproject stage (4.63 versus 4.38; p = .082). Once again, for this variable, the change in the perceptions

TABLE J.5
Gender Differences in Pre- and Postproject Perceptions

PERCEPTIONS OF INFORMATION SEARCH AND PROJECT COMPLETION SKILLS*

Variable			Male (n = 26)	Female (n = 30)	p Values[†]
Ability to use technology to work independently and complete unfamiliar projects	Preproject	Mean	3.80	3.41	.046
		SD	0.80	0.61	
	Postproject	Mean	4.23	4.00	.157
		SD	0.65	0.58	
Ability to use computers to analyze information and evaluate technical issues	Preproject	Mean	3.92	3.46	.038
		SD	0.97	0.81	
	Postproject	Mean	4.19	4.20	.941
		SD	0.63	0.66	
Knowledge of searching the Internet for information	Preproject	Mean	3.65	3.26	.145
		SD	1.01	1.08	
	Postproject	Mean	4.38	4.63	.082
		SD	0.57	0.56	

* This table indicates differences in perceptions for males and females at the preproject and postproject stages. The variables measure perceptions of students' project completion skills, ability to use computers to solve problems, and their understanding of the Internet as an information source. Taken together, these perceptions provide an indication of students' project completion and information search skills.

† Mann-Whitney tests were used to analyze differences in male and female scores.

from the preproject to the postproject was greater for female than male students (1.37. versus 0.73; p = .028); 4.63 − 1.37 = 1.37 (males) and 4.38 − 3.65 = 0.73 (females).

These results indicate that, while students of both genders had similar pre- and postproject technical knowledge of the Internet (see table J.2), female students indicated lower perceived ability for completing computer-related tasks at the start of the study. However, similar to prior studies, exposure to this type of Internet project improved females' perceived ability to a greater extent than for males.[44]

Comparing Students' Perceptions and Web Usage

Finally, we analyzed the results to determine if improvements in perceptions affected students' actions. Note that the internal validity of the project-completion and information search perceptions in panel A (table J.4) was reasonably high (Cronbach's α: 0.72). Therefore, these three variables were combined to provide a composite measure of perceived project-completion and information-search skills. The sample was partitioned into two groups based on a median split of the composite variable scores to separate students who have higher and lower improvements in their perceived skills. We then investigated whether the number of Web citations in students' written reports (panel A of table J.3) differed between the two groups. The results indicate no differences in Web citations of students in the low composite score group (mean = 4.05) and high composite group (mean = 4.26, Mann-Whitney Test p = .948). This indicated that students who had the greater improvements in perceptions were at least as heavy users of the Web as those who had lower improvements in perceptions.

It appears, therefore, that improvements in perceptions positively impacted the use of the Internet when the annual-report projects were written.[45]

DISCUSSION

Enhancing an existing teaching tool, like a company-analysis research project, can concurrently develop computer-based skills and improve perceptions about technology. The project assessment indicated that students improved their Internet skills over the course of the semester and showed strong interest in the project. Written assignments indicated that students utilized skills to access information from multiple sources by using both Web-based and text-based sources. Female students used more Web-based sources in their written project reports than did male students. Analysis of perceptions indicated that students improved their perceived ability to use the computer to analyze a technical problem, to complete an unfamiliar project successfully, and to increase their understanding of various Internet sources. Furthermore, female students showed greater improvements than did male students on their perceived ability to use the computer to conduct research, solve problems, and complete unstructured tasks. In addition, perceived improvements in skills appeared to impact actual uses of Web-based sources in the written assignments.

The results demonstrate the value of using specifically designed assignments to develop computer-based attributes that seem difficult to teach in the classroom. The project uses minimal class time and provides a relatively simple way of building key abilities of tomorrow's accountants. While developing skills provides students with the competencies to access technology, improving their perceived abilities is vital to ensure the successful utilization of computers in the workplace. Combining strong skills and high perceived abilities should allow students to access, synthesize, and analyze timely information from various information sources when working on an appropriate independent assignment, the very competencies that are being called for by accounting recruiters.[46]

This study suggests that gender differences in accounting students' perceptions toward computer-based tasks can be narrowed through exposure to technology. The type of assignment discussed in this chapter not only helps develop vital skills but also ensures that female accounting majors improve their perceived ability and self-efficacy in performing computer-based tasks.[47] Any educational tool that reduces gender-based differences in attitudes toward computers is important.

One limitation of the study is that perceived benefits from the project might not actually translate to changes in learning. That is, the increases in perceptions could simply result from students' overall positive impressions of the Internet. However, testing on several dimensions of students' perceptions, improvements in skills, and project interest provide support for the findings. Another concern is that the sections used to evaluate the project were taught by the same instructor in two different semesters. The results, however, show that there were no differences in the pre- or postproject scores between the two sections, suggesting that both classes received the same type of instruction.

While developments in technology provide unique opportunities for educators, research suggests that the benefits of technology may be dependent upon the learning situation and the characteristics of the students.[48] This study shows that some types of technology can be used effectively to supplement the traditional education process and help teach skills and perceptions needed by future accountants. However, important characteristics such as a student's gender may mediate the benefits of computer-based teaching tools. Therefore, further research is needed to explore ways in which the use of technology in the classroom can benefit students with different psychological and other characteristics. Studies also need to investigate additional ways in which the classroom can be used to improve technology-related skills that are in demand in the workplace. The findings of such research can greatly facilitate the development of effective pedagogical tools.[49]

Notes

1. Tina Y. Mills, "An Examination of the Relationship between Accountants' Score on Field Independence and Use of and Attitude toward Computers," *Perceptual and Motor Skills* 84, no. 3 (June 1997), 715–20; M. S. Igabaria, A. Parasuraman, and F. Pavri, "A Path Analytic Study of the Determinants of Microcomputer Usage," *Journal of Management Systems* 2, no. 2 (1990), 1–14.

2. James E. Walters and James R. Necessary, "An Attitudinal Comparison toward Computers between Underclassmen and Graduating Seniors," *Education* 116, no. 4 (1996), 623–32.

3. Patricia M. Flynn and John D. Leeth, "The Accounting Profession in Transition," *The CPA Journal* 67, no. 5 (1997), 42–7. Robert K. Elliott, "Assurance Service Opportunities: Implications for Academia," *Accounting Horizons* 11, no. 4 (Dec. 1997), 61–74.

4. Raymond M. Landry, Richard L. Rogers, and Horace W. Harrell, "Computer Usage and Psychological Type Characteristics in Accounting Students," *Journal of Accounting and Computers* 12 (4 April 1997), 306; Tor Busch, "Gender, Group Composition, Cooperation, and Self-Efficacy in Computer Studies," *Journal of Educational Computing Research* 15, no. 2 (1996), 125–35; Nancy E. Betz and Ross S. Schifano, "Evaluation of an Intervention to Increase Self-Efficacy and Interest of College Women," *Journal of Vocational Behavior* 56

(2000), 35–52; D. F. Gilroy and H. B. Desai, "Computer Anxiety: Sex, Race and Age," *International Journal of Man-Machine Studies* 25 (1986), 711–19.

5. Lily Shashaani, "Gender Differences in Computer Attitudes and Use among College Students," *Journal of Educational Computing Research* 16 (1997), 37–51.

6. Ibid.; Janice E. J. Woodrow, "The Development of Computer-Related Attitudes of Secondary Students," *Journal of Educational Computer Research* 11, no. 4 (1994), 307–38.

7. Accounting Education Change Commission, "Objectives for Accountants: Position Statement No.1," *Issues in Accounting Education* (1990), 307–12; International Federation of Accountants Staff, *Information Technology in the Accounting Curriculum* (New York: International Federation of Accountants, 1995); Institute of Management Accountants, *Traditional Jobs for Corporate Accountants Will Soon Be Extinct* (Montvale, N.J.: The Institute, 1997).

8. American Institute of Certified Public Accountants, Special Committee on Assurance Services, *Composite Profile of Capabilities Needed by Accounting Graduates* (New York: The Institute, 1996).

9. Institute of Management Accountants, *Traditional Jobs for Corporate Accountants.*

10. K. C. Laudon and J. P. Laudon, *Management Information Systems* (Upper Saddle River, N.J.: Prentice-Hall, 1998).

11. Hun-Tong Tan and Robert Libby, "Tacit Managerial versus Technical Knowledge as Determinants of Audit Expertise in the Field," *Journal of Accounting Research* 35 (1997), 97–113.

12. Dan V. Stone and Vairam Arunachalam, "An Empirical Investigation of Knowledge, Skill, Self-Efficacy and Computer Anxiety in Accounting Education," *Issues in Accounting Education* 11, no. 2 (fall 1996), 345–76.

13. Walters and Necessary, "An Attitudinal Comparison."

14. F. D. Davis, R. P. Bagozzi, and P. R. Warshaw, "User Acceptance of Computer Technology: A Comparison of Two Theoretical Models," *Management Science* 38, no. 8 (1989), 982–1003; Igabaria, Parasuraman, and Pavri, "A Path Analytic Study."

15. Walters and Necessary, "An Attitudinal Comparison."

16. Mills, "An Examination of the Relationship."

17. D. Patterson and J. Yaffe, "Using Computer-Assisted Instruction to Teach Axis II of DSM-III-R to Social Work Students," *Research on Social Work Practice* 3, no. 3 (July 1993), 343–57.

18. D. A. Becker and M. N. Dwyer, "Using Hypermedia to Provide Learner Control," *Journal of Educational Multimedia and Hypermedia* 3, no. 2 (1994), 155–72.

19. James L. Morrison, Hye-Shin Kin, and Christine T. Kydd, "Student Preference for Cybersearch Strategies: Impact on Critical Evaluation of Sources," *Journal of Education for Business* (May/June 1998), 264–8.

20. Marinus J. Bouwman, "Using Technology to Improve Student Learning in Accounting: A Research Agenda" (paper presented at a research colloquium, University of Arkansas, Little Rock, 1998).

21. David R. Fordham, "Freeing Class Time: Empirical Evidence on the Benefits of Using out-of-Class Video Segments in Lieu of in-Class Reviews," *Issues in Accounting Education* 11 (spring 1996), 37–48.

22. Landry, Rogers, and Harrell, "Computer Usage and Psychological Type Characteristics."

23. Flynn and Leeth, "The Accounting Profession in Transition."

24. Elliott, "Assurance Service Opportunities"; AICPA, *Composite Profile.*

25. Gilroy and Desai, "Computer Anxiety"; Larry D. Rosen and Phyllisann Maguire, "Myths and Realities of Computerphobia: A Meta-Analysis," *Anxiety Research* 3 (1990), 175–91.

26. T. P. Cornan, P. R. Emory, and S. D. White, "Identifying Factors That Influence Performance of Non-Computing Majors in Business Computer Information Systems Course," *Journal of Research on Computing in Education* (1989), 431–43; V. A. Clarke and S. M. Chambers, "Gender-Based Factors in Computing Enrollments and Achievement: Evidence from a Study of Tertiary Students," *Journal of Educational Computing Research* 5, no. 4 (1989), 409–29; G. Premkumar, K. Ramamurthy, and W. R. King, "Computer Supported Instruction and Student Characteristics: An Experimental Study," *Journal of Educational Computing Research* 9, no. 3 (1993), 373–96.

27. Busch, "Gender, Group Composition, Cooperation, and Self-Efficacy."

28. Deborah Compeau and Christine A. Higgins, "Social Cognitive Theory and Individual Reactions to Computing Technology: A Longitudinal Study," *MIS Quarterly* 23, no. 2 (1999), 145–59.

29. George H. Tompson and Parshotam Dass, "Improving Students' Self-Efficacy in Strategic Management: The Relative Impact of Cases and Simulations," *Simulation and Gaming* 31 (2000), 22–41; Mimi Bong, "Personal Factors Affecting the Generality of Academic Self-Efficacy Judgements: Gender, Ethnicity, and Relative Expertise," *Journal of Experimental Education* 67, no. 4 (summer 1999), 315–32.

30. Shashaani, "Gender Differences"; Woodrow, "The Development of Computer-Related Attitudes."

31. Philip Aspden and James Katz, "Motives, Hurdles, and Dropouts," *Communication of the ACM* 40, no. 4 (April 1997), 97–103; Robert K. Heinssen Jr., C. R. Glass, and L. A. Knight, "Assessing Computer Anxiety: Development and Validation of the Computer Anxiety Rating Scale," *Computers in Human Behavior* 3 (1987), 49–59.

32. Shashaani, "Gender Differences."

33. Woodrow, "The Development of Computer-Related Attitudes."

34. The participants consisted of traditional full-time students and part-time evening students. There were no dif-

ferences between the results of the part-time and full-time students.

35. One potential concern is that Internet usage experienced by students during the semester in other courses may have produced the observed results. Nine students (four males and five females) were enrolled in an Accounting Information Systems course at the time they participated in the project. That course also provided students with exposure to computers. The results for all variables were analyzed by removing the nine students from the sample, but the findings were still similar to those reported in the study. Therefore, this chapter reports the full sample.

36. Since the Kolmorov-Smirnov Goodness of Fit test showed a normality violation for the skills and the self-perception variables ($p < .05$), appropriate nonparametric tests were used for the analysis.

37. The results indicate that students started with reasonably high scores at the preproject stage and improved upon them while working on the project. The high preproject scores could be because students received some training on basic Internet usage before the project started. This was done to ensure that they had some baseline knowledge of the Internet before starting the project.

38. Note that there are significant differences between the postproject and preproject Internet knowledge scores for male students (mean = 8.19 versus 7.42) as well as for female students (mean = 7.50 versus 6.86 [Wilcoxon Matched-Paired Signed-Rank test, $p < .05$]).

39. Additional analysis was done to determine if the preproject perceptions of the students were representative of other accounting seniors. The preproject questionnaire was administered to another group of eighteen accounting seniors who did not participate in the study. Comparisons between the two groups indicate that there were no significant differences in the mean perceptions for any of the questions. This suggests that the preproject perceptions of students in the study are similar to the perceptions of other accounting seniors from the same institution.

40. Robert L. Ebel and D. A. Frisbie, *Essentials of Educational Measurement* (Englewood Cliffs, N.J.: Prentice-Hall, 1991).

41. Stone and Arunachalam, "An Empirical Investigation of Knowledge"; Mills, "An Examination of the Relationship."

42. Four additional questions tested students' general perceptions of how pleased they were at having chosen accounting as a major, if they expected and found the overall course to be interesting, and the usefulness of other data sources. There were no significant pre- and postproject differences in their perceptions for these questions (all $p > .1$).

43. Busch, "Gender, Group Composition"; Gilroy and Desai, "Computer Anxiety."

44. Shashaani, "Gender Differences"; Woodrow, "The Development of Computer-Related Attitudes."

45. Students rated their overall interest in the project on a five-point scale (1 = "not at all interesting" to 5 = "very interesting") and indicated a mean interest level of 4.18 (SD = 0.77). In fact, an overwhelming 85.7% ($n = 48$) of the students rated the project a 4 or 5, suggesting their approval for such an assignment. No significant differences in the mean interest level were observed between the male and female students.

46. See, for example, Elliott, "Assurance Service Opportunities."

47. Readers wanting copies of the data-collection instruments discussed in this paper should write the authors and request copies.

48. R. B. Kozma, "Learning with Media," *Review of Educational Research* (1991), 179–211; J. B. Butler and R. D. Mautz, "Multimedia Presentation and Learning: A Laboratory Experiment," *Issues in Accounting Education* (1996), 253–80.

49. The authors would like to thank Laurie Pant, Gail Sergenian, and participants at the Suffolk University Faculty Development Seminar.

SOME RECOMMENDED RESOURCES

There are thousands of monographs, articles, Web sites, and other resources available concerning assessment, learning outcomes, information literacy, and the role of libraries in assessment activities and practices. The following is a brief description of some of the more informative resources used while examining these issues; it is by no means exhaustive of the sources and resources consulted while preparing this manuscript or of the resources available on the topics. It is a starting place for exploring and learning about the rationale, roles, and actions of the stakeholders and players concerning assessment and learning outcomes.

WEB-BASED BIBLIOGRAPHIES OF SOURCES AND RESOURCES

Web-based bibliographies are highlighted because of their ease and convenience of access. All links were current as of dates indicated; some of the bibliographies are more comprehensive while others are more current. All are included because of their utility concerning the topics covered.

Ad Hoc Information Literacy Committee of the Wisconsin Association of Academic Librarians. Information Literacy and Academic Libraries. Available: http://www.wla.lib.wi.us/waal/infolit/links.html. Accessed 16 July 2001.

    All but one source included in this unannotated bibliography is a Web link to the identified source. Categories include directories, terminology, competencies, programs, organizations, conferences, bibliographies, and recent articles and papers.

Blixrud, Julia. Association of Research Libraries. Organizational Performance: Reading and Sites. Available: http://www.arl.org/stats/newmeas/orgperfbib.html. Accessed 21 March 2001.

    List of print and Web-based resources concerning organizational performance and libraries, higher education, general organization, and general Web sites.

Brenenson, Stephanie. Florida International University. Information Literacy on the WWW. Available: http://www.fiu.edu/~library/ili/iliweb.html. Accessed 23 March 2001.

    A briefly annotated bibliography of Web resources arranged into sections including general sites about information literacy; competencies, standards, and outcomes; associations; accreditation; programs in colleges and universities; and papers, presentations, and research on information literacy.

California Polytechnic State University, San Luis Obispo. General Education Assessment Library. Available: http:// www.calpoly.edu/~acadprog/gened/library.htm. Accessed 21 March 2001.

    Listing of materials in the "GenEd" library of an actively involved, assessment-oriented institution. Identifies general sources, methods of assessment, preparations for outcomes assessment programs, portfolios, tests, and software.

Council for Higher Education Accreditation. Assessment and Accreditation in Higher Education: Bibliography. Available: http://www.chea.org/Commentary/biblio.cfm. Accessed 21 March 2001.

A well-done bibliography of print sources. Categories include history, theory/philosophy, methodology, assessment, higher-education context, standards, quality assurance, and general resources.

Grassian, Esther, and Susan E. Clark. Information Literacy Sites: Background and Ideas for Program Planning and Development. Available: http://www.ala.org/acrl/resfeb99.html. Accessed 21 March 2001.

A 1999 annotated bibliography of Web-based resources including directories, guidelines and reports, programs, tutorials, discussion groups, electronic journals, articles, and organizations and associations.

Institute for Information Literacy. Recommended Readings for Librarians New to Instruction. Available: http://www.ala.org/acrl/nili/readings.html. Accessed 16 July 2001.

An annotated bibliography of print resources based upon each of its current and former IIL advisory board members recommending "three readings of any kind on information literacy" for new instruction librarians.

Library Instruction Committee, SUNY Librarians Association. Annotated Selected Bibliography on the Evaluation of Library Instruction. Available: http://library.lib.binghamton.edu/sunyla/sunylabia.html. Accessed 16 July 2001.

Most, but not all, of the numerous print sources identified are well-annotated. Unfortunately, this list has not been updated in two years.

Lindauer, Bonnie Gratch. City College of San Francisco. Assessing the Impact of IC Learning Opportunities: Selected Documents. Available: http://fog.ccsf.cc.ca.us/~bgratch/asessing_impact_IC.html. Accessed 21 March 2001.

An unannotated bibliography of print and Web-based resources. Categories include selected readings for assessing student learning, assessment methodologies and strategies, information literacy standards and assessment models, assessment teaching, and selected resources for current awareness and ideas.

North Carolina State University. Internet Resources for Higher Education Outcomes Assessment. Available: http://www2.acs.ncsu.edu/UPA/assmt/resource.htm. Accessed 21 March 2001.

The most comprehensive Web-based annotated bibliography available concerning assessment. Provides descriptions of and links to discussion groups, forums, archives of articles, assessment handbooks, assessment

of specific skills or content, individual higher education institutions' assessment-related pages, and accrediting agencies.

North Central Association of Schools and Colleges, The Higher Learning Commission. Available: http://www.ncahigherlearningcommission.org/resources/assessment/asres97.pdf. Accessed 21 March 2001.

An unannotated list of assessment print resources provided to members of the North Central Association of Schools and Colleges. The bibliography lists colleges with assessment documents, publications and other materials dealing with assessment such as testing, and selected organizations and instruments for assessment.

Office of Institutional Assessment and Testing, Western Washington University. Links to Valuable Assessment Resources. Available: http://www.ac.wwu.edu/~assess/airlinks.htm. Accessed 21 March 2001.

An annotated bibliography of Web links to other bibliographies and lists of topic-related links. Although there are fewer than twenty links on this page, it rightfully states: "Links from these central sites connect you to just about every known assessment site."

The Pennsylvania State University, Center for Excellence in Learning and Teaching. Reviews and Annotations. Available: http://www.psu.edu/celt/reviews.html. Accessed 21 March 2001.

An annotated bibliography of print and Web teaching resources in subject areas including general resources, assessment, learning and cognitive theory, and testing and grading.

Phoenix College, Student Academic Achievement. Assessment in Higher Education. Available: http://www.pc.maricopa.edu/intranet/committees/assessment/assessOnweb.html. Accessed 21 March 2001.

An annotated bibliography of Web-based resources on assessment activities of selected higher education institutions, accrediting bodies, and other assessment stakeholders. Web-link categories include general education, classroom assessment techniques, professional organizations, student development, general assessment, studies and reports, and methods and measures.

State Library of Florida, Tallahassee. Planning and Evaluation. Available: http://dlis.dos.state.fl.us/bld/Research_Office/BLD_Research.htm. Accessed 19 Sept. 2001.

This section of the library's Web site provides the Library Services and Technology Act Outcome Evaluation Plan developed by Sadlon & Associates, Inc., and a forty-seven-page Workbook: Outcome Measurement of Library Programs (September 2000). There are also hyperlinks to the home pages of associations and organizations that engage in outcomes assessment.

Standards and Accreditation Committee, Association of College and Research Libraries. Sources of Information on Performance and Outcome Assessment. Available: http://www.ala.org/acrl/sacguid.html. Accessed 22 March 2001.

An excellent annotated bibliography of print resources discussing performance and outcomes assessment.

Troy, Mark. Texas A&M. Outcomes Assessment Resources on the Web. Available: http://www.tamu.edu/marshome/assess/oabooks.html. Accessed 22 March 2001.

An unannotated listing of Web sites including university assessment pages, general resources, assessment agencies and organizations, instruments and techniques, papers and reports, commercial resources, benchmarking performance, and software.

MAJOR ORGANIZATIONS CONCERNED WITH ASSESSMENT

These organizations are among the most important catalysts for encouraging the incorporation of assessment practices in the effort to support and prove institutional accountability. Some encourage assessment by applying standards; others make available or provide access to important information sources for support, assistance, and guidance.

American Association for Higher Education (AAHE). Available: http://www.aahe.org. Accessed 21 March 2001.

The AAHE sponsors the Assessment Forum, "the primary national network connecting and supporting higher education stakeholders involved in assessment."

Association of College and Research Libraries. Available: http://www.ala.org/acrl. Accessed 21 March 2001.

A division of the American Library Association, ACRL is the major player concerning information literacy for academic libraries in higher education institutions. Among its written documents and reports is the *Information Literacy Competency Standards for Higher Education.*

Council for Higher Education Accreditation. Available: http://www.chea.org. Accessed 21 March 2001.

The accreditor of the regional accrediting agencies.

ERIC Clearinghouse on Assessment and Evaluation. Available: http://ericae.net. Accessed 21 March 2001.

The online library includes links to more than 400 full-text sources.

ERIC Clearinghouse on Higher Education. Available: http://www.eriche.org/main.html. Accessed 20 March 2001.

Search the ERIC database for abstracts of documents and journal articles.

Institute for Information Literacy. Available: http://www.ala.org/acrl/nili/nilihp.html. Accessed 21 March 2001.

Sponsored by ACRL, the Institute's stated goals are to "prepare librarians to become effective teachers in information literacy programs; support librarians, other educators, and administrators in playing a leadership role in the development and implementation of information literacy programs; and forge new relationships throughout the educational community to work toward information literacy curriculum development."

National Forum on Information Literacy. Available: http://www.infolit.org. Accessed 21 March 2001.

The Forum was created in 1990 as a response to the recommendations of the American Library Association's Presidential Committee on Information Literacy. It pursues activities in four primary areas. Through its member organizations, the Forum examines the role of information in our lives and integrates information literacy into its programs. It also supports, initiates, and monitors information literacy projects both in the United States and abroad. Much of the effort appears to be in K–12 schools; however, membership includes higher education organizations such as EDUCAUSE.

Regional Higher Education Institutional Accreditation Associations:

Middle States Commission on Higher Education. Available: http://www.msache.org. Accessed 23 March 2001.

New England Association of Schools and Colleges, Commission on Institutions of Higher Education. Available: http://www.neasc.org/cihe/cihe.htm. Accessed 23 March 2001.

North Central Association of Schools and Colleges, The Higher Learning Commission. Available: http://www.ncahigherlearningcommission.org. Accessed 23 March 2001.

Northwest Association of Schools and Colleges, Commission on Colleges. Available: http://www.cocnasc.org. Accessed 23 March 2001.

Southern Association of Colleges and Schools, Commission on Colleges. Available: http://www.sacscoc.org. Accessed 23 March 2001.

Western Association of Schools and Colleges, Accrediting Commission for Senior Colleges and Universities. Available: http://www.wascweb.org/senior/wascsr.html. Accessed 1 Sept. 2001.

United States Department of Education. Available: http://www.ed.gov. Accessed 21 March 2001.

Besides recognizing the Council for Higher Education Accreditation as the umbrella agency of the regional accrediting bodies, the U.S. Department of Education is directly or indirectly involved in almost every education and library issue in the United States.

BOOKS, ARTICLES, AND REPORTS

Thousands of books, articles, and reports, published or otherwise, are available concerning assessment, learning outcomes, and information literacy. To keep current on materials available, utilize library holdings catalogs; review information from publishers; search journal and report indexes; visit Web sites of libraries and institutional research, planning, and assessment offices, regional accrediting bodies, and organizations involved in assessment; and, occasionally, conduct keyword searches on Web-based subject directories. Following is a very select list of such resources.

American Association for Higher Education. Nine Principles of Good Practice for Assessing Student Learning. 25 July 1996. Available: http://www.aahe.org/assessment/principl.htm. Accessed 21 March 2001.

A list and description of nine values to apply when developing and conducting assessment activities.

Angeley, Robin, and Jeff Purdue. Western Washington University. Information Literacy: An Overview. Available: http://www.ac.wwu.edu/~dialogue/issue6.html. Accessed 21 March 2001.

An online paper that straightforwardly discusses the rationale for the role of the library and higher education institution in information literacy.

Angelo, Thomas A., and K. Patricia Cross. *Classroom Assessment Techniques: A Handbook for College Teachers.* 2d ed. San Francisco: Jossey-Bass, 1993.

For many faculty, this is the definitive book on descriptions of applicable classroom assessment techniques. Also includes the Teaching Goals Inventory used to help faculty identify and rank the relative importance of their teaching goals.

Association of College and Research Libraries. *Information Literacy Competency Standards for Higher Education.* Chicago: American Library Assn., 2000. Available: http://www.ala.org/acrl/ilcomstan.html. Accessed 21 March 2001.

An excellent effort describing the skills and abilities of the "information literate" person. The standards are designed to be applicable institutionwide, not just in academic libraries.

Association of College and Research Libraries. "Standards for College Libraries 2000 Edition." *College and Research Libraries News* 61, no. 3 (March 2000), 175–82. Available: http://www.ala.org/acrl/guides/college.html. Accessed 21 March 2001.

The current standards for college libraries. These standards define inputs, outputs, and outcomes and discuss expectations concerning planning, assessment, and outcomes assessment.

Association of College and Research Libraries Task Force on Academic Library Outcomes Assessment. *Report.* Chicago: American Library Assn., 1998. Available: http://www.ala.org/acrl/outcome.html. Accessed 21 March 2001.

One of the best discussions of outcomes assessment available. This report provides more definitions, rationales, and details concerning outcomes assessment than ACRL's *Information Literacy Competency Standards for Higher Education* and "Standards for College Libraries 2000 Edition."

Dervin, Brenda, and Kathleen Clark. *ASQ: Alternative Tools for Information Need and Accountability Assessments by Libraries.* Belmont, Calif.: The Peninsula Library System, July 1987.

An early effort at public library outcomes assessment by applying user surveys to measure community use providing data useful "in translating library experience and potential beyond counts of library inputs and outputs and the sheer movement of nonhuman materials into the terms of human experience that speak eloquently to voters and policy makers."

ERIC Clearinghouse on Assessment and Evaluation and the Department of Measurement, Statistics, and Evaluation at the University of Maryland, College Park. Practical Assessment, Research & Evaluation. Available: http://ericae.net/pare. Accessed 21 March 2001.

A free peer-reviewed electronic journal of articles concerning assessment, research, evaluation, and teaching. The excellent search engine facilitates searching the seven volumes (and growing) for content.

Gradowski, Gail, Loanne Snavely, and Paula Dempsey. *Designs for Active Learning: A Sourcebook of Classroom Strategies for Information Education.* Chicago: Assn. of College and Research Libraries, 1998.

Fifty-four instructional-session plans covering basic library instruction, searching indexes and online catalogs, search strategies for the research process, evaluation of library resources, and discipline-oriented instruction. While not as detailed as Angelo and Cross's classroom assessment techniques, these session plans could be effectively used to support learning outcomes, and many can be measured and assessed.

Lindauer, Bonnie Gratch. "Defining and Measuring the Library's Impact on Campuswide Outcomes." *College & Research Libraries* 59, no. 6 (Nov. 1998), 546–70.

An inspiring article, the author identifies key institutional outcomes to which academic libraries contribute; specifies practical, measurable library performance indicators; and provides a framework of assessment categories that emphasize library teaching roles.

Smith, Drew. University of South Florida, Tampa. Directory of Online Resources for Information Literacy: Definition of Information Literacy and Related Terms. Available: http://www.cas.usf.edu/lis/il/definitions.html. Accessed 21 March 2001.

Provides definitions of terms used in information literacy endeavors and includes a Web link to the source of the definition.

Smith, Kenneth R. University of Arizona. New Roles and Responsibilities for the University Library: Advancing Student Learning through Outcomes Assessment. Available: http://www.arl.org/stats/newmeas/outcomes/HEOSmith.html. Accessed 21 March 2001.

An important May 2000 paper prepared for the Association of Research Libraries. Smith places student learning outcomes assessment into an academic library perspective, encouraging librarians to develop instructional "offerings" in a proactive approach of collaboration with faculty to accomplished shared assessment needs.

INDEX

Peter Hernon is professor at the Graduate School of Library and Information Science, Simmons College, where he teaches courses on research methods, the evaluation of library services, and government information. He received his Ph.D. from Indiana University in 1978 and is the author of 37 books and more than 160 articles. He is the editor-in-chief of the *Journal of Academic Librarianship* and the coeditor of *Library & Information Science Research*. Hernon is also the recipient of the 1993 Saur Award for the best article in *College & Research Libraries* and the 1999 recipient of the Highsmith Award for *Assessing Service Quality* (ALA, 1998) and its "outstanding contribution to library literature."

Robert E. Dugan is the director of the Mildren F. Sawyer Library, Suffolk University, in Boston. In his 28 years in libraries, he has been an associate university librarian, a state librarian, head of statewide library development, a public library director, and a reference librarian. He has contributed more than 50 articles and reviews primarily concerned with information policy and the practical management and deployment of technologies, and has coauthored two other books.